The NFL's
Greatest Day

The NFL's Greatest Day

*Roger Staubach, Franco Harris
and the Story
of Immaculate Saturday*

BRAD SCHULTZ

McFarland & Company, Inc., Publishers
Jefferson, North Carolina

ISBN (print) 978-1-4766-7689-0
ISBN (ebook) 978-1-4766-3788-4

Library of Congress and British Library
Cataloguing data are available

On the cover: Photographs of Roger Staubach (12) and
Franco Harris (32) by Jerry Coli (Dreamstime)

Printed in the United States of America

*McFarland & Company, Inc., Publishers
Box 611, Jefferson, North Carolina 28640
www.mcfarlandpub.com*

Acknowledgments

The author wishes to gratefully acknowledge the help of Liz Wright at the Detre Library and Archives with the Heinz History Center in Pittsburgh. And major thanks to Skip Vanderbundt, Roger Staubach and Barry Pearson for their invaluable time for interviews and the materials they donated. All three have become extremely successful business executives, yet were more than accommodating and helpful.

As a fan, the experience of talking with them was almost surreal. I remember getting an autographed picture of Staubach as a kid and watching him play at Texas Stadium (including the first game ever played there). I've written several books now and interviewed dozens of famous people, but there's still that point at which you think to yourself, "I'm talking to Roger Staubach." That would have been impossible to imagine as a 10-year-old. Maybe this book is part of an attempt to bring some of that back.

Dallas receiver Drew Pearson once said of Staubach, "There's nothing I would or could ever say bad about Roger. He's the only player I played with who everything they say about him is true."[1] What a wonderful feeling to know that the player you watched from afar in 1972 turned out to be exactly the person you always believed him to be. If for no other reason that alone is worth a trip back to December 23, 1972, to visit our youth and the heroes we grew up with.

Table of Contents

Preface

On January 20, 2019, the NFL staged two memorable conference championship games. In New Orleans, the Rams rallied late to tie the Saints and then won on a 57-yard field goal in overtime, 26–23. Later that evening in Kansas City, the Chiefs kicked a late field goal to force overtime, only to see Tom Brady and the Patriots score a touchdown to win, 37–31. Never before had both the AFC and NFC conference championship games both gone to overtime on the same day, and immediately many sportswriters, fans, and experts began calling it the most exciting day in NFL history. "The NFL's final four looked exciting on paper and delivered in real life," wrote ESPN's Bill Barnwell. "The Patriots and Chiefs had four lead changes in a 38-point fourth quarter. The Rams battled back to tie the Saints twice and didn't lead until Greg Zuerlein hit a 57-yarder to win the game in the extra period."[1]

Exciting? Certainly. Compelling? Absolutely. The best ever? Not so fast. The games were almost immediately overshadowed by a series of questionable penalties that had more people talking about the officiating rather than the excitement. The *New Orleans Times-Picayune*, casting aside all pretense of objectivity, called the officiating in the Saints–Rams game "unbelievable" and said the upcoming Super Bowl would be "tainted." As for the Chiefs–Patriots game, as good as it was, old-timers would say the 1971 Christmas Day playoff game between Kansas City and Miami was even better.[2]

When you start arguing about NFL players and records, newer always seems to be better. There is no doubt that the modern NFL player is superior to the one who played only a few years ago—bigger, stronger and faster. In the 1970 season, the year of the merger between the NFL and AFL, and a year often considered the beginning of the "modern" NFL, the

Baltimore Colts won the Super Bowl with an offensive line that averaged in size 6'3" and 240 pounds. When the Philadelphia Eagles won the Super Bowl after the 2017 season, they had bookend offensive tackles that were 6'6" and 320 pounds. Every member of their line weighed more than 300 pounds, except for center Jason Kelce, who weighed 295.

Records from that bygone era seem to shrink in significance as well. When Johnny Unitas set a record by throwing a touchdown pass in 47 straight games, it was considered a record as unbreakable as Joe DiMaggio's 56-game hit streak or Cy Young's 511 career wins as a pitcher. Yet, the Unitas mark was broken three times in just a matter of a few years— by Tom Brady, Peyton Manning, and by current record holder Drew Brees, who threw a touchdown pass in 54 consecutive games. Unitas himself, once routinely considered in any discussion of the greatest quarterbacks of all time, today is usually mentioned far down the list behind Manning, Brady and Brees, if at all.

Unitas, and other players from the 1960s and 70s, seem to belong to a somewhat prehistoric era of professional football, and their exploits captured on grainy film images hardly seem relevant in a digital age. The pictures of Red Grange and Jim Thorpe in cartoonish leather helmets and earflaps must have seemed like ancient history to the NFL players of the 1970s; so too do the 1970s seem musty and outdated to the players and fans of today.

By almost any measure, the NFL game of today is considered better than it was nearly 50 years ago, but "better" is an immeasurable concept. Bigger, faster and stronger, certainly, but that does not always mean better. The average cost of an NFL ticket today is nearly $100, and for a family of four to go to a single game—tickets, parking, souvenirs and food—now averages more than $500 at most NFL stadiums.[3] A ticket for Super Bowl I in 1967 had a face value of $12; by Super Bowl LIII in 2019 the price had risen to $2,500 and ticket brokers were asking for and getting much more.[4]

Would the NFL fan of today trade that to return to a time when tickets could be bought with pocket change and many could be purchased by walking up to the stadium the day of the game? Don't forget that many of the stadia from that time period were older and often rundown, and certainly didn't offer amenities such as multi-million-dollar scoreboards.

Physicality and practicality play an important part in the NFL experience, but increasingly so too does memory. The league celebrated its 100th season in 2019, which is certainly long enough to build a significant institutional history. Grange, Thorpe and their contemporaries are beyond the recall of even the oldest NFL fan, but not so with the men and moments of the 1970s. The name Lombardi still carries a powerful presence not only of coaching greatness, but of a seemingly bygone football era of discipline, toughness and family.

Part of the Lombardi iconography is the mystery—what would have happened if he had not died so young? Lombardi barely even made it to the 1970s, dying of cancer at age 57. How many more Super Bowls would he have won? How far would his greatness have reached?

Memory and mystery—two powerful forces that came together on December 23, 1972, in a day that was not just better, but the best. It was the greatest single day in NFL history.

It certainly did not start out that way. In an era of defense, the playoff game in Pittsburgh between the Steelers and Raiders was a plodding affair for the first 58 minutes. Then, two lightning bolts—a late touchdown that put Oakland in the lead, followed by a later touchdown that put Pittsburgh in the history books. Fans barely had time to digest the Immaculate Reception, when Roger Staubach came off the bench to win a playoff game for Dallas in San Francisco. The Steelers and Franco Harris touched the gods once in the final seconds; Staubach and the Cowboys did it three times in the final quarter, with his last-minute touchdown pass erasing a 15-point deficit.

A once-in-a-lifetime comeback that happened twice in an afternoon. Through six hours of drama—from the opening kickoff in Pittsburgh to the final gun in San Francisco—national television audiences stood open-mouthed, watching in disbelief. Not in the long history of the NFL had anyone seen anything like it. And with all due appreciation of Saints–Rams and Patriots–Chiefs in 2019, no one has seen anything quite like it since.

While much has been written about the Immaculate Reception, much less has been written about the Dallas–San Francisco game, and no current work has attempted to combine these events and assess their relationship to one another, and their importance to the NFL. In that sense, this work is unique. It is also unique in that it brings together rigorous research in the field of sports history with a compelling narrative that helps make the events come alive.

The book includes appropriate research on the names, dates, and events, but goes much deeper to tell personal stories of how that day affected different people. One such story is about Jim Baker, the young insurance salesman who reportedly has the ball used to score the winning touchdown in the Immaculate Reception. Baker still has the ball, now kept as a family heirloom to honor the son born just a few hours before the game kicked off. It is a story of both heartache and courage.

Another story is on Preston Riley, the unfortunate San Francisco receiver who fumbled a late onsides kick that helped Dallas come back. Like many athletes who find themselves in the wrong place at the wrong time, Riley's career and life eventually spun out of control. His story is one of tragedy, as is that of offensive lineman Forrest Blue. Blue became one of the many casualties of concussion-related injuries, the scope of which is only now becoming fully known.

Memory and mystery. What is the truth behind the Immaculate Reception? Was it an illegal pass? Did Franco really catch the ball? Did the officials conspire to rob the Raiders of a game they rightfully deserved? How exactly did Staubach, who had hardly played all year because of injury, come off the bench and bring the Cowboys back? What would have happened if Craig Morton had stayed in the game at quarterback? Did the loss end any hopes of a budding 49er dynasty?

This book can't answer all of those questions, but then again, no one really can. It's the debate, the arguments, and the speculation that make it fun and enjoyable.

So enjoy a long-ago afternoon of football that is still considered an NFL classic. Not just classic, but arguably the greatest day in NFL history.

CHAPTER 1

A Football for Sam

It stands to reason that the Pro Football Hall of Fame in Canton, Ohio, would have more than its share of famous footballs. On display are footballs from every Super Bowl, the Dolphins' perfect 1972 season, and from the "Greatest Game Ever Played," the 1958 NFL Championship in which the Colts beat the Giants 23–17 in overtime. The Hall has the football used by Brett Favre to break the career passing record, the ball used by Peyton Manning to break Favre's record, and the ball used by Drew Brees to break Manning's record.

But perhaps the most famous, mysterious, and valuable football of all—*Sports Illustrated* once estimated its worth at $80,000[1] and offers for it have gone into the triple digits—is not in the Hall. It sits safely tucked away in an insurance company vault in suburban Pittsburgh.

Or does it? Like most things connected to the Immaculate Reception, one can never really know for sure.

What we *do* know for sure is this:

The insurance company, the vault, and the football are in West Mifflin, Pennsylvania, a suburb a few miles southeast of Pittsburgh along the Monongahela River. The imposing name, "Baker Insurance and Investment Services," does not seem to fit the modesty of the neighborhood or the company's small, green brick building. Jim Baker started this company in 1976, four years after he attended the most famous football game in Pittsburgh and maybe the most famous game in NFL history.

December 23, 1972, was a big day for Jim and wife Mary, as they were bringing their newborn son Sam home from McKeesport Hospital. No sooner than he had gotten his new family settled in, Baker rushed off to pick up his nephew and head downtown to Three Rivers Stadium where the Steelers would play the Raiders in the first round of the AFC playoffs.

While some might fault Baker for leaving his family on such an important day, to others the Steelers *were* family. Baker and other fans had suffered through 25 straight seasons without any glimpse of a championship, and they were not about to miss this opportunity. The two had pretty good seats—around the 30-yard line behind the Raiders' bench.

The game moved along uneventfully—lots of penalties, punts and incompletions—until the last two minutes. Pittsburgh trailed 7–6 and faced fourth down with only twenty-two seconds to play. The season seemed lost. Suddenly, a pass ricocheted into the arms of running back Franco Harris, who galloped into the end zone for the winning touchdown with only five seconds left. "Even before he hit the end zone, people started jumping off the dugout running down to the field," Baker says. "I grabbed my nephew and we jumped off the dugout and we watched what was going on as we ran down onto the field."[2]

Baker and thousands of Steeler fans rushed the field, overwhelming a small security force mainly comprised of local policemen. Most of them seemed content to mob Harris and celebrate with other Steeler players. Baker had eyes only for the football, which Harris had left in the end zone and which now, in the total chaos on the field, stood ignored and unattended.

It took five minutes to restore order and clear the field for the extra point. As Baker and several other fans crowded around the sidelines and the back of the end zone, he noticed the same football was put back into play. "The whole time, I've got my eye on that ball," he said. "They put it down for the extra point, and all I'm thinking is, 'I want that ball.'"[3] Roy Gerela kicked the point—there were no nets behind the goal posts in those days because kickers didn't have the leg power they do now—and the football clanged off a stadium wall and bounced back toward the field.

Now, another wild melee erupted as fans jockeyed for the ball. At the time, NFL footballs were considered like foul balls in baseball—finders, keepers. Stadium officials would sometimes try to get them back, but if a fan was persistent and lucky he got to go home with a souvenir. On this day, Jim Baker was both.

"I jumped on the ball as it squirted around and a lot of people fought [for it]," said Baker, an avid runner and athlete, but someone who stood only five feet, five inches tall. He managed to get control of it and when someone wrestled it away from him, Baker somehow was able to get it back. "I tore a jacket, ruined a camera, but I came off the bottom of the pile, grabbed my nephew, stuffed [the ball] under my coat and ran as hard as I could because I was afraid of a big guy taking the ball from me."[4] Officials brought in another ball, Pittsburgh kicked off, and five seconds later the game was over.

Baker was still afraid as he left the stadium—afraid the NFL, or the Steelers or a policeman—would find out that he had the ball and want it back. He approached a couple sitting in the parking lot, listening to the pandemonium on the radio because they couldn't get tickets to the game, and asked for a ride across the bridge where he had parked his car. Hiding the ball under his jacket the entire time, he made it safely home an hour later and back with an incredible story to tell his new family. Before the night was out, the play would come to be known as the "Immaculate Reception," and Baker had the football from perhaps the most famous play in NFL history.

Or did he? Much like the end of the game itself, the football is shrouded in controversy, legend and myth. There is no authentication of the ball; no sports memorabilia company has come forward to give its stamp of approval—*provenance* in the language of the industry—to Baker's football. Neither the NFL nor the Steelers have ever claimed, or shown much interest in claiming, that this was indeed the football that Franco Harris ran into history. There is no spot waiting for it in the Hall of Fame. It is simply Baker's word against the world.

But that seems to be enough.

In 2016, the Smithsonian Channel ran a segment on the football as part of its show *Sports Detectives*, which tries to locate famous sports items. Other episodes tried to track down the basketball used by Wilt Chamberlain to score 100 points in a game, Muhammad Ali's gold medal in boxing won in the 1960 Olympics, and the flag draped over the shoulders of goalie Jim Craig after the U.S. won the Olympic gold medal in hockey in 1980. Private investigator Ken Barrows, a former FBI agent, called Baker's claim an open and shut case. "In my mind," he says, "it is the real thing."[5]

"The old stuff we really have to do the homework on," says Anne Madarasz, "and you've got to believe some of the story. When you meet Jim Baker, you believe the story. He has never told any [other] story but the one he's telling." Madarasz is director of the Western Pennsylvania Sports Museum and also its chief historian. As a historian, she too is satisfied with Baker's story and the authenticity of the ball. "One of the things that makes Jim's story believable and verifiable is from the very second that he ran out of Three Rivers Stadium with that ball underneath his shirt, he talked about it."[6]

And how Baker has talked about it. He's given scores of interviews to NFL Films, national news organizations and documentary film producers. He takes the ball out of the vault on many occasions for speaking engagements, banquets, children's groups, and even to toss around with his family. Never once has he changed the details of the story.

The first night that four-day-old Sam Baker spent in his new home, so too did what appears to be the Immaculate Reception football. They were joined by Jim Baker's brother-in-law Bob Pavuchak, a photographer for both newspapers in Pittsburgh, the *Post-Gazette* and *Press*. Pavuchak took a picture of the family with the ball that ran in the *Press* a few days later. He, and anyone who has ever met or talked with Jim Baker about it, is convinced that the ball is genuine. "Throughout the years, Jim's never made a secret of the fact that he had the ball," says Madarasz. "There is evidence from the beginning that this is the Immaculate Reception game ball."[7]

"That particular week," Baker recalls with no small amount of satisfaction, "I'm the father of a newborn son, my second son. The following few days later, baby Jesus was born. I get the Immaculate Reception football. You put it all together, it's tears of happiness. I'm one of the luckiest persons in the world."[8]

*   *   *

In March of 2015, *USA Today* ran an article on what the newspaper called the most exciting day in the history of the NCAA basketball tournament. On March 19, five games were decided by a single point, with the decisive scores coming on a three-pointer, a disputed goaltending call, a shot in overtime, and another basket that sent the winning coach falling out of his chair off the bench. The paper noted, "This is the first time this many games have been this close in a single day in all of tournament history."[9]

On September 28, 2011, six major league baseball games would determine the final two wild card playoff spots on the last day of the regular season. The finishes to those games—including dramatic rallies and home runs, all within a span of seemingly a few minutes—sent the Rays and Cardinals to the postseason, while crushing the hopes of the Red Sox and Braves. "You couldn't have written a script with a game in Baltimore and a game in Tampa all happening within three minutes," said Bud Selig, baseball's commissioner at the time. "The night was absolutely extraordinary. There's nothing that was even close. Only baseball could produce a night like this."[10]

It gets tricky when one starts talking about "the greatest day" in any-

Five days after the Immaculate Reception, 1972, Jim Baker lets his son Benjie try a kick at the famous football with wife Mary and newborn son Sam looking on. Sam arrived home from the hospital just a few hours before the football did. *Photograph by Bob Pavuchak. © Pittsburgh Post-Gazette, 2019. Reprinted with permission.*

thing, because there is so much room for interpretation. A baseball fan might argue for May 17, 1979, when the Cubs and Phillies met at Wrigley Field with the wind blowing out. The teams combined for 45 runs, 50 hits and 11 home runs—three by Dave Kingman—as Philadelphia won in ten innings, 23–22. The Phillies led 7–0, 15–6 and 21–9 before the Cubs rallied to tie the game in the eighth. "We were up in the booth laughing at each other," said Philadelphia radio broadcaster Andy Musser. "We'd all had wild games at Wrigley Field, but we couldn't believe what we were seeing."[11]

Typically, NFL greatness isn't measured in single days, but rather in individual plays ("The Music City Miracle," "Miracle at the Meadowlands"), games (the Ice Bowl, various Super Bowls), or players (any examples of which would be inherently controversial because of the difficulty of comparing players of different positions).

The Immaculate Reception usually makes almost any list of great games or individual plays. Depending on which source you use, the play almost certainly ranks in every top five. "Can you imagine if the NFL used instant replay in 1972?" asked the *New York Daily News*, which ranked the play number one. "The most memorable play in NFL history would still be under review."[12] Oakland Raiders coach John Madden came to the same conclusion, and after more than 40 years of looking at replays says he still can't tell what happened.

The mystery is part of what makes the Immaculate Reception so memorable all these years later. Did Jack Tatum or Frenchy Fuqua touch the ball? Did Franco Harris catch the rebound before it hit the ground? Did the game officials conspire to cover up the real events of the play as the Raiders still believe today? While conspiracy theories abound, the official version shows that Harris caught the fourth down deflection and rambled into the end zone to give Pittsburgh a miracle win over Oakland in the first round of the playoffs.

Almost everyone remembers the details of the game, which took place on December 23, 1972, at Pittsburgh's Three Rivers Stadium. The first 58 minutes of the game were somewhat unspectacular as two Steeler field goals accounted for the only scoring and a 6–0 lead. Oakland quarterback Ken Stabler made a dramatic 30-yard touchdown run with less than two minutes to play to give the Raiders a 7–6 lead. That led to the controversial 60-yard pass from Terry Bradshaw to Franco Harris that essentially won the game with only five seconds remaining.

The play might be the most dissected in NFL history, and it certainly has been one of the most discussed. Documentaries, newspaper and magazine accounts, and television shows have all chronicled the event, as have special anniversary celebrations. For the Steelers, and to a lesser extent the Raiders, the play has become a defining "where were you" moment, much like the Kennedy assassination. On the 40th anniversary in 2012, the Steelers organization hosted a special weekend that featured the return of several players, the unveiling of a monument at the stadium, a panel discussion, and a special observance at halftime of the game that Sunday. "It's amazing as time goes on, you know what they say, the fish gets bigger," said Harris. "But in this case the fish really does get bigger, so much bigger than we ever thought it would."[13]

In San Francisco, the big fish is a play they call "The Catch." On January 10, 1982, Dwight Clark's leaping, acrobatic grab in the back of the end zone propelled the 49ers to a 28–27 comeback win over Dallas in the NFC Championship. "The image of Clark out-leaping Dallas defender Everson Walls—especially captured by photographer Walter Iooss, Jr. for the cover of *Sports Illustrated*—has become one of the most instantly recognized moments in NFL history."[14] The play launched a 49er dynasty that would win four Super Bowls in the 1980s, and destroyed another, as Dallas began a slow, painful decline. "Cowboy mystique died a little," according to sportswriter Skip Bayless. "Metallic-blue tradition was tarnished ... and all of [team vice president Tex] Schramm's computers and all of [coach Tom] Landry's men couldn't put it back together again."[15]

For the record, the play to Clark was called "Sprint Right Option," and Freddie Solomon was the intended receiver. When he was covered, quarterback Joe Montana looked to Clark and made history. In Pittsburgh, the Immaculate Reception's official name is "66 Circle Option"[16] and obviously, Franco Harris was not the intended target, but neither was Frenchy Fuqua. The play was originally designed for rookie receiver Barry Pearson. The beauty of miracles is their randomness.

The intended receiver didn't get the ball on "83 Pass," but no one in San Francisco wants to remember that. The play was the last in a series of miracles arranged by providence and Roger Staubach to beat the 49ers in a 1972 playoff game. Originally designed as a sideline to Billy Parks, Staubach saw Parks was covered and in the face of a blitz, launched the game-winning pass to Ron Sellers to culminate a 17-point fourth quarter rally. The 30–28 win sent Dallas to the NFC Championship game and San Francisco into nine seasons of playoff purgatory.

The date of that Cowboy comeback was Saturday, December 23, 1972. Yes, the same day as the Immaculate Reception and in fact, only about three hours apart. It's doubtful the NFL has ever seen a single afternoon with such high drama, all packed in a space of only six hours. In an era when national television coverage was still a big deal, both games were telecast across the nation—Pittsburgh–Oakland starting at 1 p.m. in the east and Dallas–San Francisco at 4—and they mesmerized millions. Unfortunately, that audience did not include anyone in Pittsburgh or San Francisco thanks to NFL policies that blacked out the game in a 75-mile radius.

Hundreds of thousands, if not millions, claim to have seen the Immaculate Reception in person, despite the fact that the stadium held just over 50,000. Virtually no one in San Francisco will now lay claim to having been at the Cowboys–49ers game, even though attendance there (61,000-plus) was actually greater than for the Immaculate Reception. Believing the game was safely in the bag for the Niners, fans began leaving Candlestick park midway through the fourth quarter. As the Cowboys rallied, many turned around the came back for the ending, much to their disappointment.

So on an unparalleled day of NFL excitement that featured two of the most fantastic finishes in playoff history, one game is revered while another is scorned. Had the venues been reversed—had the Immaculate Reception taken place in Oakland and the Staubach rally in Dallas—perhaps the perceptions would be different and today everyone would be talking about the Cowboys game. "In many ways, that game was more exciting than the Immaculate Reception game," says sportswriter Vito Stellino, who has covered the NFL for more than 50 years. "But there was no controversy and no nickname, and the game is now just remembered as another Staubach comeback."[17] Aesthetically, at least, the Cowboys–49ers game was much more interesting with more points, turnovers and general changes in momentum compared to Pittsburgh and Oakland. If the first 58 minutes of the Steelers and Raiders was monochromatic—black and white, just like the teams' colors—then the first 58 minutes of the Cowboys and 49ers was a Jackson Pollock painting.

Some connoisseurs may prefer the Old Masters, while others may like the more modern approach. The beauty of "Immaculate Saturday" is that there was a little something for everyone.

*   *   *

The offers for his prized possession started coming in even before Baker got to his house. "I did stop on the way home at a prominent auto body shop," he remembers. "I knew the owner real well, and he was a big Steelers fan. He always carried his money—and a lot of money, not just peanuts—in a briefcase. He got his briefcase out and said, 'I'll give you $1,000 right now.'"[18]

No sale.

Baker would not put a price on his special piece of Immaculate Saturday, even when the offers got up into six figures. As the legend of the game and the moment continue to grow, one wonders exactly how much Baker could get for his football, even without authenticity.

Maybe even in the neighborhood of Babe Ruth. Of the fifteen most expensive sports memorabilia items of all time, six belong to Ruth—from his 1933 jersey for which a collector paid $657,250, to a 1920 jersey that sold at auction for $4,415,658.[19] "You come to me with $2 million, and I'd say no," Baker said. "There's a reason for that."[20]

That reason is Sam. The four-day-old baby who arrived at the Baker home just hours before the Immaculate football did, died at the age of 33 from something called adrenocortical carcinoma. It affects only about one in every two million people, but by the time doctors found it in Sam it was already stage-four. "He took it the way God meant it to be," said Jim, his eyes misting over with tears as they often do. A picture of Sam hangs in his living room and he greets it good morning every day. "He didn't go out weak. He went out strong. He knew he was passing. He hugged his kids all the time, and his wife. He asked me if I'd help take care of them."[21]

As so he has. And he also takes care of the football, now a powerful reminder of a son and a relationship that ended much too soon. Tourists show up at Jim Baker's house, strangers stop and point, and church groups will troop in to hear the story of Pittsburgh's most famous football. They end up with a story that's so much more.

"I get to tell the story or remember my son daily," Baker says. "I don't care what family member you lose, very few people get to do that. With that ball, I get to talk about him every day. Every day."[22]

"I understand that emotional attachment between a father and a son," said the man who caught the football, Franco Harris, "and I would like Jim to feel that the whole Steeler family is connected with him. When you think about Jim and his boy, and that connection the ball brings to them, that makes it pretty special."[23]

That's why the ball will likely stay with Baker until the day he dies. He tried one time to trade it to the Steelers for lifetime season tickets, but the team turned him down. It was for the best, he decided, because it made him realize how close he came to losing something so important to him. Now, it would take a monumental offer—something that would create a trust for Sam's children and grandchildren—and even then there would be a stipulation that the ball would never leave Pittsburgh.

"I've been a good steward of this ball for 40 years," he says, his voice starting to shake with emotion. "It's part of my family history, too. Especially my son Sam. It would take a lot to give it up. Even today, I get to thinking about my son, and he's gone now. But this brings his memory back."

"I don't want to see it in somebody else's living room, or somebody else's safe. I would like to see it on display forever."[24]

CHAPTER 2

The System

The road to Immaculate Saturday was a long one for the San Francisco 49ers, and even longer for the Pittsburgh Steelers. The Dallas Cowboys and Oakland Raiders did not travel quite so far or so long, but in the end all four teams ended up headed in the same direction. They were all trying to climb the mountain where the Cowboys had just planted their championship flag.

Many were convinced that the Cowboys would never get there, and in fact, their ascent had been pockmarked by several embarrassing missteps and pratfalls. Born as an expansion team in 1960, the Cowboys went winless their first season and didn't break even until their sixth. But the organization had the foresight to hire Tom Landry, a bright young assistant from the New York Giants, and give him a long-term commitment. Landry had played seven years as a defensive back in New York, compensating for underwhelming physical skills with a keen analytical approach to the game. He took over the Giants' defense while still playing, helping the team to the 1956 NFL title, and essentially created the 4–3 defense that was to become standard throughout the league.

To counteract his own creation, Landry came up with a shifting, multiple offense that presented the defense with confusing looks. Then to stop the offense, he tweaked the 4–3 into the Flex, a variation so complex that hardly any other teams bothered with it. "The term genius gets overused in football," noted NFL Films, "but Tom Landry was a gridiron savant, a brilliant innovator who unlike any coach in the modern era, changed the way football is played on offense and defense."[1]

Landry was so cool, so calculating, especially in his demeanor on the sidelines, that he was accused of lacking emotion. He never screamed or yelled like Lombardi, but instead had an icy stare that players came to dread. "It was like sticking a hundred daggers right through your heart," said a later Dallas quarterback, Danny White. "It was the most painful thing. Fine, make me run a hundred laps, but don't give me that look, whatever you do."[2]

Players openly admitted that their only relationship with their coach was a professional one, and when asked about it, Landry always had the same response. "We're all professionals," he would say. "A coach can't be buddy-buddy with his players and get the job done."[3] Nothing typified this more than Landry's complicated relationship with quarterback Don Meredith, who guided the team through the early losing years.

Meredith masked his uncertainty and insecurity in a fun-loving persona. He was the class clown who sang songs in the huddle, openly talked back to coaches, and found a lot more interesting things to do in Dallas besides quarterback the Cowboys—all of which severely tested Landry's patience. In a 1968 quarterbacks meeting, which in Meredith's mind had stretched on far too long, he began to idly twirl his lit cigar in his fingers. Meredith called it to the attention of his backup, Craig Morton.

"Hey, Curly, watch this one!"

"Don," Landry said, overhearing, "are you listening to me?"

Meredith chomped back on the cigar, but quickly realized he had the lit end now in his mouth. He spit it out, bouncing it off a chalkboard right next to Landry.

"There were ashes everywhere," Morton said later. "Ashes over Coach Landry, as Meredith is spitting and choking." Already trying to stifle a laugh, Morton lost control when Meredith stuck out his tongue to reveal a large, red blister.

"Craig," Landry said evenly, "would you like to leave the room to try and control yourself?"[4]

Another day during practice, when a player intercepted one of Meredith's passes, Meredith chased him down and jokingly threatened to bean him with his helmet. Everyone on the field laughed except for Landry. "Gentlemen," he told them in dead seriousness, "nothing funny ever happens on a football field—if we can help it."[5] Sportswriter Steve Perkins, who covered the Cowboys during these years for the *Dallas Times Herald*, summed up the troubled relationship between coach and quarterback. "Meredith finally came to believe that Landry was a football genius," Perkins wrote. "That is, he believed it intellectually. He never believed it viscerally, and this essential gap probably cost the Cowboys a couple of championships."[6]

No losses were more devastating for Meredith than the two last-second defeats to Green Bay in the 1966 and 1967 NFL title games. In the first, Meredith could not get the team into the end zone from the two-yard line to tie the game and send it to sudden death. The second was another last-second loss played in fifteen-below weather—the Ice Bowl—and Meredith played dreadfully. The Cowboys' only offensive score came on a pass from running back Dan Reeves to Lance Rentzel. "In critical moments Meredith is hampered by a death-wish syndrome," Dr. John Gunn said at the time. "He considers himself unworthy of being a championship quarterback. And when it's all there to grab, he finds a way to fail."[7]

In 1964, when the Cleveland Browns were on their way to an NFL title, the wife of quarterback Frank Ryan began to write a twice-weekly column for the *Cleveland Plain Dealer*. At the time, columns by players' wives were typically about idle gossip or recipes, but Joan Ryan was much more blunt and confrontational. When the Cowboys were playing the Cardinals one year, she noted caustically, "Don Meredith is a loser."[8]

People began to say the same thing about the organization as a whole. When a less talented Cleveland team beat Dallas the following year in the playoffs, Meredith had had enough and retired at the relatively young age of thirty-one. The Browns then came back the following year and humiliated the Cowboys again in the playoffs, 38–14, this time in Dallas. "With all their talent, if you come out and stick it to Dallas early, something happens," said Browns defensive end Jack Gregory. "If you come out fired up and attack them, it seems like they don't want to get hit."[9]

There was no Meredith to blame this time; Craig Morton played miserably in the rainy weather and was booed off the field. "People began to wonder as the Cowboys were always one heartbeat away from the ultimate triumph," wrote sportswriter Jim Murray. "It was the best team in the league, but it kept getting beat by the Cleveland Browns. The Packers kept beating it, too, on things like 'second effort' and 'love' and all the things you couldn't find in the Cowboys' playbook."[10] The team, like its head coach, was said to have a fatal flaw—it lacked that heartbeat of a champion.

Part of the heartbeat may have arrived in 1970 when the Cowboys traded for former Packers defensive back Herb Adderley, and the next year acquired another Packer, tackle Forrest Gregg. Both players were on the downside of Hall of Fame careers, but having played so long and so well for Vince Lombardi, they brought an important intangible to the Cowboys. When they hugged in the Dallas locker room upon their reunion—a black man and a white man in a segregated southern city—mouths dropped open. According to Dave Robinson, a Packer who heard the story from Cowboys defensive back Mel Renfro, "[Renfro] knew right then and there that Dallas would never win the championship until they got that kind of relationship between the black and white players."[11]

Adderley brought a swagger to the team, showing off his championship rings and telling his new teammates what they had to do to get one. The Cowboys responded in 1970, salvaging a seemingly lost season by winning seven straight to end the season, including their first-ever NFC title. But after a last-second 16–13 loss to the Colts in Super Bowl V, a game the Cowboys could have and *should* have won easily, the emotional scars were reopened. "That hurt more than the losses to Green Bay," said perennial All-Pro defensive tackle Bob Lilly. "If we were beaten by forty points, you could just say we were whipped. But we had every opportunity to win."[12] After the game ended, Lilly threw his helmet thirty yards in disgust. Sportswriters derisively called it the best Dallas throw of the day.

Called "Next Year's Champions," and "The Team That Couldn't Win the Big One," Dallas seemed to be going nowhere again in 1971, stuck at 4–3 midway through the season. Craig Morton had taken over for Meredith and quarterbacked the team to Super Bowl V, but injuries and a poor performance had opened the way for a competition with Roger Staubach. Landry—the ultimate system coach—figured it didn't matter who played, and in the Bears game alternated the two quarterbacks on every play, like ships passing in the night. "I think he was saying to himself," noted Staubach, "'They are just two people. They can pass and hand off. The system is fine.' He didn't consider that our styles are different, or that the team needed one player to look to, or how we felt about it."[13]

"Landry had an unbelievable explanation for alternating us," said Morton. "He said, 'You'll be right next to me, so when the next play starts we'll talk before you go in.' First of all, he doesn't have a clue what the next play is going to be because he doesn't know yard and distance. And then you don't have the time to talk about it, because you only have 25 or 30 seconds to get the play off. It was so dumb."[14]

Dumb and futile as it turned out, as Dallas lost the game and Landry was criticized as wishy-washy, out of touch and indecisive. Don Meredith, now safely away from Landry and a bona fide star on *Monday Night Football*, was especially harsh. "It's Landry's responsibility as head coach to pick a quarterback," he said. "Now after he's spent this long with them and he doesn't have any idea which one is best, then get another goddam coach."[15]

"As far as the offensive linemen are concerned, we need a clear-cut quarterback," said offensive tackle Ralph Neely. "We need to know who's back there, so we'll know his tendencies. When you have a 260-pounder trying to run you over, you need to know the guy you're protecting, not wonder who's back there."[16] When sportswriters pressed Neely as to his preference, he said bluntly, "Either damn one. At this point, I don't care."[17]

In the face of mounting criticism from fans, the press and his own players, Landry had to make a decision. But even in defeat, he *still* believed his alternating system would work. "There's nothing wrong with the two-quarterback system," he said after the Chicago game. "It would have worked today if we hadn't made so many mistakes."[18]

But after the loss, Landry threw in the towel and finally made up his mind. In a decision that would impact the NFL for the next decade, launch a dynasty, and create an American hero, he went with Staubach. The former Heisman Trophy winner, naval officer and Vietnam veteran became "Captain America," a clean-cut embodiment of hard work, self sacrifice and moral living. Staubach energized the team with his daring runs out of danger and led Dallas to ten straight wins. The last came in Super Bowl VI against Miami as the Cowboys dominated every phase of the game in a 24–3 victory. "Free at last!" read the headline the next day in the *Dallas Morning News*, as the Cowboys finally exorcised their demons. Tom Landry, the tin man coach with no heart, was smiling broadly as players carried him from the field. "This is a successful end to our 12-year plan," Dallas owner Clint Murchison, Jr., deadpanned in the locker room after the game.[19]

Even as Dallas enjoyed its new success, situations were developing that threatened to topple the team from its perch. Something would have to be done with troublesome running back Duane Thomas, who despite all his talent had become a divisive figure in the Cowboys' locker room. Craig Morton was only twenty-nine years old, and with Staubach entrenched as the starter and Super Bowl hero, was unlikely to accept another year on the bench. "He will ask to be traded and he probably is justified," said Landry. "We will never trade unless we get value, but I can't imagine us not getting value for him. He's at the point where he could be a great quarterback."[20]

Already the Super Bowl champions were starting to break apart and reform. Uneasy is the head that wears the crown.

Dick Nolan had shared almost all the frustrations the Cowboys suffered without much of the success. Nolan played with Landry in New York, and then became a player-coach on the early Cowboy teams. When injuries forced him to retire, Nolan took over full-time as Landry's defensive coordinator, laying the groundwork for the Flex and helping create the team's famous "Doomsday Defense." He spent six years absorbing Landry's system before heading off to San Francisco as head coach in 1968.

It was a team desperate for success after twenty-three years of mostly mediocre football. The 49ers had their individual stars—Y.A. Tittle, Hugh McIlhenny, and Joe "The Jet" Perry—but never could figure out a way to get those stars to challenge for a championship. Symbolic of the team's misfortune was the 1957 season. In October, team founder and owner Tony Morabito suffered a heart attack watching the team play the Bears and died in the stands at Kezar Stadium. "He had lived for the day when the 49ers would hold first place," read newspaper reports, "then missed seeing it by less than an hour."[21]

San Francisco rallied to beat the Bears, take over first, and tie Detroit in the Western Conference with an 8–4 mark. In a special playoff game with the Lions, the team jumped out to a 24–7 lead and was whooping it up in the halftime locker room. "They were very confident that they were going to be opening the champagne," said the Lions' Jack Christiansen, "and their wives had already spent the championship money for fur coats and houses."[22] Instead, Detroit rallied from 20 points behind in the second half, the largest come-from-behind playoff win at the time, and San Francisco lost, 31–27. "Who knows how?" asked Ron Fimrite, then a young fan growing up in San Francisco and later a writer for *Sports Illustrated*. "We were all too stunned to remember. All over the stadium beer cans dropped from the hands of disbelieving fans. It all seemed to happen with a terrible inevitability. And it kept on happening."[23]

That same year the Niners drafted quarterback John Brodie, a great passer from Stanford, and tried to turn him into a runner. In 1961, coach Red Hickey devised the shotgun, a variation of the old single-wing, with the quarterback taking the snap a few yards behind center and then having the option to pass or throw. Brodie alternated with Tittle and Billy Kilmer, and the combination almost blew away the league—49–0 over the Lions, 35–0 over the Rams and 38–24 over the Vikings. "You start to get one quarterback figured out," lamented Detroit linebacker Joe Schmidt, "and another comes in who does something else."[24]

Of course, like most things associated with the Niners, it ended disastrously. In a 31–0 loss to Chicago, the Bears jammed the shotgun by moving their middle linebacker over the center and disrupting the timing. "Everybody said what killed the shotgun was the Bears lining up Bill George on our center," said Hickey, "but that had nothing to do with us losing that game. We fumbled a couple of times and things started to get out of hand. We beat ourselves."[25]

Bears coach Clark Shaughnessy told Hickey after the game not to give up on the shotgun, but the team didn't listen. The Niners traded away the aging Tittle, who went on to New York and led the Giants to three straight Eastern Conference titles. Hickey and the shotgun were both gone after 1962.

Nolan scrapped all that nonsense when he got to San Francisco in 1968. "The chemistry began to change when Dick showed up," said Brodie. "He was as tough as any man I've ever known when it comes to effort expended. If you could measure success by time invested in getting a job done, Dick would be at the top of the list. He drove himself relentlessly."[26] Nolan began by installing Landry's complicated defense, and while it took some time for the system to take hold, by 1970 the team was ready to challenge for the NFC West. Brodie had a sensational season, leading the league in passing and winning NFL MVP honors. The Niners won the NFC West, upset favored Minnesota on the road in the playoffs, and then returned home to host the NFC Championship in the last game at Kezar Stadium.

Standing in their way was Tom Landry and the Dallas Cowboys. The pupil would try to beat the teacher with his own blackboard.

The teams knew each other intimately. During the summer the Cowboys trained at California Lutheran College in Thousand Oaks, while the Niners were in Santa Barbara. They scrimmaged at least twice a year and had played in the regular season the year before. "We knew those guys pretty well," said Niners linebacker Skip Vanderbundt. "My old coach Tommy Prothro once said you play your best games against your enemies and your friends. It's the guys you don't know that you better be afraid of."[27]

"This game will be the only time all year in a college game, high school game, semi-pro game or pro game where you will see both defenses in exactly the same alignment," said Cowboys assistant Ermal Allen. "San Francisco and Dallas may do things differently out of that alignment, but they will line up exactly the same way."[28]

Nolan faced the same challenge against Landry that Landry did against Vince Lombardi. Once both assistants with the Giants—Landry on defense, Lombardi on offense—the two had gone on to successful head coaching careers. But Landry never could beat Lombardi when it mattered most, namely in the playoffs, and those failures set the tone for the NFL in the 1960s—Lombardi and the Packers a dynasty; Landry and the Cowboys a bridesmaid.

Now as the 1970s dawned, it was Landry trying to hold off his former protégée. "Dick Nolan ran the same defense as we did," said tight end Pettis Norman, "and I think that made it easier for us, because we had to run against our own defense in scrimmages. And I felt very confident against the 49ers. The whole team did."[29]

Dallas intercepted Brodie twice to set up touchdowns, and won the game, 17–10 to advance to the Super Bowl. The following year, San Francisco again won the division and faced the Cowboys in the NFC Championship, this time in Dallas. It was another close, defensive game, described by the Niners' Earl Edwards as "an alley fight with white dinner gloves."[30] Once again, a Brodie interception played a key role. In a scoreless game in the second quarter, and back by his own goal line, Brodie threw a screen pass right to the Cowboys' George Andrie who lumbered down to the two. It set up a decisive touchdown as Dallas won, 14–3.

"We had a blitz on, and it was my job to head upfield and contain wide," Andrie said afterwards in the locker room.

Overhearing the comment, linebacker Dave Edwards replied, "George, we didn't have a blitz on."

Believing that Edwards was kidding him, Andrie turned to another linebacker, Chuck Howley.

"Hey, Chuck," he yelled. "Didn't we have a blitz on?"

Howley shook his head no.

"Then what was I doing upfield?" Andrie wondered.

"I guess," laughed Edwards, "that it was the pure instinct of a veteran pro."[31]

Over in the other locker room, Brodie contemplated his miserable line for the afternoon—30 passes attempted, 14 completed, and three intercepted.

"Were the Cowboys taking something away from you?" writers asked him.

"Yeah," Brodie answered. "Points."[32]

Points figured to be hard to come by in 1972 as Brodie turned 37 years old and injuries started to become more of a problem. But with a defense that remained stout, and division competitors that didn't look appreciably better, San Francisco figured to have at least one more good shot at the Super Bowl.

Chapter 3

The Blessed Virgin Is Proud of Me

On January 14, 2018, the Minnesota Vikings and New Orleans Saints playoff game featured an ending that would rank with any in NFL postseason history. The Saints had just kicked a field goal to take a 24–23 lead with only 25 seconds to play. With only ten seconds left, Minnesota had no time outs and the ball on its own 39-yard line. Surely, New Orleans defenders would knock down a desperation pass, advancing the Saints to the NFC Championship game the following week.

Instead, quarterback Case Keenum and wide receiver Stefon Diggs hooked up on a play that transformed reality into surreality. Diggs caught the ball some thirty yards from the goal line with the idea of immediately getting out of bounds for a field goal attempt. But when a Saints defender whiffed on an attempted tackle, Diggs turned around and saw no one between him and the end zone. He sprinted for the winning score as time expired, and then rifled his helmet across the field.

"Unbelievable!" yelled broadcaster Joe Buck, calling the game on national television.

"Unbelievable!" said Vikings defensive end Everson Griffen." This is the first time I'm ever out of words."[1] Diggs had no trouble finding words in the exultant Minnesota locker room, except when someone asked him about 1975.

"1975?" he said. "I think I was still swimming at the time."[2]

1975?

The Hail Mary.

"I actually got a call from a reporter," said Roger Staubach, "and I don't know how he got my home number, but he was calling from the Vikings' locker room after that play [the Diggs touchdown]. He was talking about the ending and if I thought it made up for the Hail Mary pass. To get a call like that tells you how much people remember it."[3]

Staubach's fingerprints are all over the Hail Mary. He drew it up, executed it and named the play that along with the Immaculate Reception stand as the greatest playoff endings in NFL history. Dallas had the ball on the 50-yard line trailing Minnesota 14–10 in a 1975 divisional playoff game. Only 32 seconds remained when Staubach improvised a desperation heave that Drew Pearson somehow caught on his hip for the winning touchdown.

To this day, the Vikings believe Pearson pushed off defender Nate Wright and should have been called for pass interference. Fans in the stadium vented their anger by throwing bottles on the field, one of which hit an official in the head and knocked him out of the game, and their anger has not cooled in forty-plus years. For many, the play became a symbol for the team's frustration and failure, headlined by blowout losses in four Super Bowls. That Vikings team never got a chance in the Super Bowl, even though coach Bud Grant called it the greatest he ever had in Minnesota.

"After the game I said I just closed my eyes and said a Hail Mary, so now it's known as the Hail Mary game," said Staubach. "The term played a role in it. Before then, it was the bomb or the alley oop. The Hail Mary is at the top of the list as far as a memorable term. As a Catholic kid, I think the Blessed Virgin is proud of me."[4]

It was perhaps Staubach's most memorable comeback, but not his first. That would take place on Immaculate Saturday in San Francisco.

Having sat out most of the year with a separated shoulder, Staubach had played only bits and pieces of games late in the season, usually in mop-up relief of Craig Morton. He fully expected to watch the 49er playoff game from the sidelines. "When I came back I didn't say I wanted my job back," he remembered. "Of course, I did, but Craig was playing well and I supported him. When coach Landry made the decision to put me in the game, I really think he thought we had lost."[5]

Entering the game late in the third quarter with his team down 28–16, Staubach engineered three scoring drives that brought Dallas back from the dead to win, 30–28. Two touchdowns came in the final two minutes of play. "I just remember all the players going crazy. We had a lot of close games, but there was nothing like the enthusiasm on the sidelines at the end of that game. Guys were jumping up and down, rolling on the ground."[6] Many Cowboys would point to that moment—not the Hail Mary—when the legend of Roger Staubach was born. From that day on, the team believed that no matter how dire the circumstances, Staubach would somehow find a way to win.

Staubach's will to win and competitive nature burned long before his eleven-year NFL career, and would continue long after. It was that will that led him to a Heisman Trophy at the Naval Academy and kept him focused on a football career during a four-year tour of duty in Vietnam. In Vietnam, Staubach wired the Cowboys to send more footballs because he kept wearing them out in passing drills. Toward the end of his tour, he took his two-week furlough to attend training camp and find out if he could still play competitively. "I remember Staubach coming in," said backup quarterback Jerry Rhome. "[Camp] is just starting, so we're out there in shorts, taking it easy. And here comes Roger Staubach, fully dressed; he's got his helmet, shoulder pads, the whole works. And I turned around to [Don] Meredith and say, 'We're in trouble, man.'"[7]

Flash forward thirty or forty years and the competitive fires still burn. Staubach launched a successful commercial real estate business after his football career ended. It became a multi-billion dollar company by 2008 when it merged with financial giant Jones Lang LaSalle, where Staubach still works as an executive chairman. He's also still on the field, and every Thanksgiving takes part in a Turkey Bowl flag football game. It used to feature a lot of former Cowboys like Pearson and Cliff Harris, but now the 77-year-old Staubach is usually quarterbacking against guys half his age. "Roger is the gold standard," says former Cowboys quarterback turned broadcaster Babe Laufenberg. "He wins the Heisman, graduates from the Naval Academy, serves the country, comes back, wins the Super Bowl, wins another, goes on to have a multimillion-dollar international real estate company, and he's in the Hall of Fame. I said to Roger one day, 'Roger, do you ever get tired of accomplishing things?'"[8]

For so many fans, his greatest accomplishment remains his eleven-year NFL career. Twenty-four times he helped the Cowboys win a game when trailing in the fourth quarter, including the last regular season game he ever played. On the final weekend of the 1979 regular season and with the NFC East title on the line, Staubach actually led two comebacks against the Redskins. Dallas trailed 17–0 in the first half, and then 34–21 in the fourth quarter. That last deficit was overcome when Staubach engineered two touchdowns in the final two minutes, including a game-winning touchdown pass to Tony Hill with less than a minute to play. "I have a confidence that I will never quit until the game's over," he said. "I've lost quite a few games where I thought we could come back, but I also think I've been successful as an athlete by having a strong, never quit attitude. When I'm the quarterback and I walk on the field, I know that some way, somehow, we are going to walk off the winner."[9]

They might have the next week too, except that Staubach could not pull off one last miracle. In a playoff game against the Rams, he threw a late touchdown pass to Jay Saldi that gave Dallas a 19–14 lead, but paid the price for it. Linebacker Hacksaw Reynolds drove Staubach into the ground, causing a concussion. After the Rams went ahead 21–19, there was time enough to come back, but Staubach couldn't ride to the rescue and Dallas lost.

Dallas lost the game, its season, and its quarterback. The concussion, coming off a season in which he suffered several others, convinced Staubach it was time to retire, even though he was coming off a great year. He visited a concussion specialist who told him that the next one could cause serious problems. In light of what's known about concussions, brain injury and CTE—especially among players of the 1960s and 70s—Staubach knows he made the right decision. "I'm still healthy and functional," he said in 2018, "but I do worry about it. I've got friends and teammates that are in really bad shape—teammates at Navy and the Cowboys with some serious dementia problems that need full time care. That's why they keep guys out of the game now. If they had kept me out for a week after I got knocked out, it would have made a difference. Because after I got knocked out I felt OK and played the next week, but the brain hasn't had time to heal yet."[10]

Among those former teammates are Hall of Famers Tony Dorsett and Mel Renfro. Dorsett had a brain test in 2009 that revealed possible CTE. He was just relieved to find a diagnosis for his memory loss and outbursts of anger. "It's like a fog," he said. "That's the only way I can explain it. I can't get out of it, and I know—it's just a weird feeling and that can make me get real frustrated, if I'm not careful."[11] That's the way it was described by teammate and defensive back Mel Renfro, who estimates he suffered nine concussions in a fourteen-year career. When a concussion began to clear toward the end of one game, Renfro sat on the bench unaware of who or where he was.[12]

Healthy and active as he nears 80, Staubach has no such problems, and by all accounts has led a blessed life. He's been married for more than fifty years, has a loving family, is a multi-millionaire many times over, and is an NFL Hall of Famer. No wonder Staubach has been called "Captain America," and more than thirty years after his retirement is still considered an American legend. "Roger Staubach was and is my hero," said former teammate and linebacker Thomas "Hollywood" Henderson, who credited

Staubach with saving his life from drug addiction. "You may grow up wanting to be like a lot of people, but if you're lucky in life, you will be in the presence of somebody who is exactly what you want to be, but you don't even know it."[13]

Even Staubach admits that his signature moment as a player came in the Hail Mary game in Minnesota, not on Immaculate Saturday in San Francisco. If not the greatest Staubach comeback, the win over the 49ers was the first—something like being the first Model T to roll off the assembly line or the first Macintosh computer born at Apple. "It isn't as well known because we lost the championship game the next week to the Redskins," said Staubach. "The Redskins just shut us down, and that took a lot of enthusiasm out of it. If we had gone on to beat the Redskins and gone on to the Super Bowl, then the game would have become much bigger than it was."[14]

CHAPTER 4

Rooney U

While the Niners had suffered twenty-three years before getting their first taste of glory, Pittsburgh wandered in the playoff desert for forty years, and like Moses, wondered if it would ever get to see the Promised Land.

One of the oldest franchises in the NFL, the Steelers came to epitomize the term "lovable loser." The lovable part came from owner Art Rooney, Sr., who founded the team in 1933. Rooney was a lifelong resident of Pittsburgh, growing up and living in the same northside neighborhood his entire life. The avuncular Rooney had a penchant for glad-handing, smoking cigars and picking winners at the track, and it was his winning horse bets that helped finance his entry into the league. He really never left the track, even while running the Steelers. When the team had the number-one draft choice in 1970 and used it to select quarterback Terry Bradshaw, Rooney stayed for the announcement and then promptly left. "After the first choice, the other choices are like the races they run after the Kentucky Derby," he said. "Everybody goes home."[1]

Rooney's "hail fellow well met" personality earned him the lifelong loyalty of friends, and the admiration and respect from the few enemies he had. Unfortunately, it proved a detriment in running a professional football team. Rooney ran the Steelers much like a neighborhood bar, hiring friends and cronies as coaches and executives, and then holding on to them far too long out of loyalty. His biographers noted that Rooney "never hired coaches with the same cool calculation he picked horses. As a result, the fate of the Steelers rode on men of wildly uneven skills. Art lived more and more in the familiar habits and friendships that had always sustained him."[2]

From 1933 through 1971—a span of thirty-nine seasons—the Steelers had a winning record exactly seven times. One of those seasons, 1943,

World War II forced the team to merge with the Philadelphia Eagles, a combination that sportswriters mockingly called the "Steagles." (When the team also briefly merged with the Chicago Cardinals during the war, the team was officially known as "Car-Pitt." Of course, cynics began calling them the "Carpets.")

The franchise always appeared to be on the brink of disaster, both on the field and off. In 1938, Rooney's team had so many injuries—not unusual at a time when there were only thirty men on a roster—that he petitioned the league to postpone a game against Cleveland. The other teams felt such an embarrassment would hurt the NFL's credibility, and one owner moved to get the franchise revoked and Art kicked out of the league. Rooney tried to make up for the shortages by buying players, trading away first-round draft picks in 1939 and 1941. The trades always seemed to work out better for the other teams, in this case the Bears, who used those picks to acquire Hall of Famers Sid Luckman and George McAfee.

Art was also a boxer in his younger days and perhaps he transferred some of that pugnacity to his franchise. Ernie Stautner was an undersized Hall of Fame defensive tackle who earned a justified reputation for violence and toughness. During one game, he suffered a compound fracture of his thumb. "I'm figuring now he's going to ask for the doctor, and he may have to go to the hospital because this thing could get infected," said teammate and linebacker Andy Russell, "and he says, 'Give me some tape.' So they throw him some tape and he just starts taping this huge ball. He plays the entire game. Never misses a down. I'm just astounded, and he's using this hand that is broken as a club. He's beating people with it. After the game, we go into the locker room and he says, 'Hey Doc, I think I got a problem.'"[3]

With men like Stautner, Pittsburgh got the reputation as a brutally physical team that could punish the opposition but usually come out on the wrong end of the score. When the rest of the league went to the explosive T-formation in the 1940s, the Steelers doggedly stuck with the old single wing until 1951. "The single wing takes too much out of your players," Bears owner George Halas told Rooney in 1950. "You do kick the hell out of the opposition physically, but the opposition is still getting points and beating you. Remember, the other team takes that beating once; your team takes it every week."[4] Switching to the T, Pittsburgh promptly sank to fourth place.

Beginning in 1951, Pittsburgh finished in third place or lower for eleven straight years and nineteen of twenty. So often were the Steelers outclassed that newspapers began calling the team "Rooney U," suggesting that they were nothing more than college boys in over their heads against the pros. After a 38–10 pasting at the hands of the New York Giants in 1956, coach Walt Kiesling called the effort "disgraceful," said that most of the players were simply amateurs getting paid for pretending to be pros, and promised a get-tough attitude the rest of the season.[5] It didn't help, as the Steelers finished at 5–7.

By the late 1950s, Art's children were getting old enough to help him run the team. Dan, John, and Patrick would eventually join Art in running the franchise, and while Tim took to his father's penchant for the horses and focused on harness racing, he still suffered with the rest of the family. "When I needed a haircut," he said, "I'd sit down and I'd start praying, *'Please. Don't ask me about the football team. Please don't ask me about the football team.'* Or I'd pray nobody recognized me."[6]

The situation got so bad that in 1959 Art asked the Pittsburgh Public Auditorium Authority to release the team from its two-year lease at Pitt Stadium because of low attendance. There were whispers that Rooney was entertaining offers to move the team out of Pittsburgh, and that pushed the city to help finance what became Three Rivers Stadium. Even when Rooney signed a forty-year lease for the new stadium in 1964, the agreement had an escape clause that would let the team leave after 13 years. Rooney loved his hometown, but it was a love tinged with the reality of losing.

It was a fourth-place finish in 1968 that finally turned around the franchise. When Rooney decided not to retain coach Bill Austin he turned to his son Dan rather than go to his old-boy network. After preliminary discussions fizzled with college coaches Ara Parseghian and Joe Paterno, Dan Rooney settled on Baltimore Colts assistant Chuck Noll. It looked like a disastrous hire when Noll won just one game in his first season and lost thirteen in a row. When a reporter asked Rooney Sr., if hiring Noll was a mistake, Art answered with an emphatic no. "Chuck never once lost his poise and he didn't lose the ballplayers. I turned to my sons and said, 'Well, you've got yourselves a coach. This guy's got it.'"[7]

Pittsburgh's 1–13 record tied Chicago for worst in the league, and the Steelers won a coin flip with the Bears for the overall number one draft pick, which they used on Bradshaw. Coupled with the first round selection of defensive tackle "Mean" Joe Greene the previous year, it gave the team a solid foundation of future Hall of Famers to build around. Noll's first three drafts produced an incredible haul—Hall of Famers in Greene, Bradshaw, Jack Ham and Mel Blount, along with solid starters in L.C. Greenwood, Jon Kolb, Ron Shanklin, Dwight White, Gerry Mullins, and Frank

Lewis. Previous Steeler coaches had tried to rebuild with veterans and traded away many of the team's draft picks, a practice Noll stopped. "Any time you upgrade yourself anyplace, you do it," he said. "You build a great football team in bits and pieces. One guy doesn't come in and make that much of a difference."[8]

Infused with new talent, and guided by Noll, the Steelers began to see daylight. In 1970, transferred to the new American Conference after the NFL-AFL merger was finalized, the team went a respectable 5–9 and actually had a chance to win the weak AFC Central with two weeks to play. The next season, they upped the win total to six and showed drastic improvement on defense. With no teams standing out in the mediocre division, Pittsburgh suddenly became a trendy pick to contend in 1972. "One would defy history and flatly predict a division championship for the long-suffering Pittsburgh Steelers," wrote *Sports Illustrated*, "whose rebuilding program has now prevailed through six U.S. Presidents, 16 head coaches and 40 haggard years."[9]

"I thought we should have won in 1971," said Noll. "The team failed in the stretch when it counted most. Most of our young players have the experience now. I am very optimistic."[10]

"It's been said, 'This is the year' so many times before that it doesn't mean anything," added Bradshaw. "We want to do it, not talk about it. We'll prove ourselves when the season starts."[11]

Much like the Steelers, the Raiders were dominated by the force of personality of one man. But unlike the personable Rooney, Al Davis was brash, pugnacious and confrontational, befitting his youth spent on the streets of Brooklyn. While Rooney might extend a warm hand of friendship and a cigar, Davis might offer a handshake while sticking a knife in the back with the other hand. And if he offered a cigar, best to check it for explosives.

Oakland floundered as an original AFL franchise and got progressively worse its first three seasons, capped with a 1–13 record in 1962 when the Raiders finished last in offense and next-to-last in defense. Fans mostly ignored the team and stayed away from Frank Youell field, a tiny, decrepit structure named after a local undertaker. "There were no lights," remembered the Raiders' quarterback and later coach Tom Flores. "There were a few shower heads. The water was hot if you got in early."[12]

Davis changed everything when he arrived as coach and general manager in 1963 after serving as an assistant with the Chargers. He changed the colors to the now-iconic silver and black, installed a new long passing game and found the players to run it. In came men like massive defensive lineman "Big" Ben Davidson, 6'8" and 275 pounds, known as much for piling on after the whistle as sacking quarterbacks. In came quarterback Daryle Lamonica in a trade with Buffalo, and he immediately began executing Davis's vertical passing game. Lamonica threw 30 touchdown passes in 1967 and another 34 in 1969, efforts that earned him AFL MVP honors both seasons, and an enduring nickname—"The Mad Bomber." "Our philosophy was attack, attack, attack," Lamonica noted. "If you had a weakness we would go right after it. Most teams couldn't keep up with us."[13]

Most importantly, Davis changed the team's image and personality. The Raiders became an extension of Davis on the field—"pro football's Hells Angels"[14]—combative, aggressive, and willing to cut corners when necessary to win. "They'll break your jaw with an elbow," observed one sportswriter. "They knock you down, step on your face with a cleated shoe and then pivot. They are proud of being the game's bully, the roughneck who will bust up the saloon at the toss of a coin."[15]

The results were almost immediate, as the Raiders went 10–4 in Davis's first year, and starting in 1965 embarked on a streak of sixteen straight winning seasons. Oakland left Youell Field in 1966, moving into the brand-new Oakland Coliseum, and record crowds began to show up. Davis relinquished the coaching duties that same year to briefly become AFL commissioner, but he remained managing general partner and the team kept winning. The Raiders went 13–1 in 1967, and even a Super Bowl loss to the mighty Green Bay Packers could neither diminish their success nor cloud their future.

Many more championships were expected, but while the Raiders rang up victories and division titles, they could not return to the Super Bowl. Oakland lost three straight conference championships—to the Jets in 1968, the Chiefs in 1969 and the Colts in 1970—and each time the team that beat them went on to win the Super Bowl. Davis changed coaches in 1969, figuring young John Madden could get the team over the final hurdle, but the Raiders always seemed to fall just short. Particularly galling was the loss to the bitter rival Chiefs in the last AFL Championship game in January 1970. Oakland had beaten Kansas City twice during the regular season and was playing at home, but Lamonica threw four interceptions in a 17–7 defeat. "They couldn't play it safe," said Chiefs linebacker Willie Lanier. "When they're ahead of you, they whipsaw you, but when they're behind, they're a very predictable team."[16]

The Raiders did not play poorly in 1971 but shockingly missed the playoffs for the first time since 1966. Lamonica dropped to only sixteen touchdown passes and key injuries hampered the Oakland defense, especially in a three-game slide late in the season that cost the team a playoff spot. Another key loss was receiver Warren Wells, a two-time Pro Bowler and Lamonica's primary deep threat, who was charged before the season with violation of parole on a previous attempted-rape conviction and never played again in the NFL. The Raiders still could have made the playoffs by beating Kansas City in a showdown game on December 12 but lost to the Chiefs, 16–14.

While certainly not in crisis mode, the Raiders entered 1972 with plenty of issues. Deep threat Wells was gone, and the offense needed a compliment to stretch the field for the sure-handed Fred Biletnikoff. They tried to address that in the draft by taking Mike Siani in the first round and Cliff Branch in the fourth. Even more troubling was a growing concern at quarterback, where Lamonica seemed to steadily be losing his effectiveness. His passing numbers—completions, percentage, yards, and touchdowns—had dropped for three straight years, and at age thirty-one he was becoming more injury-prone. It was an injury early in the 1970 AFC Championship that may have cost Oakland the game and a trip to the Super Bowl. Behind Lamonica on the depth chart were the ageless George Blanda, good in spots but not a serious long-term option, and the untested Ken Stabler.

But Oakland had a lot of everything else, and going into the season most experts saw them retaking the division crown from Kansas City. "They have depth, striking power, defense, a good kicking game and a tradition of winning," boasted *Sports Illustrated*.[17] They also still had Al Davis, still plotting and scheming, trying to figure out a way to return the team to his personal credo—"Just Win, Baby."

Oakland, Pittsburgh, Dallas, and San Francisco would rate as strong favorites not only to win their divisions but also contest for the Super Bowl. Coming off a Super Bowl season, Dallas was once against expected to win the NFC East, although the Cowboys would get a challenge from George Allen's surprising Washington Redskins. In just his first year in 1971, Allen had taken a moribund franchise to its first playoff game in more than a quarter century. The Redskins had lost that opening round game in San Francisco, but had served notice that Allen's "The Future Is Now" strategy of building around aging veterans would make them dangerous.

Allen had come to the Redskins from the Rams, a talented team that like Dallas typically stumbled in the playoffs. The Rams still had former league MVP Roman Gabriel at quarterback and they expected to fight it out with the Niners in the NFC West. The NFC Central seemed to be locked up by the Minnesota Vikings, a team coming off four straight division titles. Minnesota had a rugged defense, but had struggled in recent years with poor quarterback play. The Vikings looked to solve the problem in the off-season by reacquiring former star Fran Tarkenton, whom they had traded away five years earlier. Detroit was a possibility in the Central, but Green Bay still languished in the post–Lombardi era.

The AFC West figured to be another dogfight between Oakland and Kansas City, just as it had for the past six years. The teams had finished first or second in the division every year since 1966, with the Chiefs' last-second win over the Raiders in the next-to-last game of the 1971 season giving them the title. Even with Kansas City's double-overtime loss to Miami in the playoffs—helped in no small part by two shocking field goal misses by reliable Jan Stenerud—the 1972 AFC West looked to come down to a December meeting between the Chiefs and Raiders in Oakland.

Miami was clearly a team on the rise, and coach Don Shula had performed a miracle almost as quickly as George Allen. Born in 1966, the Dolphins had a losing record for four straight years, including a 3–10–1 mark the year before Shula arrived. Shula transformed that to 10–4 and a playoff berth in 1970, and then an AFC East championship and Super Bowl berth in 1971. Much of it was discipline and hard work, and while the players grumbled about it, such as Shula occasionally conducting four-a-day practices in training camp, they also realized they were getting better. "It's 90 degrees, and guys are just at their wits' end," said running back Larry Csonka of the practices. "But it's Coach Shula and he's working just as hard, sweating just as much as we are, so you just kept going."[18]

The Dolphins had shut out Baltimore 21–0 in the 1971 AFC Championship game, and after winning a Super Bowl just two years before, the Colts expected again to contend, but many of its championship stars were aging, including quarterback Johnny Unitas, who would turn 39 a week before the season kicked off. Baltimore collapsed in 1972 and won only five games, its first losing season in sixteen years and the last one for Unitas in Baltimore.

Pittsburgh fans couldn't help but wince every time they thought of Unitas, for he was a hometown guy drafted by the Steelers in 1955, but let go in training camp. With four quarterbacks fighting for three jobs, Unitas was the odd man out, in part because team officials thought "he was too dumb to remember the plays."[19] Coach Walt Kiesling took the blame for that, but in turn blamed Rooney and the front office. All Unitas did was win three NFL titles, three league MVP awards, and end up in the Hall of

Fame. While the Steelers searched for years to find a quarterback, they couldn't help but look at Unitas and wonder, "What if?"

Now, with an improving Bradshaw at the helm, Noll at coach, and with a bevy of young talent, Pittsburgh was a trendy choice in the AFC Central. The primary competition would come from Cleveland where the Browns were traditional powers and defending division champs. The Browns did make the playoffs again, but a December visit to Pittsburgh most certainly convinced them that these were not the same old Steelers.

Pittsburgh would open the season at home against Oakland, a game that would certainly provide the young Steelers with a barometer for their championship hopes. San Francisco figured to have an easier time at home with a rebuilding San Diego team, while in Dallas the Cowboys would begin defense of their championship against the Eagles with yet another quarterback change. This time, it was a decision completely out of the hands of Tom Landry.

CHAPTER 5

Rivalry—Part I

There is no reason that the Cowboys and 49ers ever should have developed a rivalry. They were not connected by geography, history or divisional alignment. When the Cowboys began play in 1960 they were placed in the same NFL West as San Francisco, but the next year moved into the East and created rivalries with teams they played twice a year such as the Eagles, Redskins and Giants.

Under new head coach Tom Landry the expansion Cowboys were a rag-tag bunch built around castoffs from other teams. They were allowed to select from the other NFL teams a group of players that had not been protected—mostly, the old, the lame and the halt. The prize was receiver Frank Clarke who came from the Browns, a team with so much talent at the time that it couldn't hide it all. Clarke went on to have an outstanding eight-year career with the Cowboys, leading the NFL in receiving average and touchdown catches in 1962, even though he missed the last two games with injuries.

From San Francisco, Dallas picked up defensive lineman John Gonzaga, end Fred Dugan and linebacker Jerry Tubbs. Gonzaga and Dugan lasted only one season with the Cowboys before moving on, but Tubbs played seven seasons at middle linebacker, earning Pro Bowl honors in 1962. The former University of Oklahoma All-American became a mainstay, holding down the position until Lee Roy Jordan was ready to become a full-time starter.[1]

Like most expansion teams the Cowboys struggled mightily in their first season. While competitive in most of its games, the team lost eleven of twelve and managed only a tie with the Giants. On November 20 in the season's ninth week, the Cowboys hosted San Francisco at the Cotton Bowl and played another strong game. When Eddie LeBaron threw a 76-yard scoring pass to Clarke, the Cowboys took a 14–9 lead in the fourth quarter. But the problem with that Dallas team was defense and as happened so often that season, the lead did not hold up. San Francisco scored seventeen straight points and won the first-ever meeting between the teams, 26–14. The 49ers finished the year at 7–5, just a game behind Green Bay in the NFL West. The Cowboys ended at 0–11–1.

Dallas had improved significantly when the teams met again in 1963, just two weeks before President Kennedy's assassination. Before the season, *Sports Illustrated* took notice of the Cowboys' growth and talent and predicted Dallas would win its division, noting that "the youngest club in the Eastern Division may very well be the best."[2] Instead, the team dropped its first four games and six of its first seven. When the teams met at Kezar Stadium, the Cowboys again took a second-half lead and again gave it away. Journeyman quarterback Lamar McHan burned Dallas with three touchdown passes as San Francisco held on to win, 31–24.

If things had just broken a little differently, McHan might have been known as the quarterback of the Packers' dynasty. At Green Bay in 1959, Vince Lombardi's first year, he actually beat out Bart Starr for the starting job. "McHan was big and strong and athletic and could throw a football through a brick wall," said receiver Gary Knafelc. "He was strong in his beliefs and confident, but he had a temper and a short fuse if things didn't go his way."[3]

They certainly didn't go McHan's way after a shoulder injury to end the year. That opened the door for Starr, who took over for good at halftime of the Steelers game in 1960. Upset at getting pulled, McHan had a little too much to drink on the plane ride back home and wanted to confront Lombardi. Teammate Paul Hornung tried to talk him out of it, but McHan found Lombardi and his assistant coaches at a local restaurant. "If Mac had not spoken up, I'm sure Vince would have started him the next week," said Hornung. "He never started another game and was traded soon after. No one told coach Lombardi what to do."[4]

Dallas got its first-ever win over San Francisco in week nine of the 1965 season, a game that might have been the most pivotal in the history of the franchise up to that point. The Cowboys were once again expected to contend in the NFL East, but five straight losses, climaxed by a 22–13 defeat to lowly Pittsburgh, had the franchise and Tom Landry on the brink of disaster. In his first five-plus seasons in Dallas, Landry had won only 24 games and local fans and media were calling for his head. After the Pittsburgh loss, Landry addressed the team in the locker room. "In the six years I have been with the Cowboys," he said, "this is the first time I've felt truly ashamed of the team's performance." Landry's voice was cracking, but he tried to continue. "Maybe the fault is the system, with the approach we..." and at that point, the supposedly unemotional Tom Landry began to cry.[5]

He fully expected to be fired, but the scene became a watershed moment in the franchise's history. The next week at the Cotton Bowl, Dallas rallied from behind in the fourth quarter to beat the 49ers, 39–31. It triggered a five-game winning streak that pushed the Cowboys to their first-ever post-season appearance. Over the next twenty seasons, Dallas failed to make the playoffs only once. "We saw the real man that day," said defensive tackle Bob Lilly. "He was crying because he felt he had let us down. We never forgot that moment. It was the turning point for the Dallas Cowboys."[6]

It was also a turning point in the Cowboys–49ers series. After losing three of four games against San Francisco through 1967, Dallas didn't lose to San Francisco again for more than a decade. Most of the games were close and usually decided by a touchdown or less. Even in 1977 when a dominant Cowboys team went on to win the Super Bowl, the game at Candlestick Park was a wild 42–35 affair not decided until the very end.

The closest the 49ers could get was a 24–24 tie on Thanksgiving night in 1969, a game the Cowboys rallied to tie with a late touchdown. The Niners were on their way to a dismal 4–8–2 season, in part because of some horrendous kicking problems. In his last of his eleven years with the team, Tommy Davis kicked half the season and made only three of ten field goal attempts. The 49ers then turned their placekicking over to a Yugoslav import named Momcilo Gavric.

Gavric came to America in 1967, lured by the fledgling North American Soccer League, and soon became a fan favorite for his athleticism and full-throttle playing style. He eventually won championships with the Oakland Clippers and Dallas Tornadoes, and it was while playing for Oakland that Gavric came to the attention of the kicking-starved 49ers. After signing a deal through the rest of the season, "Gabbo" became the oldest rookie in NFL history at age thirty-one.

On Thanksgiving night, Gavric made both of his extra points and a fourth-quarter field goal that gave San Francisco a brief lead. But on the whole, he fared even worse than Davis, hitting only three of eleven field goals on the season, none of them over forty yards, and actually missing a couple of extra points. The 49ers had seen enough and traded for Bruce Gossett in the offseason, ending Gavric's brief career.

Gavric worked installing carpets for a couple of years before heading back to pro soccer as a player-coach with the San Jose Earthquakes, and then coached for several more seasons. Although he landed with the first wave of the foreign-born, soccer-style kickers that would revolutionize the league, Gavric is now little more than a footnote in NFL history, as in 2007 punter Sal Rocca broke his record as the NFL's oldest rookie at age thirty-three. "The team was not so good," Gavric said of his brief stint with the Niners. "If they got within 40 yards of the end zone, I would need to try a field goal. Not many tries were close."[7]

The 49ers were just as bad in 1979 and possibly much worse, winning only two of fourteen games in Bill Walsh's rookie coaching season. About the only attraction that season was the return of O.J. Simpson.

Simpson was a native of the San Francisco area and former Heisman winner who had smashed all sorts of rushing records during his ten seasons in Buffalo. But O.J. had accumulated a lot of mileage on a thirty-one year old body and injuries had slowed him considerably. The Bills saw how his rushing totals had declined precipitously the past three seasons and were looking for a graceful way to unload the future Hall of Famer, if only they could find a team willing to take O.J. off their hands.

Enter "Trader" Joe Thomas.

Thomas earned his reputation honestly after he dismantled the championship Colts teams of the late '60s and early '70s. "If you're going to spring clean," he said, "you have to do it from top to bottom."[8] His brusque, heavy-handed approach forced the exit of such legends at Tom Matte, Jerry Logan, and the seemingly untouchable Johnny Unitas. "Thomas doesn't talk with anybody on this team," Unitas said shortly before he was cut loose in a trade to San Diego. "He says what he wants done [and] he gives the orders."[9] Such moves earned him the enmity of Colts fans, but in the end they proved successful. The draft picks the team acquired helped the team rebound from 2–12 in 1974 to division titles the next three seasons.

Fired by the Colts, Thomas came to San Francisco as general manager in 1977 still wheeling and dealing. One of his biggest moves was the trade that brought Simpson back to the Bay area at a staggering cost—five draft picks, including a number-one, two number-twos, a number-three and a number-four over the next three seasons. "I was a 49er fan when I was a kid and I've never stopped being a 49er fan," said an ecstatic Simpson at the time of the deal. "Hopefully I can get here what I couldn't get there, and that is a championship."[10]

It was not to be. One year removed from knee surgery and suffering from arthritis, Simpson was barely able to practice, much less play. Thomas could not duplicate his success in Baltimore and lasted only two seasons, in part because he gave up so much to get Simpson. O.J. signed a three-year deal, but made it only through one; the 1979 season was his last in San Francisco and the NFL. His totals for the year were a depressing 460 yards rushing with three touchdowns.

One of those touchdowns came in the week two loss to Dallas. Simpson ran over from a yard out in the second quarter and finished with 43 yards, but the Cowboys went on to win, 21–13. At the end of the season San Francisco's two-year mark stood at 4–24, the worst stretch in franchise history. But with Thomas and Simpson gone, and Walsh now in control, better times were ahead. "That 1978 team might have been one of the worst NFL teams ever," said 49er center Randy Cross. "But the 1979 team might have been one of the best 2–14 teams ever."[11] The ground was being laid for a dynasty.

But first, the Niners had to endure one more beating from the Cowboys. In 1980, the teams met in Dallas and San Francisco was humiliated, 59–14. The Cowboys led at halftime 38–7 and never stopped scoring, finishing with 573 yards of total offense. The only bright spot for the 49ers came on two touchdown catches by Dwight Clark. As Bill Walsh finished the second of two straight losing seasons, there was talk that maybe the former Stanford coach was in over his head.

Much has said and been written about the 49ers' transcendent 1981 season that led them to their first Super Bowl and launched a dynasty. Some of it was Walsh, some of it was Joe Montana, who became the starting quarterback, and some of it was a continuing infusion of talent, headlined by an all-rookie defensive backfield with future Hall of Famer Ronnie Lott.

Things didn't seem much different as the team opened by losing two of its first three, but that was followed by a seven-game winning streak. The most important game in that stretch—the game that convinced the young 49ers that they were *really* good—was a 45–14 beat down of the Cowboys at Candlestick Park. Clark caught a long touchdown pass and Lott returned an interception for a score, as the Niners gained a measure of revenge for what happened the year before in Dallas. "That game kind of pushed us over the edge," said Montana, "to get us to believe that we were now at that level where we could compete for a championship."[12] San Francisco went on to its best-ever season up to that point, winning twelve of thirteen and finishing 13–3. Dallas won twelve games and the NFC East.

The teams met again, of course, in the NFC Championship, a rubber game of sorts after the NFC title games of 1970 and '71. Long suffering

49er fans, denied three times in the playoffs by the Cowboys, dared to get their championship hopes up again. "I was driving down the freeway, and a fan was yelling at me," said Lott, "and I literally thought it was road rage. Finally, I realized he was saying, 'Frickin' beat Dallas!' That was an unbelievable moment. I don't think people realize how, for some people, beating that team *was* the Super Bowl."[13]

It almost didn't happen, if not for Clark's miracle touchdown reception with less than a minute to play. The 28–27 win created one dynasty and destroyed another. San Francisco won four Super Bowls in the 1980s, while Dallas slowly faded from powerhouse to contender to punching bag. The intersection was a play now known throughout the NFL as "The Catch." After Clark's touchdown, Dallas defensive end Ed Jones turned to Montana and said, "You just beat America's Team." Montana replied, "Well, you can sit at home with the rest of America and watch the Super Bowl."[14]

The Dallas decline was almost as fast and surprising as the 49ers' ascendancy. The Cowboys missed the playoffs in 1984, had losing records in 1986 and 1987, and then saw the bottom drop out in 1988, falling to 3–13. Just as it had it 1965, the heat turned up on Landry and this time there would be no locker-room turning point to save him. The winner of two Super Bowls and the third-winningest coach in NFL history was canned in 1989 after Arkansas oilman Jerry Jones bought the team. One could argue that just as Landry may have driven Dick Nolan out of the league, Walsh and the 49ers may have done the same to Landry.

Jerry Jones hired his college teammate Jimmy Johnson to coach the Cowboys, a move that raised more than its share of laughs around the league, especially when the team went 1–15 and 7–9 the first two seasons. But like Walsh, Johnson began stockpiling draft picks and young talent. In 1991 the team made the playoffs; by 1992 it was ready to contend for a championship.

Standing in the way was San Francisco. Walsh had retired and Montana had left for Kansas City, but the franchise looked just as dominant now coached by George Seifert and quarterbacked by future Hall of Famer Steve Young. In 1992, the team went 14–2 while Dallas had a record of 13–3. The two best teams in football were set to meet again for the NFC Championship in San Francisco.

It was just about as thrilling as the 1981 title game. On a muddy, soggy field at Candlestick Park, the teams went back and forth, with Dallas holding a tenuous 24–20 lead late in the fourth quarter. Backed up in their own end of the field, the Cowboys decided not to play it safe, and a 70-yard completion from Troy Aikman to Alvin Harper ultimately sealed the 30–20 win. "How 'bout them Cowboys!" Johnson roared afterwards in the locker room.

The win might not have been possible without some help from the 49ers. Earlier in the season, the team was looking to unload disgruntled defensive end Charles Haley, who was considered locker room poison. Dallas gladly took the future Hall of Famer off San Francisco's hands in a trade that help push the Cowboys over the top. Dallas crushed Buffalo in the Super Bowl, the first of three championships in four years.

Jimmy Johnson majored in industrial psychology in college and put his skills to good use when Dallas and San Francisco met again in the 1993 NFC Championship. On a radio talk show the week of the game, Johnson flatly predicted a Dallas win. "We will win the ballgame," he said. "And you can put it in three-inch headlines. We will win the ballgame."[15]

Whether to motivate the Cowboys or enrage the 49ers, the act achieved its purpose. San Francisco players tried to start a pregame scuffle and normally mild-mannered receiver Jerry Rice was so fired up he drew an unsportsmanlike conduct penalty during warm-ups. "For them to have such a negative response to my off-the-cuff comment on a radio show, and for Jerry Rice to get a penalty," Johnson said, "I believe it had an effect on their play."[16] Despite losing Aikman to a concussion, the Cowboys easily won the game, 38–20 and went on to win a second straight Super Bowl.

It was a desperate 49er team that met Dallas for a third straight year in the NFC title game in 1994. "There was no 'maybe,'" said defensive back Eric Davis. "There is not a player that understands what it means to be a Niner that could have survived losing that game."[17] There was also no Johnson, who parted company with Jerry Jones in a clash of egos that resulted in Barry Switzer coaching the team. Spurred by an interception return for a touchdown by Davis, the Niners jumped to a quick 21–0 lead and held on to win, 38–28. "We had a great team, and they had a great team, but somebody had to lose," said Dallas defensive back James Washington. "I know the 49ers will have a good time in the Super Bowl. Looking at this game, the Super Bowl is a done deal."[18]

And so it was. Steve Young threw a record six touchdown passes as San Francisco crushed the upstart Chargers, 49–26. The Niners passed Dallas for number of Super Bowl titles, five to four.

The Cowboys retied it the following year. Although San Francisco won a surprisingly easy game over Dallas in November, the team was knocked out of the playoffs by Green Bay. Dallas went on to beat the Packers in the NFC Championship and then the Steelers in the Super Bowl.

Both teams remain stuck at five Super Bowls apiece and have not met in the playoffs since the 1994 season. Yet the rivalry lives on. In 2000, with both teams headed to dismal seasons, they met for a regular season game at Texas Stadium. After catching a second-quarter touchdown pass, 49er receiver Terrell Owens ran to the Cowboys' blue star logo at midfield and raised both arms in triumph. A few moments later, Dallas running back Emmitt Smith scored on a short run and he too ran to the star, helmet in hand, and slammed down the ball.

Then it was Owens again. After he caught a fourth-quarter touchdown pass that essentially put the game away, Owens ran to the star to repeat his earlier celebration. However, he was interrupted by Dallas safety George Teague, who sprinted to midfield and leveled Owens with a blindside hit. The hit may have restored some Cowboy pride, but it made little difference in the 41–24 final score.

"It all comes from having pride and getting our butts kicked over and over," Teague said. "I think it will help us in the long run to be able to not feel that way and not want to feel that way anymore."[19] Owens, who was fined and suspended by his own team, never felt Teague was trying to "protect the star," but only wanted to get back at him for a vicious block earlier in the game. "Go to the star, give your thanks to God, because he's watching down on this game, and show him who's the best player today," Owens said in explaining his actions. "And that's what I did. It had nothing to do with me taunting my opponent. But the media, that's what they say it is."[20] Naturally, Owens joined the Cowboys later in the decade, and in 2008 caught a 75-yard touchdown pass that helped Dallas beat San Francisco, 35–22.

In a rivalry filled with heated confrontations, close games and playoff memories, perhaps the most poignant moment came in a 2017 regular season game in San Francisco. Dwight Clark, suffering from amyotrophic lateral sclerosis, Lou Gehrig's disease, and with less than a year to live, returned to be honored by his 1981 Super Bowl teammates, including Joe Montana and Jerry Rice. "It was a heartwarming, yet heartbreaking day for us all," said another former teammate, Mike Schumann. "You want to be there for him, as when you win a championship like we did together. You are bonded for life with this team on and off the field."[21]

Dallas won the game, 40–10, but that hardly mattered. Back and forth the rivalry ebbs and flows, and will continue.

"It was competition at the highest level," said Eric Davis. "Living it, being a part of it, breathing it, it truly was one of those almost sibling rivalries. It was built on a certain respect, but it was a fight—and it was about blood."[22]

CHAPTER 6

A Season Begins

Less than three weeks after Dallas beat Miami in Super Bowl VI, the new season began with the NFL Draft. The draft, seventeen rounds at the time, took place over two days starting on February 1 at the Essex Hotel in New York. Pittsburgh had the 13th overall selection and badly wanted a running back to take the pressure off of Terry Bradshaw. The team had searched for years to find a headline back but had failed miserably with top picks that had turned out to be disappointments—Bob Ferguson in 1962, Dick Leftridge in 1966 and Don Shy in 1967. The team had also been burned with Bobby Campbell of Penn State, a fourth-round pick in 1969 who lasted only one season.

Chuck Noll was understandably gun-shy as another Penn State back was under consideration. While Steeler scouts and scouting director Art Rooney, Jr., raved about the potential of Franco Harris, Noll had his eye on University of Houston fullback Robert Newhouse.

"Newhouse is faster," Noll kept saying.

"Harris is big and fast," replied Rooney Jr. "The big guys have long and more consistent careers than the little guys."

While a wild story circulated that the scouts had to lock Noll in a closet in order to keep him from drafting Newhouse, the truth is that he eventually came around.

"All right," he told Rooney Jr. "I'll go along with you on Harris, but you better be right."[1]

Drafted in the second round by Dallas, Newhouse went on to a solid twelve-year career. Franco Harris became a legend.

In addition to Harris, Pittsburgh added starters in offensive tackle Gordon Gravelle (second round) and tight end John McMakin (third round), along with quality defensive line depth with Steve Furness (fifth round).

43

It was a bountiful draft for the Steelers, and while not quite as impressive as the 1974 haul that yielded four Hall of Famers, it reinforced Noll's philosophy of how he wanted to rebuild the team. "We will have to make up our mind about Harris after he's been in camp awhile," Noll said of his number-one pick. "I will try him at both running back positions. We know he can catch passes and he has speed. We drafted him first because we think he's a great pro prospect, but only time will tell."[2]

The Raiders added almost as much quality as did the Steelers, with the real value coming after first round receiver Mike Siani. Oakland landed offensive tackle John Vella (second round), receiver Cliff Branch and center Dave Dalby (fourth), and defensive back Skip Thomas (seventh round). All would become starters and eventually Super Bowl champions.

San Francisco may have had the weakest draft of the four teams from Immaculate Saturday. Number-one pick receiver Terry Beasley helped Pat Sullivan win a Heisman Trophy at Auburn and brought that same confidence to San Francisco. "I feel, pound for pound, I'm as tough as anyone in pro football," he said.[3] The problem was that he just didn't have many pounds, weighing only 186 and standing only five feet, eleven inches. That, combined with a reckless disregard for his own safety, led to a series of injuries, including multiple concussions, which forced him out of the league after three unspectacular seasons. None of the other picks made much of an impact, meaning that the 49ers would have a strong, but significantly aging team in 1972. "No doubt, we had some bad drafts," said San Francisco linebacker Skip Vanderbundt, "and that definitely had an effect."[4]

With the luxury of drafting for depth and not necessarily for need, the Cowboys took Boston College running back Bill Thomas with their first pick. Dallas had introduced computerization and data analysis into the drafting process to create a dynasty, but this time got its wires crossed. Thomas played for three different teams in a three-year career and didn't get so much as a single carry in his only season in Dallas. But the fact that the Cowboys took Thomas and Newhouse with their first two selections suggested that they were deeply concerned about the other Thomas in their backfield—Super Bowl hero Duane Thomas.

Thomas led the league in rushing average his rookie season in 1970, and with quarterback Craig Morton hurt and having difficulty passing, he almost single-handedly carried the offense to the Super Bowl. In 1971, he may have played even better, starring in a Dallas backfield that set a then–Super Bowl record of 252 yards rushing in the win over Miami. In just two seasons, his power, speed and elusiveness drew comparisons to Hall of Famer Jim Brown. "He wasn't a power runner," said Dallas defensive back Mel Renfro, "although he was strong and could break tackles and elude, but he was just like a big antelope, just those giant powerful steps, and the way he'd weave in and out. I just loved to see him run."[5]

But all that talent came with heavy baggage.

Thomas came to the Cowboys as a naïve idealist, often described by other Cowboys as hardworking, polite and a perfect teammate. A year later, discouraged by what he considered the dehumanizing elements of pro football in general and the Cowboys organization in particular, Thomas was being described in starkly different terms, including difficult, troubled, and enigmatic. Even before his rookie season ended, Thomas began to show disturbing signs, and a telling incident took place at Super Bowl V in Miami. A few days before the game, reporters found Thomas barefoot and alone on the beach behind the team hotel, his gaze fixed on the Atlantic Ocean.

"What are you thinking about?" they asked.

"Where I am," Duane said.

"You mean on a beach in Fort Lauderdale?"

"No," Duane said. "I mean where I am." His nostrils flared slightly.

"Where's that?"

"Just now I was thinking about New Zealand."

"Oh?"

"It's a good place to retire."

"A rookie shouldn't be thinking about retiring."

Thomas gave them his curious poor-devil look and said, "It's the best time."[6]

After a key Thomas fumble contributed to the Cowboys' loss to the Colts, Thomas refused to meet with the media and essentially vanished for six months. He reappeared at training camp demanding the team renegotiate his contract, and when the Cowboys refused, he lashed out at team officials, including Tom Landry. "The problem in general is that I'm black," he said. "Had I been a white player, they would have not done me such an injustice. They've done this to all black players and have exploited black players all along. I'm tired of being treated like a stupid animal, and I think these people have been trying to crook me."[7]

Less than two weeks after the Super Bowl win, Thomas and his brother were stopped in Greenville, Texas, for marijuana possession, an incident some suggested was a setup, and he received five years probation. When training camp began in July Thomas was a no-show, but he sent in his place a friend who said he wanted to try out for the team. "So we had this little passing drill," said Roger Staubach, "and it was the weirdest thing I ever saw. He was out there running routes in sweats and combat boots. Then [Cowboys vice president] Gil Brandt came out, and said, 'Get that guy the hell off the field,' and we never saw him again."[8]

When Thomas eventually reported four days late he maintained his separation from the team. At meal times, while teammates ate together, he would climb through a dining hall window, scoop up a handful of fruits and vegetables into his shirt pockets, and disappear back to his room to eat in solitude. "As long as he can carry the football, we don't have to be buddy-buddy," noted linebacker Lee Roy Jordan.[9]

But with new running backs in camp, and now having the pressure of winning a Super Bowl removed, team executives took a harder line and began talking trade. In fact, the team had actually traded Thomas during training camp the year before, sending him to the New England Patriots. But Thomas got in hot water with his new team, ignoring coaches and refusing to take a physical exam. "I felt compelled," said Schramm, "both from a moral and ethical standpoint, to effect a solution that would not work an undue hardship on either club."[10] The deal was cancelled and the running back returned to Dallas.

A year later to the day, August 1, 1972, Schramm traded Thomas again and this time made it stick. San Diego gave the Cowboys two promising young players—receiver Billy Parks and running back Mike Montgomery— in exchange for Thomas in an unusual deal that was "unconditional," meaning that Thomas was not coming back under any circumstances. The Chargers tried everything to get Thomas on board, including giving him a substantial pay raise, letting him work on his own timetable, and having him shadowed by a psychiatrist, Dr. Arnold Mandell.

It was November, eight weeks into the season, before Thomas showed up for practice, and in the one game for which he was activated—ironically, against Dallas—he warmed up apart from the team and then never got off the bench. He left San Diego and football for awhile, resurfaced briefly with the Redskins, and was then gone for good by age twenty-seven. Thomas eventually made peace with his past, but in 1972 his departure from the Cowboys was as mysterious as it was tragic. "Tom Landry's attitude was one of bewilderment," said Dallas assistant general manager Al Ward. "Tom couldn't believe that [Thomas] couldn't be reached and helped. What a crime to see all that talent go to waste. Tom would just shake his head and say, 'Why couldn't I reach him? Where did I fail?'"[11]

The departure of Thomas was not Landry's most pressing problem in the off-season, especially considering that former rookie of the year Calvin Hill reclaimed his starting role and by the end of the season would become the first Dallas back to rush for more than 1,000 yards. Instead, the concern was for starting quarterback Roger Staubach, who refused to give up his scrambling ways. Staubach's willingness to run out of the pocket reflected his highly competitive nature—he was willing to sacrifice his body if it meant a couple of important yards. "If someone did one hundred sit-ups, Roger was going to do one hundred and one," said teammate Walt Garrison. "If somebody ran a mile in six minutes, Roger would do it in five fifty-nine. If someone threw the ball sixty yards, he was going to throw it sixty-one."[12]

It was hard to argue with Staubach's running when it carried Dallas to ten straight wins and the Super Bowl title, and Landry never specifically told Staubach to stay put. But he cringed every time Staubach left the pocket, certain that his quarterback was courting disaster. "We have no plays where Staubach is supposed to run," said Landry. "He runs enough without any plays."[13]

Dallas opened its preseason on July 29 in a match against the College All-Stars in Chicago,[14] and Staubach had to be pulled in the second quarter of a 20–7 win. A scramble left him temporarily scrambled after a blow to the head. "Apparently, I didn't do very well," said Staubach, trying to clear the cobwebs.[15] No sooner had Landry exhaled than Staubach tempted fortune once more. Two weeks later against the Rams, he ran out of the pocket and decided to try for the goal line rather than run out of bounds. The result was a collision with linebacker Marlin McKeever that separated Staubach's right shoulder. The injury would require surgery and put Staubach on the shelf for most, if not all, of the season. "I knew it was bad," he said. "As I lay on the ground I was thinking, 'I wish could get up for one more play and drop back in the pocket and get hurt in the pocket,' because I knew everybody was going to criticize me for getting hurt running."[16]

He was also criticized for wearing smaller shoulder pads that made it easier for him to throw but didn't offer as much protection. From that point on, Staubach would wear the bigger pads, but for 1972 it was too late. "How do you feel when you're on top of the world and it crashes?" Landry asked rhetorically. "You can't run over big guys. You've got to run out of bounds."[17]

The Cowboys' season, for better or worse, now dropped in the lap of Craig Morton, who thankfully for Dallas, had not followed through on a trade demand. Back in the lineup, Morton played like a condemned prisoner who had just received a reprieve from the governor, throwing three touchdown passes against the Rams and leading Dallas to a league-best

6–1 preseason record. "Why not?" he said after taking over the reins. "I took the Cowboys to a Super Bowl once before, and this team has always performed well for me."[18] In an era when exhibition games were treated seriously and starters played most of the way, Pittsburgh finished the pre-season 4–1–1, while Oakland went 5–1, handing Dallas its only loss. San Francisco broke even at 3–3.

The regular season opened on September 17 and Morton continued his hot hand. After falling behind at home to the Eagles, 6–0, Dallas scored four straight touchdowns to win its eleventh straight game, 28–6. Morton threw a pair of touchdown passes, including the first for Ron Sellers as a Cowboy, while Newhouse added his first pro touchdown on a one-yard run. "Catching that first pass helped a lot," said the former New England star who came to Dallas in an off-season trade. "I was nervous being [in] my first regular season Cowboy game. The only other time I've been that nervous was at my wedding three years ago."[19]

It sure beat the feeling Sellers had the first time he had played in Texas Stadium the previous year when the Patriots and Cowboys chris-tened the new facility. "I was going out on a pattern and Cornell [Green] hit me in the eye with his hands balled in a fist," said Sellers. "Blood hem-orrhaged in my eyeball and I missed five games. I got to see a lot of Texas out of one eye from a window in Baylor Hospital."[20]

In its season opener, San Francisco had an easy time in a 34–3 home rout of the Chargers. John Brodie threw three touchdown passes, all in the first half to Gene Washington, and the 49er defense had four intercep-tions.

A sellout crowd of 50,141 nervously jammed sunny Three Rivers Sta-dium in Pittsburgh for the opener between the Steelers and Raiders. Pitts-burgh had improved in every one of Chuck Noll's three seasons, and now there was whispered talk of perhaps a championship. If Pittsburgh could somehow beat a traditional power like Oakland, the Steelers could stamp themselves as legitimate contenders.

On the first possession of the new season, Bradshaw fumbled, and even though the Steelers recovered, the play killed the drive. Pittsburgh pressured Oakland quarterback Ken Stabler immediately, forcing a high throw that bounced to Chuck Beatty, who returned the interception to the Raider 38-yard line. With a chance to grab the lead, the Steelers instead returned the gift as Bradshaw threw right into the hands of Jack Tatum at the five-yard line. In the early going it looked like a typical, ragged season opener, and fans began to mutter about the "Same Old Steelers."

Oakland fans watching back home were also muttering and wondered why the team's two veteran quarterbacks were sitting on the bench. Under former coach John Rauch, Daryle Lamonica was the unquestioned starter, and he led the team to the Super Bowl following the 1967 season. When John Madden took over in 1969, Lamonica still started, but George Blanda began to see more action, and in 1970 he came off the bench to rally the Raiders to a win or tie in five straight games. The streak helped Oakland win its fourth straight division title, and made the 43-year-old Blanda the talk of the nation. "The attraction has been George Blanda, basically," said an NBC executive trying to explain a spike in the TV ratings for the games that fall. "These are games people don't want to walk away from. They can't leave for fear that George will do it again."[21]

After a year on the Raiders practice squad, and another playing in the minor Continental League, Ken Stabler joined the team for good in 1970 and mostly watched as Blanda and Lamonica jousted for headlines and playing time. "How can you possibly compare these two guys?" Stabler asked. "They make one helluva combination, don't they? I haven't played much this year, maybe eight or ten minutes, but I wouldn't take anything for the education I'm getting."[22] When Blanda told Stabler that he would get more playing time in 1971 because Blanda was 90 percent sure he was going to retire, Stabler answered back, "Yeah, George; it's that other ten percent I'm worried about."[23] Stabler, who had gotten Blanda's autograph as a young boy, more often addressed his older teammate at "sir" during his rookie year.

Of course, Blanda did return in 1971, but even then Stabler saw more action and threw the first touchdown pass of his career. He got even more playing time during the 1972 preseason, leading the team in attempts, completions and touchdowns, and on that basis Madden took a chance and named him as the starter for the Steeler opener. "He's just a natural quarterback," Madden said of Stabler. "He always knows where the open men are."[24] Blanda would kick and be first quarterback off the bench. The Pennsylvania native would also be honored during pregame ceremonies celebrating his 45th birthday. Family and friends from his hometown of Youngwood would be on hand for Blanda's first game in Pittsburgh since he played in 1958 as a member of the Chicago Bears.

Blanda would get his chance early in the second quarter. By that time, Stabler had thrown two more interceptions, one of which directly led to a Pittsburgh touchdown when Bradshaw ran a quarterback sneak twenty yards untouched into the end zone. Henry Davis blocked, scooped, and ran back a punt for a score as the Steeler lead ballooned to 17–0. By the time he departed, Stabler's miserable passing line for the day read five of twelve for 54 yards and three interceptions.

Unbelievably, Blanda fumbled attempting a handoff on his first play. But when Oakland got the ball back, the birthday boy warmed up, hitting tight end Raymond Chester with two passes, the second of which resulted in a touchdown that cut the Steeler halftime lead to 17–7.

The brief success did not carry over and the Oakland comedy of errors continued in the third quarter. Another botched Oakland punt, this time a dropped snap by punter Jerry DePoyster, set up a Pittsburgh field goal, and then Bradshaw scored on another quarterback sneak. Delirious fans almost rubbed their eyes in disbelief looking at the scoreboard which now read 27–7.

At this point Madden, who had developed the curious strategy of subbing his quarterbacks almost like a baseball manager changed relief pitchers, had seen enough of Blanda and went to his bullpen for Lamonica. The third quarterback proved to be the charm as the "Mad Bomber"—known for his penchant for the deep pass—hit two long touchdowns to rookie Mike Siani. But by that time Bradshaw had also thrown for a score to Ron Shanklin and the deficit was too great to overcome. Lamonica had hit on eight of ten passes for 172 yards and two touchdowns, all in the fourth quarter, but Pittsburgh held on to win, 34–28. "I suppose we relaxed," said Davis. "It was a hot day and we were tired. Lamonica came in and made us look bad."[25]

Afterwards, some suggested that had Madden started Lamonica the outcome would have been different. "The second guessers can go —— themselves," Madden answered reporters caustically. "Any time you play with two or three QBs, you're bound to bring the second-guessers out of the woodwork. I have no regrets. I think I know what I'm doing."[26]

In Madden's defense, rotating quarterback was not all that unusual up to that time. The Rams won an NFL title in 1951 with Hall of Famers Norm Van Brocklin and Bob Waterfield splitting the snaps. Sid Gillman switched between John Hadl and Tobin Rote when the San Diego Chargers won the AFL championship in 1963. "It's just like baseball," said Gillman. "When your starting quarterback is off with his control, you bring in another man from the bullpen right away."[27] But early in the week after the Pittsburgh loss, Madden quietly promoted Lamonica from reliever and announced that he would start the following Sunday against Green Bay.

In the Pittsburgh locker room, players and coaches were obviously happy, but the late Oakland rally, turning a blowout into a barnburner not decided until the Steelers recovered a late onside kick, had taken some of the shine off the win. "I played stupid football at times," said Bradshaw, who finished with the one touchdown pass but also three interceptions. "Hell, yes, we were lucky," Noll admitted. "I'd rather be lucky than smart."[28] The most appropriate comment may have come from defensive end Dwight White, "I won't say we're the best...." He then paused and smiled. "But we can play with the best."[29]

No matter how hard the Steelers tried to tap the brakes on the euphoria, fans and the media wanted to go full speed ahead. In its headline following the game, the *Pittsburgh Press* boldly asked, "Could '72 Be the Year of the Steelers?" and columnist Phil Musick gushed, "The longest prayer vigil in the history of football may have ended yesterday. This long suffering burg can get off its knees—apparently, life can begin at 40, at least in the National Football League."[30]

It took awhile for the Raiders to get off their knees, winning just one of the first three games, and standing at 4–3–1 past the midway point of the season. But the team then closed out the year with six straight wins, albeit over pretty weak competition aside from the rival Chiefs, and won the AFC Western division title at 10–3–1. While Stabler and Blanda would make occasional appearances the rest of the way, they combined for only five touchdown passes compared to Lamonica's eighteen. It was very much Daryle Lamonica's team as the Raiders prepared to return to the playoffs.

Pittsburgh followed its win over Oakland by losing to Cincinnati and beating St. Louis. Then came another significant test for the young Steelers—a road game against the Cowboys. Dallas had won two of its first three games, losing to eventual NFC Central champ Green Bay. Morton cooled considerably, playing unexceptionally in a win over the Giants, and then throwing three interceptions against the Packers. Making matters worse, he was consistently booed at home, with venom from the Dallas fans seemingly increasing each week. In their minds, Staubach had taken the team to the Promised Land; Morton was the bungler who cost the team Super Bowl V. "I don't understand it and really don't know what to say about it," Morton confessed of the fans' anger. "I'm not going to let it get me down ... but I certainly hear it. Hell, a deaf man could hear those people."[31]

Perhaps Morton should have remembered a conversation he had with Don Meredith a few years earlier. Dallas fans had booed Meredith mercilessly for his failures in the playoffs, and they would often chant for Morton to replace him. "So [Morton] went over to him and said, 'I'm sorry, Don, I hate hearing this.' He said, 'Hey, don't worry about it, Curly. It's going to happen to you.'"[32]

Now it was happening to Morton and it affected him deeply. Blessed with enormous physical gifts, including a rocket arm and 6'4" frame, he was nonetheless tormented by injuries and self-doubt. Hampered by an injured throwing shoulder, Morton played dreadfully in the playoff loss to Cleveland in 1969 and again in the Super Bowl a year later. With his confidence shot, Morton began seeing a hypnotist during that 1970 season. Edward Pullman was a retired furniture designer who had founded the Southwest Hypnosis Research Center. "I knew I was dealing with one million dollars worth of ballplayer, and I'm no coach," he admitted. "But you can clear away distractions that may be preventing an athlete from performing to his full potential. It's like a file drawer in which all the papers are filed out of order. Hypnosis can put the papers back in order."[33]

The treatments started before a big win over Kansas City, and every week thereafter Pullman would call Morton and give him the key phrase "black salt" to induce a brief hypnosis. Morton played very well against the Chiefs, and even admitted he felt better physically, but his effectiveness waned as the season progressed. "How can you measure it?" he responded when asked if the treatments helped. "It is supposed to work on the subconscious, which is unmeasureable. But you really have to believe in it for it to work."[34]

Ever since the hypnosis stories had come out the year before, many in Dallas, including the press covering the team, had written off Morton as a head case; not so much in the mold of Duane Thomas, but certainly someone not capable of withstanding the pressures required of a championship quarterback. Now, after the first loss of the year to the Packers, reporters were quick to try and reignite the quarterback controversy.

"What do you do when Staubach is ready to come back?" was one of the first questions asked of Landry after the Green Bay game.

"I don't know," Landry confessed. "It would be hard to change a winning combination. Right now, I'd stay with Morton."[35]

Landry stayed with Morton against the Steelers, but the sloppiness continued for both teams on October 8 in Texas Stadium. The Steelers and Cowboys combined for six turnovers, fifteen penalties and enough bizarre plays to keep the game in doubt until the last moments. Pittsburgh scored its only touchdown in the second quarter when Bob Hayes fumbled an end-around and Mel Blount scooped it up and ran 35 yards for a 13–3 lead. Dallas countered with Calvin Hill, who scored on a short run and then threw a 55-yard touchdown pass to Ron Sellers for the go-ahead score. Hill may have had the best Dallas arm on the field as Morton completed only eleven of 29 passes with two interceptions.

"We made enough mistakes today to lose the next three games,"[36] moaned Landry, and the Cowboys would have lost except that Pittsburgh made just as many errors. Bradshaw completed only twelve of 39 passes with an interception. He was not helped when Frank Lewis dropped a perfect fourth-quarter bomb that would have given the Steelers the lead. Then the Steelers saved the strangest mistake for the finish. With less than two minutes to go and trailing by four, Bradshaw was sacked on his own 15-yard line and fumbled. The ball bounced right to Franco Harris who scooped it up and ran all the way down to the Dallas two-yard line, but the 77-yard gain was wiped out by a holding call on tackle Gerry Mullins. "I let [Tody Smith] just run over me because I knew Franco was right behind me," said Mullins. "But I was so tired by then I might have grabbed him. I don't know."[37]

It was still not over because the Cowboys kept trying to hand the game back to Pittsburgh. Cornell Green intercepted a desperation fourth-down pass by Bradshaw and returned it for an apparent clinching touchdown, but it too was negated by penalty. Given another chance, Bradshaw drove the Steelers down to the Dallas 22-yard line, where four straight passes, including the last play of the game just beyond the reach of Lewis in the end zone, fell incomplete, handing the game to Dallas, 17–13.

"If I tell you it was the sun, what does that sound like?"[38] Lewis snapped afterwards when asked about the drop on Bradshaw's long pass. He may have lost the pass in the unusual shadows of Texas Stadium, which was covered except for an opening over the playing field. Bob Hayes had dropped a similar pass in the season opener against Philadelphia, and both plays were in bright sunshine on almost exactly the same spot on the field. "There's no such thing as a good loss," Noll groused, refusing to make excuses. "Our coming back at the end was encouraging, but we have to move the ball. The defense was tough, but we have to score."[39]

The scoring problem would never be entirely solved, but it did get some help. An army was about to ride to the rescue.

CHAPTER 7

Soul Brother
with Italian Legs

They began arriving in the mid–nineteenth century; most of them Poles, Slovaks and Germans, but also a lot of Irish and Italians. Between 1880 and 1910, more than seventeen million immigrants poured into the U.S., and many of those found their way to Pittsburgh. Enticed by the area's growing industrial strength and the possibility of work, by 1910 they had made Pittsburgh the eighth-largest city in the country with more than a quarter of its population foreign born.[1]

Some came to farm, and Germans in particular spread beyond Pittsburgh into the fertile lands in Ohio, Indiana, and Iowa. Others, like the Irish family of Art Rooney, had seen enough of farming in the potato famine and came for jobs in Pittsburgh's steel mills. The Irish primarily settled in the city's North Side, while the Germans went to Millvale, the Slovaks to Munhall, the Hungarians to Hazelwood, the Italians to Bloomfield, East Liberty, and Morningside, and the Ukrainians to the South Side. Each area was culturally distinct and remained so for decades. "For my parents," said Donald Warhola, a third-generation Pittsburgh Slovak, "it was always an emphasis to stick your heritage as much as possible."[2]

The one thing that helped bring together the disparate communities was sports. Blacks, Irish, and Italians among others fought against each other on the city's sandlots. "These teams battled on the playing field, with fights spilling into the stands," noted Art Rooney's biographers. "But their clashes created a larger social solidarity. For immigrants, sport provided a near-meritocracy in a country otherwise pinched by tightening intolerance."[3]

The Irish focused on boxing, baseball and football, in contrast to the vastly outnumbered Italians, who stuck mainly with bocce. Italian immigrants created a "BGI Club," in which members would play the courts and speak the native language when interlopers would approach "because they didn't want you hearing what they were talking about."[4] The BGI Club is gone, but bocce is alive and well, especially in Morningside, which has the city's highest percentage of Italians, and where new courts were built and then renovated. Nearby Bloomfield still advertises its neighborhood as Pittsburgh's "Little Italy."

But in the first half of the twentieth century, no area in Pittsburgh had more Italian immigrants than East Liberty, an area to the northeast of Pittsburgh between the Allegheny and Monongahela Rivers. It was between the Italian enclaves of Bloomfield to the east and Larimer to the west, and the Larimer Avenue boundary featured dozens of Italian-American shops, markets, and stores. "It was so ethnic back then, you had nothing to do but be Italian," said Anthony Amen, a second-generation Italian-American who grew up on Larimer Avenue in East Liberty. "It's more like a family than a neighborhood. It had that magic to it. They didn't say you were from East Liberty, you were from Larimer Avenue. You were Italian before you were an American."[5]

Another of those second-generation Italians was Tony Stagno, whose family came from Spigno Saturnia, a village midway between Rome and Naples in south-central Italy. As a young boy, Stagno began working in his father's bakery, and in time he became acquainted with another East Liberty baker, Al Vento, whose family ran a pizzeria. Beyond their heritage and occupations, the men found they also shared a love of the Steelers. They began going to games first at Pitt Stadium and then at Three Rivers Stadium. While Pitt Stadium was more rowdy and raucous, the new facility seemed more sterile and antiseptic.

"We were at a game and noticed there were no banners, no enthusiasm," said Stagno, early in the 1972 season. "Someone around us said, 'It's going to take an army to move this crowd.' So we said, 'OK, we'll be an Italian army.'"[6] Stagno and Vento became its founding generals, although Stagno outranked his friend with four stars instead of three. With officers in place, the army now needed a focal point.

Franco Harris was searching, too, during his rookie season. He was still getting used to the NFL, and his early-season rushing totals reflected it—28 yards against Oakland, 35 against Cincinnati, and just 16 against Dallas. He was also still getting used to a new city, having settled into an apartment in Bloomfield. It was not a conscious decision on his part that Harris ended up in one of the strongest Italian-American neighborhoods in the area, but it did reawaken at least part of his heritage. Harris grew up as one of nine children of an Army enlisted man and an Italian war bride. "I've never seen anyone like you before," a man once told him. "You've got a Roman nose, you've got Roman eyebrows, you've got a Roman face, but you're black. I don't understand."[7]

Harris had long before come to understand his mixed heritage and always claimed to embrace both ethnicities. While working at an Italian restaurant as a teenager, he made the decision to accompany his mother on a trip back home to Pisa, Italy. There he discovered a family tree with roots back to the year 1250. "If you have any black blood in you, you're considered black," he said. "I basically grew up in a black neighborhood and I've always considered myself black. [But] I became more conscious of my Italian background when the Italian Army started."[8]

When Stagno and Vento learned of Harris's half–Italian heritage, they decided to build their army around him. They tentatively approached a security guard at the stadium who was in charge of the Steelers' locker room and asked him to pass the invitation on to Harris. "They really didn't know how to approach me, but they finally did and asked me about starting it," Harris said, "and I said, 'I like that.' And it was incredible. They were so into it and having so much fun."[9]

It didn't hurt, either, that about that time Harris had started to find his rushing legs. After the October loss in Dallas, the Steelers rebounded with five straight wins, thanks mainly to the rushing of Harris—115 yards against Houston, 138 against Buffalo, and 101 in the game against Cincinnati. By the time Kansas City arrived for a November 12 game, the Army was ready to make its debut.

Stagno, Vento, and a few of their friends and co-workers came to the stadium in full regalia—army helmets, Italian flags, and plenty of food. They had spent the morning at Vento's Pizza to prepare hoagies of prosciutto, capicola, and provolone. And of course, there was the wine, smuggled in hollowed-out loaves of bread. By the following season, there was so much food that the Army had to buy two additional season tickets just to get it all in.

There was also the Italian whammy that included a *corno* (horn) and *malocchio* (evil eye). Stagno began bringing a small red plastic pepper that inside it had an ivory carving of a hunchback. The Army would use the malocchio to put the evil eye on opposing teams and the corno to protect the Steelers from evil spirits.

All of this commotion took Harris somewhat aback when he came on the field before the game. Facing him was a large red, white and green banner inscribed "Franco's Italian Army" in large letters, and behind it Stagno, Vento and the Army. Later would follow small individual Italian flags and a banner that read, "Run, Paisano, Run." "I laughed," said Harris of seeing the banner for the first time. "I've got a fan club, and that's really fine."[10] The Army witnessed another outstanding performance, as Harris rushed for 134 yards and a touchdown in a 16–7 victory over the Chiefs.

The spirit and popularity of the Army began to catch on. Stagno and Vento began an active recruiting campaign and put up a booth outside the stadium with a sign that read, "Enlist now ... join Franco's Italian Army."[11] Even though it was a traditionally male club, women were invited to join as well into a special "Nurse's Division." Other ethnic fan clubs quickly sprouted up. "Dobra Shunka" loosely translated in Polish and Slovak as "Good Ham," supported linebacker Jack Ham. "The Green Babushkas" were a smaller group that wore colored scarves in honor of Joe Greene. And while not necessarily ethnic, "Gerela's Gorillas" supported kicker Roy Gerela, with Bob Bubanic dressing in full gorilla costume and dancing on top of the dugouts. "Those [are] my people," said Gerela. "I didn't know them when they adopted me, but now we're all drinking buddies."[12]

But not everyone was on board. Much of the city's black fan base resisted the Army, believing that the Italian-Americans were trying to "steal" their emerging hero. A Black Nationalist group in Pittsburgh discussed the issue and advocated creating its own group and regalia. While nothing came of the proposal, it did reflect the tension between the city's black community and the Italian-Americans, which had simmered for decades.

Stagno tried to defuse the situation. "We have blacks, Poles, Italians, every nationality in the Army," he said. "We don't see color. Our bakery shop borders a black area of the city. In fact, a black man made the first banner."[13] Still, some resentment remained on both sides. After Harris smashed over a would-be tackler in the win over the Bengals, several black waiters in the stadium's Allegheny Club yelled, "Thata way, Soul Brother! Get it on!" Rocky LaCascio, a stadium security guard, replied, "He may be a Soul Brother, but his legs are Italian."[14]

Despite such feelings, Franco's Italian Army became the rallying point for the Steelers sudden surge into prominence. Even as Pittsburgh temporarily fell into a first-place tie with the Browns after a heartbreaking last-minute 26–24 loss in Cleveland on November 19, the Army marched proudly into the Browns' Municipal Stadium. "We'd march in with 80 or 100 people, everybody with khaki shirts and helmet liners," said Al Vento, Jr. "My dad and Tony Stagno would lead us in and start a cadence."

During the 1972 season Franco's Italian Army helped unite the city's disparate black and Italian communities under one banner. *Courtesy Detre Library and Archives, Sen. John Heinz History Center, Pittsburgh, Pennsylvania.*

> Bam, bam, we got Ham!
> One-Two-Three-Four
> Dwight White, he's all right!
> One-Two-Three-Four[15]

When the Browns returned to Three Rivers Stadium two weeks later for the rematch, the Steelers and the Army were ready. Stagno, Pat Signore, Armen Zottola and the rest of the Army brought their pepper and hunchback, and "put the 'evil eye' on the Browns," said Stagno. "It's the 'big maloccio,' imported from Italy."[16]

With Stagno and the Army putting the whammy on the Browns, and Harris rushing for more than a hundred yards in his sixth straight game to tie Jim Brown's NFL record, Pittsburgh crushed Cleveland, 30–0, to take sole possession of first place. If it wasn't the most important win in franchise history, it was certainly one of the most impressive. "We owed them that shutout," said Dwight White. "The Cleveland writers helped get us up by writing how good the Browns were and how mediocre we are. And the Browns even warmed up in our usual spot on the field trying to intimidate us. But we didn't get upset, did we? Boy, I wish we were playing them in the next two games."[17]

Instead, Pittsburgh went to Houston, where the Oilers stopped Franco's hundred-yard rushing streak, but the Steelers managed to survive, 9–3 on three Gerela field goals. With the Browns also winning, the team would have to win the division on the last day of the season in San Diego.

The team flew out the week of the game and headquartered in Palm Springs to get out of freezing Pittsburgh and acclimate to the three-hour time change. Myron Cope, the legendary Pittsburgh sportswriter turned radio broadcaster who would later introduce the "Terrible Towel," went to California with a mission—find Frank Sinatra. Stagno and Vento had asked him to track down Sinatra and induct him into the Army. Cope, who by this time had been made a one-star general, figured he had at least an outside chance. Sinatra was obviously Italian, living in Palm Springs at the time, and reportedly liked to bet on football. Cope put out feelers all over town, but with no luck.

One night at dinner, Cope was eating with a team contingent at a swanky restaurant when Sinatra and his retinue walked in. Cope quickly wrote out an invitation on a cocktail napkin and had it sent to Sinatra's table. To sweeten the pot, the note mentioned that Franco was from New Jersey just like Sinatra. After some convincing, the waiter dutifully presented the note to Sinatra, who amazingly came to Cope's table with his group, which included a bodyguard, baseball manager Leo Durocher and pro golfer Ken Venturi.

Pat Livingston, the longtime sports editor of the *Pittsburgh Press*, described the meeting between Sinatra and the excitable, squeaky-voiced Cope as one between "the best voice and the worst voice in the English-speaking world."[18] Sinatra's first question was about the health of Terry Bradshaw, arousing Cope's suspicions about the football betting. When Cope mentioned that he wanted to induct Sinatra into the Army, Sinatra promised to attend practice and then departed, leaving several bottles of wine as a parting gift.

Cope called back to Pittsburgh telling Stagno and Al Vento to get to Palm Springs so they could personally induct Sinatra. It was Stagno's first-ever plane flight and he was treated royally upon arrival. While doing a radio interview, Stagno was told, "Franco has a fan club in every high school. He has more fan clubs here than any of the Chargers."[19]

Meanwhile, Cope had several problems the next day, including a hangover. He had no way of knowing if Sinatra would actually show, and he had already run afoul of both Dan Rooney and Noll who had gotten wind of the plan.

"What's this I hear, you're planning a distraction at my practice?" Noll asked Cope.

"Look," Cope replied, "I have this terrible headache. You're only two years younger than me, kid, so I know you were as big a Sinatra fan as I."[20]

Practice ran as scheduled and had just about ended with no sign of Sinatra. Steelers traveling secretary Jim Boston made the announcement to the gathered reporters that Sinatra was a no-show, and added, "Cope's a loser again." Suddenly, Boston felt a tap on his shoulder from a man in an orange cardigan sweater and porkpie hat. Sinatra had been watching inconspicuously from the stands, not wanting to disrupt the practice.

"When Sinatra says he'll show," the singer said, "he shows."[21]

While Cope was overjoyed and rushed out onto the field to stop practice, Harris was hesitant. "Who would ever have thought this?" he said later, admitting he was extremely shy at the time. "A kid from New Jersey and here's Frank Sinatra."[22] Only when Noll barked at him to join the gathering did the rookie make his way over. Apparently, Cope's earlier talk with Noll had the desired effect.

Stagno greeted Sinatra warmly, inducted him as a Colonel with an official Army helmet, and then passed around wine, cheese and prosciutto. Plenty of pictures were taken of Sinatra with Stagno and Harris, and the beaming matchmaker Cope called it the biggest thrill of his career. For Tony Stagno, it was a life-changing moment. "Honey, it was for real," he told his wife Patsy over the phone from California. "I kissed him on both cheeks. It was like kissing God."[23]

After that, the game against a poor San Diego team was anti-climatic. Earlier in the day, Cleveland knocked off the Jets, so Pittsburgh had to win in order to take the division outright. Harris didn't hit a hundred yards, but with area sailors waving "Franco's Italian-American Navy" signs, he did score a short touchdown. The man Steeler scouts had to practically beg Chuck Noll to draft, and didn't start until the sixth game of the season, finished with 1,055 yards rushing, was named to the Pro Bowl, and easily won Rookie of the Year honors.

The Pittsburgh defense played fanatical, forcing seven turnovers and limiting the Chargers to 178 total yards. It would have been a shutout if not for an early safety given up by the offense, but the Steelers still cruised to their first-ever championship, 24–2, and carried Noll off the field in

"When Sinatra says he'll show, he shows." Frank Sinatra surprised a Steelers practice in Palm Springs, California, in order to be inducted into Franco's Italian Army. Flanking Sinatra are the Army's founders, Al Vento (left) and Tony Stagno. *Courtesy Detre Library and Archives, Sen. John Heinz History Center, Pittsburgh, Pennsylvania.*

celebration. Art Rooney entertained the press after the game in his usual restrained way. "I'm not jumping up and down because that's not the way I am," he said. "But inside, I'm bubbling like a volcano. It took a long time, but we did it. [The wait] was worth it."[24] As Harris pulled off his uniform he received a telegram that read "Go Steelers Go." It was signed, "Colonel Francis Sinatra."[25]

Rooney handed out cigars in the locker room, and then on the plane ride home he walked the aisles, thanking each player for his contribution to the season. Defensive captain and linebacker Andy Russell got on the intercom and gave the game ball to the team owner. "I don't want to sound maudlin or sentimental," said Russell, "but I speak for every member of this team when I say this ball goes to a great guy. It's always been a pleasure to play for this man."[26] The Steelers patriarch choked up on receiving the ball, and it appeared tears were coming down his cheeks. "I knew we'd win if I lived long enough," said Rooney. "I did get kind of worried as I got into my later life."[27]

If Rooney got emotional on the plane, he had more in store for him back in Pittsburgh. The flight did not get home until around one in the morning, yet some 5,000 were there to welcome the Steelers home. Thousands more were already standing in line, some for more than twenty hours, at Three Rivers Stadium trying to get playoff tickets. No doubt many of those same fans were dreaming of another ticket queue—this one for the Super Bowl. If fan support could get them there, the Steelers were well on their way to Los Angeles.

CHAPTER 8

Fight to the Finish

The 49ers record fell to 2–2 after a dispiriting 31–7 loss in Los Angeles, their ninth loss in ten tries against the Rams. Los Angeles punished the Niners with 303 yards rushing, including 142 yards from unknown reserve back Bob Thomas. The team that may have looked the best that weekend was Oakland, which wiped out Houston on *Monday Night Football*, 34–0, holding the Oilers to a franchise low 89 yards of total offense. So dominant was the Oakland victory that the Astrodome had mostly cleared out by the fourth quarter. When ABC cameras panned the thinning stands looking for crowd shots, an obviously irritated Houston fan flipped the bird to a national television audience. After a pause, ABC commentator Don Meredith laughed and added, "They're number one in the nation."[1]

San Francisco was not even number one in its own division after the debacle in Los Angeles, trailing the first-place Rams by a half-game. Rushing defense, as evidenced by the Rams loss and another loss to Buffalo in which O.J. Simpson ran for 138 yards, was the primary culprit, but the offense was also wildly inconsistent. After throwing for three touchdowns in the opening win against San Diego, John Brodie had as many interceptions as completions against Buffalo—one—before giving way to backup Steve Spurrier. Brodie returned to throw a pair of touchdowns in an easy win over New Orleans, but in the Rams game it was no touchdowns and two more interceptions.

Week Five brought the Giants to San Francisco and it dealt another blow to the staggering Niners. A wet, sloppy day made the synthetic surface at Candlestick Park like a Slip-N-Slide, as the teams combined for eight fumbles, two interceptions, and seven turnovers. One turnover that didn't count cost the Giants a touchdown, when Vic Washington clearly fumbled a kickoff return that Willie Williams ran into the end zone. The officials blew the play dead ruling an inadvertent whistle. San Francisco gladly accepted the break and took a 17–13 lead with six minutes to play when John Brodie threw his second touchdown pass to Gene Washington.

After a field goal cut the lead to 17–16, Pete Athas intercepted Brodie and ran it back into Niner territory. A few plays later, Charlie Evans put New York ahead 23–17 on a touchdown run with less than two minutes to go. With only thirty-eight seconds left, Brodie had San Francisco at midfield, but he was then sacked awkwardly by Jack Gregory. For the first time in his long career Brodie was unable to walk off the field, and as a stretcher carried him off it seemed to be taking the team's title chances with it. The former league MVP and heart of the offense was out up to eight weeks with a severely sprained ankle. "To tell you the truth, I don't know how long he'll be out," said coach Dick Nolan. "I keep hearing different reports. I can only say I was told he would be ready to play against Green Bay" on November 12.[2]

Backup Steve Spurrier came in, but his desperation throw into the end zone was intercepted by Athas as San Francisco dropped to 2–3. The team appeared to hit rock bottom the following week, salvaging a tie with the winless Saints on a late field goal by Bruce Gossett. Spurrier filled in for Brodie with two touchdown passes but also threw three interceptions. "Spurrier's personality seemed depressingly devoid of spark, marked with a coolness that bordered on the lacksidasical," *Sports Illustrated* said of the backup now forced into a starting role. "His arm was also suspect, for Spurrier's passes ... flutter as if filled with helium."[3] Hurt, dispirited and in third place in the division, San Francisco's season seemed to be slipping away.

If one play could be described as having turned around a season, it may have come the following week in Atlanta where Vic Washington returned the opening kickoff 98 yards for a touchdown. Spurrier threw three touchdown passes as San Francisco smashed the second-place Falcons, 49–14. After a loss to Green Bay he passed for two touchdowns in a win over the Colts and then five more in a 34–21 rout of the Bears. The Chicago game was played in driving rainstorm and Spurrier limped on his own sprained ankle, but he still tied a team record for touchdown passes in a game. San Francisco climbed to 5–4–1 and into a first place tie with the Rams. "I don't put too much stock in records," Spurrier said after being named NFC offensive player of the week. "Touchdown passes are just a matter of circumstance."[4]

That brought a Thanksgiving game against Dallas in Texas Stadium, where the Cowboys had never lost. San Francisco had all kinds of odds stacked against it, including a sidelined Brodie, a short week to prepare for a road game, and the psychological frustration of having lost the last two NFC Championship games to the Cowboys. The team flew directly to Dallas from Chicago and began studying the Cowboys' game films. The more they watched, the more worried they got, concerned they would not have enough time to get ready.

"We were so confused on defense," said Vanderbundt, "that some of the veterans went to Nolan and said, 'Let's simplify the game plan. Let's just play them. Line up man to man and play them straight up.' And he said, 'If that's what you guys want to do, we'll do that.' That showed me a lot for a head coach to do that."[5]

Playing straight up, San Francisco quickly fell behind on a Walt Garrison touchdown. Then with Dallas threatening to add to its lead in the second quarter, the Niners almost outfoxed themselves. Middle linebacker Ed Beard called for Vanderbundt to make a weak side blitz. When Dallas shifted away from Vanderbundt, Beard called for strong side linebacker Dave Wilcox to blitz. Then the Cowboys sent a man in motion back toward Vanderbundt, who picked that up as a signal to blitz. But Beard didn't catch it and never said anything, which meant now that both linebackers would be blitzing.

No one saw the move coming, including Garrison, who couldn't figure out who to block, and including Craig Morton, who nearly had his head taken off as Wilcox came clean and forced a fumble. The ball popped into the hands of Vanderbundt who raced 73 yards for an unmolested touchdown. "The ball took one bounce and there it was," said Vanderbundt. "I just scooped it up and ran. It may have looked like I was trotting, but I was running for my life."[6] The sudden turnaround energized the Niners, who took a 14–10 halftime lead.

Defensively, they made life miserable for Craig Morton, who was sacked nine times and suffered two interceptions, the second of which Vanderbundt returned for a 21-yard touchdown after he guessed correctly and jumped a sideline route. "I broke my shoulder pads in the first quarter," explained Vanderbundt, "and they fixed me up with some wide receiver pads. I figured if I'm going to dress like one, I'm going to score like one."[7]

A month earlier, Vanderbundt had returned an interception against the Falcons for a touchdown. Having never scored before, he now had three touchdowns in five games. They were the only touchdowns in a ten-year

NFL career, but the outburst won Vanderbundt conference defensive player of the week honors. "Statistically, the Thanksgiving game was my best," he said, "and obviously it was a great game for me. But I actually graded out higher in other games than I did the Dallas game."[8]

San Francisco won, 31–10, and for the moment had exorcised its Dallas demons. More importantly, the Niners now stood alone in first place. "They are sometimes superb, occasionally impossible, frequently inept," observed one sportswriter, "and despite it all, suspiciously still contending for the Super Bowl."[9]

True to form, the inconsistent Niners went out the following week and lost to the Rams again, falling back into a first-place tie. Spurrier did not play nearly as well, throwing two touchdowns, but also three costly interceptions. By now, Brodie was back in uniform and in his mind, ready to play. Nolan, however, perhaps out of a sense of loyalty to Spurrier, kept Brodie on the bench, where he slowly seethed in frustration. The relationship between Brodie and Nolan had always been difficult. After two championship game losses to Dallas, Tom Landry observed, "I'm afraid Dick thinks Brodie let him down."[10] Now, it deteriorated to the point that they communicated primarily through quarterbacks coach Jim Shofner.

"There was animosity between [Brodie and Spurrier] from day one because they are such highly competitive people," said Vanderbundt. "John didn't like to lose at anything and Spurrier absolutely hated to lose. Both felt they should be playing. Nolan didn't want to upset the apple cart and tried to keep the ball rolling."[11]

Spurrier threw infrequently in another easy win over Atlanta, which set up a decisive season finale against the Vikings in San Francisco. A win over Minnesota would clinch the division title, while a loss could open the door for either Atlanta or Los Angeles and leave the Niners out in the cold. Minnesota was having a down year and already out of the playoff race at 8–7, but the Vikings were still dangerous. When reporters asked him the day before the game if he would like to play, Brodie demurred. "If I go in tomorrow," he said presciently, "it will probably be because we are behind."[12]

It didn't take long for San Francisco to fall behind, in no small part because Spurrier played miserably, throwing three interceptions in the first three quarters, as San Francisco suffered seven total turnovers. Down 17–6 entering the fourth quarter and with the season slipping away, Nolan finally turned to Brodie, who later admitted, "When Shofner told me Dick wanted me to go in, the first thing that came into my head was to tell him to take a hike."[13] Instead, Brodie fared little better than Spurrier, throwing interceptions to kill his first two drives.

Still down 17–6, Brodie began the third possession at his own one-yard line after a Minnesota punt. Six plays and four completions later he capped a 99-yard drive with a 24-yard scoring pass to Gene Washington, cutting the deficit to 17–13. San Francisco held again, and Brodie got the ball back one more time on his own 34-yard line with only 1:30 remaining. A critical pass interference moved the ball to Minnesota's 26, and from there Brodie hit Vic Washington down to the Vikings' two-yard line with only forty seconds to play. Two incompletions brought up third down with but thirty seconds to go. Brodie rolled to his right, directed traffic, and then found Dick Witcher open in the back of the end zone for the improbable go-ahead score. "Dick's had about six touchdowns called back by penalties the last few years," said Brodie. "I turned around and looked for a flag."[14]

He saw no flags, but only a jubilant celebration in the end zone. Witcher, who lost his starting job midway through the season to Preston Riley and was only in the game as an extra tight end, caught his only touchdown pass of the season. "John motioned me to stop," said Witcher. "I couldn't see that there was nobody behind me and he could. It's the greatest thing that ever happened to me, both personally and as a team thing."[15]

It still wasn't over. Minnesota got down to the San Francisco 36 with enough time for one play. The Vikings had a decision to make—go for broke and a possible win or kick a field goal and settle for a tie? Barring a fake or some other type of miracle, as soon as the kicking team came on the field, the Niners had the playoffs clinched, as only a loss would have eliminated them. "We don't give a damn about knocking them out," said Minnesota coach Bud Grant, who wanted the tie to give his team a winning record on the season. "We're in business to help ourselves. I would do it all over again."[16] Fred Cox made the argument moot when he missed the 43-yard try wide left as time ran out, and San Francisco had its third straight division title, 20–17.

San Francisco finished at 8–5–1 and would meet Dallas for the third straight year in the playoffs, this time at home. Even though Dallas had a better record at 10–4, the Cowboys qualified as a wild card team behind division winner Washington and would have all their playoff games on the road. Dallas did not play poorly during the season but had developed the frustrating habit of building big leads in the first half of games and then having to hold on for dear life. The Cowboys led San Diego, 31–0,

Opposite: The 1972 San Francisco 49ers. Just 25 years old and in his third season, Preston Riley (#85, third player from left in the third row) took over the starting wide receiver role from veteran Dick Witcher. Riley seemed to have a bright future in San Francisco, but it all came crashing down in the playoff game against Dallas. Standing to Riley's left is linebacker Skip Vanderbundt (#52). *Courtesy Pro Football Hall of Fame via AP Images*

but managed only a 34–28 win. The following week, St. Louis turned a 30–10 deficit into a 33–24 final. "Our problem could be overcaution," observed linebacker Chuck Howley. "In the first half we're fresh and not afraid to take chances. Then we lay back trying not to look bad in the game films."[17]

The game films from the showdown with the Redskins in the penultimate game of the season showed a vicious crackback block that essentially ended Howley's career. On a sweep, receiver Charley Taylor doubled back on an unsuspecting Howley, who tore knee ligaments. After the game, which the Cowboys typically won by building a big lead and then surviving, 34–24, Washington coach George Allen complained that a similar crackback by Dallas receiver Lance Alworth had injured Redskins linebacker Jack Pardee. "I never hit a guy when his back is turned," answered Alworth. "I could have, but didn't. If anything was illegal, it was the block thrown on Chuck Howley."

Added Dallas receiver Ron Sellers, "Maybe they didn't like it because they didn't think of it first. I think it's only something coach Allen is doing to motivate his players if they play us again, which I hope does occur."[18] Howley, a five-time All-Pro and former Super Bowl MVP, retired after playing only one game the following season.

Just as Nolan had a difficult decision to make with Brodie replacing Spurrier, Landry was starting to at least entertain the possibility of a quarterback change. Staubach was now almost fully healed from his separated shoulder, and Landry gave him some playing time in a meaningless season-ending 23–3 loss to the Giants. While Staubach tried to shake off the rust, Morton continued his puzzling inconsistent play. "A quarterback should not have great games and bad games," Morton had said during the season. "He should have good games all along."[19]

The problem was that Morton didn't take his own advice. He threw two more interceptions against New York, giving him 21 on the season compared to just fifteen touchdowns. Those numbers ranked him in the top three in the league for interceptions thrown and in the bottom half of passer efficiency. No one on the Cowboys expressed much concern over the lackluster display in the Giants game; the team knew beforehand that win or lose it would travel the next weekend to San Francisco in the first round of the playoffs.

As Dallas ended its regular season with a thud, back at Candlestick Park the scene after the Vikings game bordered on total pandemonium. Players had engulfed Witcher after the touchdown catch, and as Cox's field goal sailed wide, fans poured on the field. They hoisted Brodie on their shoulders, tugged at his uniform, and slowly moved him toward the victorious locker room. "Nothing like that had ever happened to me, before or since," he admitted. "For a moment, I wondered whether some of the people were some of the same ones who had so often booed me over the years. But that thought just faded away, overpowered by the joy and grit and emotion from the game of a lifetime, one that had put us back in the playoffs once more."[20]

The date was December 16, 1972. Seven days later a similar scene would play out at Candlestick Park, with players joyously rolling on the field after an improbable comeback win. This time, San Francisco fans would not join in the celebration.

There was far less drama in Oakland, where the Raiders ended their season with a 28–21 win over Chicago. Even though the Bears' Bobby Douglass ran for 127 yards to set a season quarterback rushing record with 968, the Raiders won their sixth straight and wound up 10–3–1. "I told the team, 'This one's in the can,'" said Madden afterwards. "Anything we do or talk about from now on has to be for the Steelers."[21]

At 11–3, Pittsburgh would host Oakland in the first round of the playoffs, while Cleveland would travel to Miami. The Dolphins had just completed the NFL's first-ever unbeaten and untied season, going 14–0 despite losing starting quarterback Bob Griese for most of the year with a broken ankle. Earl Morrall had filled in superbly for Griese, and Miami set an NFL record as both Larry Csonka and Mercury Morris rushed for more than a thousand yards. The Dolphins also led the league in most points scored (385) and fewest points allowed (171). "I think we're a better football team this year than last year," said Don Shula. "Greater experience is a factor."[22] Famous Vegas oddsmaker Jimmy "The Greek" Snyder installed the Dolphins as 3–1 favorites to win the Super Bowl, while Dallas went off at 6–1, Pittsburgh at 7–1, San Francisco at 8–1 and Oakland at 12–1.

Many people were still not convinced. "The Dolphins played such a cream-puff schedule," noted *Sports Illustrated*, "that not one of their opponents made the playoffs, and only two of them barely scraped by over .500."[23] Shula, long known for his quick temper and lack of patience with reporters, shot back, "Who says it was soft? We certainly didn't feel it was a soft schedule when it was handed out to us, but we didn't cry about it then."[24]

Milt Richman, who covered the NFL for United Press International, went with the favorites in picking Dallas, Washington, and Pittsburgh, but also saw the Browns upsetting the Dolphins. "Every ball club in the world, even the Dolphins, has an off-day sometime," he wrote. "Call it the law of averages or whatever you like, I have a hunch Cleveland is going to knock over Miami on Sunday."[25]

"The real class of the AFC would now appear to be the Oakland Raiders," continued *Sports Illustrated*, "who have won their last six games. The odds would suggest that the winner of the 49er–Cowboys game will emerge as the NFC's Super Bowl entrant."[26]

Given the magazine's track record with cover jinxes and picking play-off results, the Steelers should have felt pretty good about their chances. "I have a hunch," added the Greek. "I don't go in for hunches, but this one strikes me as good. I think the winner of the Pittsburgh–Oakland playoff game will win the Super Bowl title."[27]

Chapter 9

Pregame

The week leading up to the NFL playoffs was a time of high drama. On December 20, two jetliners collided on a runway at Chicago's O'Hare airport, killing nine. The next day, two survivors from a Uruguayan air force plane that crashed in the Andes Mountains suddenly appeared more than two months after the accident. They stumbled out of the Chilean mountains and came upon a mule driver on a river bank near San Fernando. "I am from the plane which crashed in the mountains," read the message they tied to a stone and threw to attract attention. "I am a Uruguayan. We have been walking for ten days."[1] The two led rescuers to the crash site, where fourteen others were miraculously still alive, some having resorted to cannibalism after the deaths of twenty-nine other passengers.

The drama about to unfold in Pittsburgh and San Francisco was certainly not life-or-death, but for many it was no less intense.

Dallas, San Francisco, Pittsburgh and Oakland would all have a short week before their playoff games. The Raiders and Steelers would kick off at 1 p.m. Eastern time on Saturday, December 23, with the weather expected to be cloudy and in the 40s with a chance of rain. Pittsburgh had not lost at home all year and ranked as a two-point favorite. Dallas and San Francisco would follow at 4 p.m., also with cloudy skies but much warmer 60-degree weather. On Sunday, Washington, would host Green Bay and Cleveland would play in Miami.

Both games on Saturday would be showcased to a national audience, with Pittsburgh and Oakland on NBC, followed by Dallas and San Francisco on CBS. The NFL's controversial blackout policy became an issue the week of the games. The policy forced the blackout of all local games within a 75-mile radius of the stadium, and Steeler fans who couldn't get tickets would have to drive far enough away from Pittsburgh to watch the game in a bar or motel. Chartered buses took Moose and Elks members to watch from out of town lodges. Local newspapers advertised that the game would be carried on television in East Liverpool, Ohio, only about forty miles north and west of Three Rivers Stadium, but technically in another state for television purposes.

A similar situation unfolded in Washington where the Redskins were about to end a thirty-year home playoff drought, but those fans were not content merely to drive to nearby Baltimore to pick up a television signal. The Redskins fan club[2] filed suit against the NFL and the Redskins seeking to get the blackout lifted. "Ironically," the suit read, "the only people in the world who will not be able to view the game of December 24 are the taxpayers and owners of the stadium where the game is to be played."[3]

Representatives from other playoff cities joined in the suit, including Pittsburgh mayor Peter Flaherty, who made a personal appearance before Judge Joseph Waddy and the U.S. District Court in Washington, D.C. Embarrassingly, the original lawsuit had to be refiled because it failed to name CBS television as a defendant in the complaint. After that was settled, the suit was dismissed in Waddy's court, the U.S. Court of Appeals, and then on an emergency appeal by the U.S. Supreme Court.

One unhappy Redskins fan was President Richard Nixon, who was often in the habit of going to Camp David in Maryland to see the games. Nixon planned to spend the weekend at his Key Biscayne, Florida, retreat, which meant he could watch the two games on Saturday, but not the Dolphins and Browns on Sunday from Miami. He asked the NFL to lift the blackout and issued a veiled threat that if the league did not, he would ask Congress to "re-examine the entire antitrust stature and seek legislation that is more in keeping with the public interest."[4]

NFL Commissioner Pete Rozelle stood his ground. Back on October 4, Rozelle testified before a Senate subcommittee, warning that if the policy was lifted, football on television might suffer the same fate as boxing. "We all remember the Friday Night Fights, but how about the Wednesday Night Fights, the Saturday and the two Mondays," he cautioned. "The sport simply ate itself with overexposure."[5] Rozelle did agree to lift the local ban in the Los Angeles market for the upcoming Super Bowl if it was sold out ten days prior to the game, but that's as far as he would go.[6]

The short week put a further strain on the teams nursing injuries after twenty weeks of exhibition and regular season play. Pittsburgh expected offensive linemen Bruce Van Dyke and Sam Davis to be fairly healed from nagging injuries, and both were activated for the game, replacing Melvin

Holmes and John Brown. Starting wide receiver Frank Lewis was out with a broken collarbone suffered in the San Diego finale. Rookie Al Young would take his spot in the starting lineup and his place on the roster went to another rookie receiver, Barry Pearson.

Both San Francisco and Dallas faced injury problems. The biggest loss for the 49ers was strong safety Mel Phillips, out with a broken shoulder. The seven-year veteran had played a key role in limiting the Dallas rushing attack in the Thanksgiving Day game. "You lose something when you lose a guy like Phillips," said linebacker Ed Beard, "but nobody on this team has doubts about Windlan. He's a hitter."[7] Rookie Windlan Hall would replace Phillips and would figure in several important plays—both good and bad.

For Dallas, Running back Calvin Hill was hospitalized during the week with flu symptoms but returned to practice Wednesday. He and cornerback Mel Renfro, held out of the Giants finale, were both expected to play. However, linebacker Chuck Howley was obviously out after his knee surgery, and of even greater concern was the health of defensive tackle Bob Lilly.

The future Hall of Famer had made the Pro Bowl for the ninth straight year, but at age 33, injuries had finally begun to erode his incredible skills and he was conspicuously left off the All-Pro team. At 6'5" and 260 pounds, he could lie on his back in full pads and jump to his feet in a standing position. Offensive guard Halvor Hagen, a Dallas teammate of Lilly's for one season, was traded to New England and faced Lilly in 1971. "I got help from the center," Hagen said sheepishly after the game, "but you give that guy a crease"—he held his forefinger and thumb an inch apart—"and he's through."[8] That same year, Lilly hurdled a Buffalo guard and tackled O.J. Simpson behind the line of scrimmage. "If Bob Lilly had the weight program like they have now, I'm not sure Bob would have been controllable," said teammate Lee Roy Jordan. "And if he had a mean streak like some defensive lineman, you would have had to outlaw him."[9]

Lilly left Wednesday's practice on crutches and doubled over at the back, and then checked into Baylor Hospital in Dallas. He stayed there in traction until Friday, catching a commercial flight to join his teammates in California. "If I get up and it's like it was, I can't play," he said. "When I came in here I could hardly walk, but I got up this morning and was moving pretty good. I think, though, I'll make it."[10] Combined with a bad knee, Cowboy officials guessed that even if Lilly played he wouldn't be more than seventy-five percent. D.D. Lewis would replace Howley at linebacker, and while Lilly would play, his skill and intimidating presence were greatly reduced. The Dallas defense would enter the playoffs crippled.

San Francisco may have also entered the playoffs somewhat wounded psychologically. The Niners knew they were good enough to play with Dallas as evidenced by their Thanksgiving blowout, but they were also wary after two straight playoff losses to the Cowboys. Most of the players talked about the Cowboys respectfully, preferring to let sleeping dogs lie. "We've just got to forget what we did to Dallas back there," said Beard of the Thanksgiving game.[11] Coach Dick Nolan also brushed off the Cowboys' season-ending loss to the Giants. "Last week, they were just waiting for the playoffs," he said.[12]

Looking to gain the psychological high ground, Dallas players talked confidently, despite the lackluster way in which they finished the season. "You're always disappointed when you look that bad," said Tom Landry. "But that's not our concern now. We'll be ready for the 49ers at kickoff time."[13]

Landry admitted the obvious—that the team had to play better than it did against the Giants—but also took some verbal jabs at San Francisco. "We're still the champs," he said. "They'll have to prove they can do it in the playoffs. My team in the playoffs is capable of being a Super Bowl team."[14] "We'll prove ourselves in San Francisco," added receiver Bob Hayes. "I'll guarantee that."[15] Hayes certainly had a lot to prove after a down year that saw him catch only fifteen passes and no touchdowns—both career lows. Ron Sellers would start at receiver opposite Lance Alworth.

Were the Cowboys justifiably confident or simply trying to blow fog over the Niners? Defensive back Pete Athas of the Giants, who helped New York roll Dallas in the season finale, weighed in. "You can say a team has a tendency to be flat after clinching a playoff spot," said Athas, "but in the Cowboys' case I can't buy that. Dallas needed a win against us. You don't go into the playoffs like this. If they don't play any better against San Francisco than they did against us, they'll be playing a lot of golf pretty soon."[16] By kickoff, the game was officially listed as even by oddsmakers.

Just as Dallas had to answer questions about its play toward the end of the season, so did the Steelers. Even though Pittsburgh wrapped up the division title by winning its last two games on the road, the victories were mainly accomplished by the defense, which didn't allow a touchdown in either game. Meanwhile, the Pittsburgh offense had stalled, scoring only three touchdowns combined against the Oilers and Chargers. During the week, players and coaches heard repeatedly that the offense had to improve if the Steelers had any chance against Oakland. "We had a lot of injuries," said Noll. "We had a makeshift line without two starting guards. They judge our offense by how many yards Franco Harris gains. If he doesn't make a hundred yards in a game, it's a failure."[17]

Fans remained optimistic, snapping up tickets to make the game a complete sellout by Tuesday, and oddsmakers installed the Steelers as three-point favorites. "At full strength, Art Rooney's team can win," said Jimmy the Greek. "The edge I give Oakland is experience. I'm rooting for Pittsburgh to go all the way."[18] But not everyone was so sure. "Nuts to sentiment. Bah, humbug," wrote Pittsburgh sportswriter Charley Feeney. "It says here the Raiders will beat the Steelers at the stadium. The Steelers are young and their day will come. But [Saturday] will be the Raiders' day. Experience will win out over youth."[19]

Experience proved to be the key factor in Dick Nolan's decision on his quarterback. Nolan hedged until Thursday when he named Brodie the starter over Spurrier, citing his play in the Minnesota game and the veteran's sixteen years of NFL experience. "John came off the bench and did a great job—I can't say anything more," said Nolan. "He was our shot in the arm."[20] "Steve can't feel too bad," said linebacker Skip Vanderbundt. "He's got us this far."[21]

There was not quite as much suspense in Dallas, where as expected, Landry named Craig Morton the starter over Roger Staubach. As his shoulder healed, Staubach had played in only four games, thrown just twenty passes, and had two interceptions with no touchdowns. Statistically, it was the worst season of his NFL career. "I thought it would be Roger Staubach," Nolan said upon hearing the news, "[although] Morton's a good quarterback. He can throw the ball, and he always could."[22] Secretly, Nolan may have been delighted. Even with a bad shoulder, Staubach was much more mobile than Morton, who had suffered nine sacks in the Thanksgiving loss.

The Cowboys worked out all week at home and flew on Thursday to the team's headquarters in San Mateo. They practiced briefly at Candlestick Park, trying to get used to the synthetic surface which was different from their own at Texas Stadium. When the teams met in the NFC Championship game in 1970 it was played on the natural grass of Kezar Stadium, an intimate, smaller park that many believed provided an important home-field advantage. Because Kezar hosted high school and college games, it was often a muddy mess, patched and covered with black cinders and green paint to at least make it look like an NFL field. Fans there were some of the worst in the league, bombarding players after the game with beer cans, most of which were not empty. The city actually considered building a moat around the field to protect the players, but finally settled on a simple wire fence. "Kezar invariably brought out the worst in everyone," noted *Sports Illustrated.*[23]

On top of all that, seagulls roamed throughout the stadium, causing dread from visiting players who swore the gulls took special aim in bombarding them. "It is a wreck, a shambles, and an embarrassment," said San Francisco sportswriter Wells Twombly. "Yet, there is warmth to the joint that pretty nearly defies description. It is a beautifully eccentric way of life."[24]

Almost to a man, the Niner players loved Kezar as much as they hated Candlestick. Built primarily as a baseball home for the Giants, Candlestick Park had become one of the detestable multi-purpose stadiums that spread throughout the 1970s. There were seams where the artificial surface covered the pitcher's mound and base cutouts, causing untold ankle sprains. After winning six of seven games at Kezar in 1970, the team moved to Candlestick and went only 4–3 in 1971 and 4–2–1 in 1972. "Absolutely brutal," Vanderbundt said of playing there. "It was first-generation Astroturf and had one-inch hard foam padding laid over asphalt. It was like a wire brush and would take skin off so fast. Guys were wearing long sleeves and everything else because of that surface."[25]

The Cowboys had never played at Candlestick and came prepared, bringing four different types of shoes. "Candlestick is surrounded on three sides by water and there is no telling what kind of conditions we are going to have," said equipment manager Jack Eskridge. "We are even taking our steel tipped cleats because if the Astroturf in that stadium gets wet it's really something."[26]

Instead of its usual light workout on Tuesday, Pittsburgh went with a full-scale practice at Three Rivers Stadium. The Steelers were convinced that Daryle Lamonica would try to test them with deep passes like he did in his abbreviated appearance in the season opener, when he hit two long ones to Mike Siani in the fourth quarter. Lamonica, "The Mad Bomber," did not have the eye-popping passing numbers of previous seasons. He threw 281 passes compared to 426 three years before, reflecting the Raiders' transition to a power running game that saw fullback Marv Hubbard rush for 1,100 yards. The Raiders finished third in the league in total offense and were incredibly balanced—twenty-three passing touchdowns against twenty rushing, and 2,369 yards passing versus 2,376 rushing. "Personally, I'd like to throw the ball more," Lamonica said in a statement that surprised no one. "If you're going to win, you've got to have good passing. That's what makes the difference."[27]

Many felt Lamonica would have made the difference had he played the entire game against Pittsburgh in the season opener. The Steelers braced themselves for what they were sure would be another air raid from the Mad Bomber. "Lamonica was fresh and we weren't," said defensive end Dwight White of the first meeting. "But I won't use that as an excuse. He'll be there Saturday. So will we. Then we'll find out."[28]

White seemed particularly fired up about the playoffs, and after Wednesday's practice he called it "blood and guts time." White was one of the few Pittsburgh headliners without a fan club, and he used that as motivation during a season in which he was selected to his first Pro Bowl. "I've been an underdog, a dark horse, all my life and I don't expect it to change," he said. "That's why I'm bitter, very bitter."[29]

While Pittsburgh worked out all week at home, including a Friday practice followed by the annual Steeler Christmas party at the stadium complete with a visit from Santa, the Raiders spent a frustrating week trying to stay dry in rainy Oakland. Adding to the misery was rain and fog that delayed the team's flight to Pittsburgh by five hours, with the weary Raiders not landing until four in the morning on Friday. The team did manage to get in a short workout Friday afternoon after the Steelers' morning practice.

By that time, almost all of western Pennsylvania had lost its mind over the game. Tony Stagno and the Italian Army sold thousands of small Italian flags with the proceeds going to benefit a local children's hospital. The same hospital also benefited from a hamburger chain promotion which sold Army armbands for a buck each, with twenty-five cents going to the charity. Sporting goods stores were mostly cleaned out, with Steeler jackets, jerseys, pennants, and hats sold almost as fast as stores could get them in. "Nothing like it before with the Steelers, ever," said Paul Stajduhar, a store employee. "Everything is going like wildfire. We'd like to have ordered more things, but who could have predicted this?"[30]

Friday concluded with a raucous Steeler pep rally in Market Square that included, among others, the Italian Army, Gerela's Gorillas, and the Turtle Creek High School band. "This is our contribution to help the Steelers go to the Super Bowl," said organizer Terry Bennett. "The Steelers won't be there because they have a curfew, but they're going to know the whole city is cheering for them."[31]

The rally spilled over to the nearby Hilton hotel where the Raiders where staying and was still going strong when Oakland tight end Bob Moore and roommate Greg Slough returned from watching a movie. "We tried to squeeze through and get back to our room," Moore said. "The cops began shoving us. We told them we were Oakland Raider players and then all hell broke loose."[32] At some point, the crowd hung a Raiders dummy in effigy.

Raider coach John Madden appeared on a hotel balcony, and when the crowd started booing he responded with an obscene gesture. As he looked down on the crowd as Public Enemy #1, Madden could not have guessed that the Italian Army had jokingly discussed plans to kidnap him before the game. "There was some talk of maybe kidnapping Madden," says John Danzilli, whose title in the Army was Special Operations, "but that seemed a little extreme to me. If he's not at practices, people are going to notice, so maybe we better come up with something else."[33]

Fans started throwing things, including an object that hit a police officer. When Moore tried to enter the hotel, he apparently exchanged obscenities with another officer, and that's when Moore alleges he was attacked by half a dozen policemen. "I thought they were going to kill me," he said. "[One] hit me on the head with his stick. While I was down the other guys were kicking me in the side. Then one got on top and started swinging his nightstick at me."[34] Police Supt. Robert Colville later stated that "police ordered [Moore and Slough] to turn around and go with the crowd. They had no idea who they were, nor did the two offer any identification."[35] Moore played the game with his head heavily bandaged and later filed a lawsuit charging the Pittsburgh police with brutality. Federal judge Barron P. McCune called the incident a "riot" but ultimately dismissed the charges for lack of evidence.[36]

It would not be the last time the Pittsburgh police figured prominently in Immaculate Saturday.

CHAPTER 10

Same Old Steelers

In 1947, the Steelers tied the Eagles for first place in the NFL's Eastern Division with an 8–4 record. That set up a special playoff game between the teams to break the deadlock. The Eagles shut out Pittsburgh, 21–0 in Philadelphia, but fell the following week to the Cardinals, who won their first, and so far only, NFL championship. From that point onward, darkness seemed to settle over a Steeler franchise that in the following years became an NFL laughingstock.

Now, twenty-five years and two days later on December 23, 1972, the first home playoff game in franchise history attracted a fanatical crowd that included Franco's Italian Army, the Gorillas, and half a dozen other groups. They waved banners, sang songs and drowned out the rendition of the National Anthem. The capacity crowd was officially listed at 50,327, although in the coming years many more would claim to have been there. "The fans helped us, believe me," said Roy Gerela. "They gave us a psychological edge with their cheering. Those cheers brought the whole team up."[1]

Those who wanted in and did not have a ticket were at the mercy of the scalpers, a problem not encountered before during the team's losing seasons. A ticket in Section 644, the upper deck of the stadium above the corner of the end zone opposite the press box side, was officially listed at $10.15. Scalpers were getting four and five times that amount. "These guys are asking $35, $40, $50 each for tickets," said a local bartender near the stadium. "And maybe they'll get that much, too. Maybe more."[2] Allegheny County detectives thought so, too, and they were patrolling the area in plainclothes hours before game time.

Art Rooney went to the game directly from Mass. He chatted awhile with Raider coach John Madden and gave a quick interview to local sportswriter Gene Ward. "I'm happiest for the fans," he told Ward. "They really deserved it, and I only hope they won't be too disappointed if the Raiders beat us today."[3] He then headed to his box on the third level of the stadium, which was not as fancy as it sounds. It was bare concrete with only a couple of chairs and was not even glassed in. Rooney watched there with his personal driver and a pair of priests.

One priest not in the box but nonetheless at the game was John Duggan. Duggan had missed only two games all season, both of which Pittsburgh had lost. He had been at all the rest of them, with Pittsburgh winning eleven of twelve, including all of them at home. "You get that priest down here for every game," Art told his sons. "I don't care what it costs."[4] As was his custom, Duggan held Mass before the game.

As he stretched out on field before the game, Joe Greene thought about his rookie season in 1969. Greene and Noll were both rookies that year when the Steelers won only one game. Noll had steadily rebuilt the team with Greene, named to the Pro Bowl for the fourth straight year, as his cornerstone. "We were 1–13 four years ago," Greene marveled. "I didn't think this day would ever come. Coach Noll did a helluva job. We were in a complete state of confusion when he took over and he molded us into a championship team."[5]

The game began shortly after one o'clock with Gerela kicking the ball through the end zone giving Oakland possession at the twenty. Contrary to Pittsburgh's expectations, Lamonica did not come out throwing deep, but instead used Marv Hubbard and Charlie Smith to establish the running game. Oakland opened the game with nine straight runs good for three first downs, but when Lamonica went to the air the first time his pass was intercepted by linebacker Andy Russell.

Pittsburgh's first drive ended with a 52-yard field goal attempt by Roy Gerela that fell short. After trading punts, Oakland turned over the ball again on a fumble by Hubbard recovered at midfield by Glen Edwards. The Steelers almost immediately returned the favor, deciding to go for a fourth-and-one from the Oakland 30. Safety Jack Tatum, already regarded as one of the hardest hitters in the league, came up fast and nailed John "Frenchy" Fuqua short of the first down. "I knew the minute we were stopped that I should have kicked for three," Noll admitted later in perfect hindsight.[6]

With the emergence of Harris, Fuqua had become something of a forgotten man on the Steelers. In the prime of his career at age 26, he had led the team in rushing the past two seasons. Now Fuqua was noticed mainly for his eccentric personality and flashy wardrobe. He claimed to be an actual French count "turned black" by fallout from a nuclear test, and arrived at the playoff game sporting a feathered musketeers hat, cape, and gold cane. At one time he modeled shoes with three-inch high see-through heels and two live goldfish in each shoe. "My biggest problem was that the fish kept dying," he said. "I kept running and adding water, but that just got my socks wet."[7]

Nothing in the first half—which featured a parade of incompletions, defensive stops and punts—could match the excitement of one of Frenchy's skin-tight jump suits with knee-high moon boots. Lamonica finished the half two of eleven for 13 yards and the interception, while Oakland held Franco Harris to just 33 yards on ten carries. The teams combined for nine first downs and seven punts, and fans in Three Rivers Stadium, so enthusiastic at the start of the game, now began to wonder if the teams might set some kind of playoff record for offensive futility as the scoreless half ended.

Down in Miami, the Dolphins took a break from their playoff preparations to watch some of the Steeler game. The Dolphins would meet Cleveland on Sunday, but already they were feeling a bit uneasy about a possible AFC Championship matchup in Pittsburgh. "I had to turn off the television set," said Miami linebacker Doug Swift. "I was so nervous looking at that defense."[8]

Pittsburgh took the second-half kickoff and immediately tried to open up the game. In an eleven-play drive, Bradshaw threw eight times, completed five, and moved the Steelers to the Oakland eleven, where Roy Gerela kicked a field goal on fourth down. Finally, someone had points on the board, and the Steelers led 3–0 with just under ten minutes left in the third quarter. The rest of the quarter passed uneventfully, except for a tipped Lamonica pass that was caught by Oakland center Jim Otto. Like most other plays, it failed to produce a first down.

By the start of the fourth quarter Otto had more receptions than wide receiver Mike Siani, and Lamonica came out of the game. His stat line read just six completions in 18 attempts for 45 yards and two interceptions. Although it went unnoticed at the time, Lamonica's departure was very much a changing of the guard for the Raiders. Just thirty-one years old, the four-time Pro Bowler and former AFL MVP started but three games in 1973. The fans booed him so loudly that the Raiders stopped sending the offensive team on the field for pregame introductions. "The development of the deep zone killed Daryle," said his teammate Phil Villapiano, "because he loved to be the 'Mad Bomber.'"[9] Lamonica was out of the league by 1974.

Instead of Blanda, Madden decided to go with Ken Stabler, figuring younger legs might help against a devastating Pittsburgh pass rush. Of course, Stabler was immediately sacked by Dwight White, ending his first drive. "I was scared," he admitted later. "I felt like I was going to throw up. But I was ready, too. In those times, when the moment's right there in front of you, you've got to grab it."[10]

It got worse for the young quarterback when he fumbled on back-to-back plays the next time Oakland got the ball. The second was recovered by Mike Wagner on the Raider 35, and four straight Harris rushes brought the ball to the 22. Gerela kicked another field goal, and with just 3:41 remaining Pittsburgh had what looked to be a safe 6–0 lead.

Stabler now gave up on the running game, except for a fourth-down carry by Charlie Smith that kept the season alive with 3:06 to go. Stabler then hit Pete Banaszak for ten, Fred Biletnikoff for twelve and Siani for seven. Suddenly, the ball was on the Pittsburgh 30-yard line with 1:22 left. The crowd, almost to a man, was now standing and screaming.

The Steelers tried to stop Stabler's momentum with a blitz, and he was almost sacked by Craig Hanneman who had outside responsibility on the play. But Stabler coolly moved to his left around the overanxious Hanneman, and when he got to the corner found no one there. The Steelers had all their rushers trapped in the middle, and Stabler raced down the field untouched until he reached the goal line. "The corners ran off to the wide receivers," explained Stabler, "and there was an awful lot of room out there when I started to run."[11]

His dive into the end zone gave tied the game with 1:13 left. More than 50,000 Steeler fans shook their heads in disbelief and under their breaths mouthed the words that had come to symbolize the team over the past forty years—Same Old Steelers. "We outplayed them all day," Pittsburgh linebacker Andy Russell fumed, "[and] then we screwed up one play."[12]

From his perch in the press box, local sportswriter Al Abrams recalled a similar scene at Three Rivers just a few weeks before. The baseball Pirates had been just three outs from the World Series when disaster struck. The Reds rallied for two runs in the ninth to steal the pennant on a wild pitch that scored the winning run. "The thought struck me then," wrote Abrams, "it's not going to happen to us again."[13]

Abrams and other reporters began writing their stories for the Sunday newspapers. Larry Fox of the *New York Daily News* banged out his lead paragraph:

Pittsburgh, Dec. 23—Sub quarterback Ken Stabler scrambled 30 yards for a touchdown with only 73 seconds left to play to give the Oakland Raiders a 7–6 victory over

The first 58 minutes of the Oakland–Pittsburgh playoff game was a bruising defensive battle that saw more punts than points scored. Here, the Oakland defense moves in on a passing Terry Bradshaw. *Courtesy Detre Library and Archives, Sen. John Heinz History Center, Pittsburgh, Pennsylvania.*

the Pittsburgh Steelers in the first game of the AFC playoffs today. Oakland, champions of the Western Division, will meet the winner of tomorrow's Miami–Cleveland game in next week's AFC title clash. That game will be held in either Miami or Oakland....[14]

Jerry DePoyster kicked off and when the ball hit the goal post, Pittsburgh got possession at its own twenty with 1:13 to go. As the Steelers offense came on to the field, Art Rooney left his box seat and headed downstairs to offer condolences to the team. At the start of the fourth quarter he had recited the rosary, but now it all seemed for naught. "I figured we had lost," he said, "and I wanted to get to the locker room early so I could personally thank the players for the fine job they'd done all season."[15] Others would have to tell the team owner what had happened, although hearing the roar of the crowd in the elevator he guessed it was something good. In the Steelers' radio broadcast booth, Myron Cope also left early to get ready for post-game interviews, leaving Jack Fleming alone on the mike.

Pittsburgh hit two quick passes that moved the ball to the 40-yard line. "Have we got excitement in the Steel City today," said Mutual Radio announcer Bob Reynolds as the Steelers called timeout with 37 seconds left. "Stay tuned after this one. There's another one out on the coast that ought to be a great one—Dallas and San Francisco."[16] Bradshaw then fired incomplete three times, with Oakland's Jack Tatum making great plays to break up two of the passes. Now it was fourth down and ten, still from the Pittsburgh 40 with but 22 seconds to play.

Watching the game on television from their home was Franco Harris's family, including his mother, father and younger brothers. After the Stabler touchdown, the men in the room got very quiet. Gina Harris was a typical Italian mother, not as much into sports as she was in raising her family and keeping a clean house. "Our house was always spotless," Franco said of his childhood "I never, ever saw a speck of dirt. And yes, we had a plastic cover on the couch in that one room no one could go into."[17]

But now, Gina Harris sensed that something was very wrong. She quietly got up, went to the record player, and began playing the song "Ave Maria."

The Army was also having its problems. "We only had a few seconds left, so we took out the ivory man and he fell on the ground; we couldn't find him," said Tony Stagno.[18]

Among the many Raider fans delighted at the turn of events was a 20-year-old college junior watching from his living room in Alabama. He was also a star receiver on the Alabama A&M football team. "I was the biggest Oakland Raiders fan you could imagine," said John Stallworth.[19]

The Raiders dropped their defensive backs into a deep zone, conceding any short passes underneath. Their goal was to

Another young receiver, Barry Pearson, was in his rookie year with the Steelers. Because of an injury to starter Frank Lewis, Pearson played a key role in the Oakland playoff game and was the primary receiver on what became the Immaculate Reception. *Courtesy Barry Pearson.*

keep any completion in bounds, potentially running out the clock, and not let the Steelers reach field goal range, which was around Oakland's 40-yard line. "We put in a nice little coverage where the two inside linebackers, me and Gerald Irons, would lock up on the running backs and then have a deep zone behind us," said Raiders linebacker Phil Villapiano, "so it would be impossible to penetrate us."[20]

Jogging in from the Pittsburgh sideline with the play was rookie wide receiver Barry Pearson. Pearson had spent most of the season on the practice squad—called back then the taxi squad[21]—and had not caught a single pass all year. Activated after the injury to Frank Lewis, Pearson was now bringing in the most important play of the Steelers' season, with himself as the primary target. If he was nervous, he did not show it. "I was just glad to be out there, number one," he says. "If my name's called, my name's called, and I've got nothing to do but my job."[22]

Pearson lined up in the left slot, between receiver Al Young and tight end John McMakin, with Harris and Fuqua in the backfield. While Frenchy ran a curl and Harris stayed in to block, Young and McMakin were to clear out the middle for Pearson. The play was never designed to score, only to pick up the yardage for a first down. "I was wide open," said Pearson, "but pressure came from my side and forced Terry out of the pocket. Of course, he couldn't throw it back across his body to me, so he threw it to Frenchy."[23]

Bradshaw had scrambled right, avoiding a near-fatal sack by first Horace Jones and then Tony Cline. "I was open," Fuqua said. "I'm thinking, 'Bradshaw throw it!'"[24] Running out of time, Bradshaw did throw to Fuqua, spiraling a pass deep down the middle. "I could hear Tatum," Frenchy said. "First his footsteps. Boom, boom, boom. They sounded like a giant. And I could hear him breathing."[25]

On NBC television, broadcaster Curt Gowdy had little excitement in his voice as the final play unfolded. "Bradshaw ... trying to get away," he described, "and his pass is ... broken up by Tatum."[26] On the Steelers radio broadcast, Fleming had a little more urgency. "Bradshaw, running out of the pocket ... looking for somebody to throw to, fires it downfield, and there's a collision!"[27]

The ball, Fuqua, and Tatum all arrived at the same point on the Oakland 34-yard line, a collision that seemed to send the ball, and the Steelers' season, ricocheting to the ground. "He looks, he throws deep," said Reynolds's broadcaster partner Van Patrick, "and it is batted away."[28]

For a flickering instant, the Steelers season looked to be over.

CHAPTER 11

If Someone Goes Down, You Gotta Go

One of the beautiful mysteries of the NFL is that so often genius is born in accident. In 1932, the Chicago Bears and Portsmouth Spartans tied atop the league standings, each having won six games with only one loss. NFL officials decided to break the tie with a special playoff game set for Chicago's Wrigley Field the week before Christmas, but a crippling blizzard made it impossible to play the game outside. "The snow was waist deep when we arrived," said Portsmouth running back Glenn Presnell. "There was no way we could practice."[1]

Bears owner George Halas arranged for the game to be moved to Chicago Stadium, the home of hockey's Blackhawks. The indoor setting and smaller playing area posed challenges that required special rules, including kicking off from the ten-yard line and moving the ball back twenty yards after crossing midfield, thus forcing teams to cover 100 yards in order to score.

Perhaps the biggest change was moving the ball in from the sidelines to specially-created hash marks closer to the middle of the field. League rules at the time snapped the ball in play no matter how close it was to the sidelines, but that was impossible inside the cramped arena. The Bears won the game, 9–0, and the hash marks worked so well that the NFL adopted them for good the next season, opening up the game offensively. The game was so well received that the league also created two divisions and a yearly championship at the end of each season, essentially creating the playoffs as they are known today. And even though the game would not return indoors for decades, football under a roof proved to be competitive and exciting. "All of the sounds of human beings smashing other human beings were right there," marveled one sportswriter, "and very real."[2]

Such serendipities are sprinkled throughout NFL history, including the Immaculate Reception game. And if the famous fourth-down play—which Barry Pearson brought in from the sidelines with himself as the primary receiver—had worked the way it was supposed to, he might have a statue at the Pittsburgh airport instead of Franco Harris. "I'm glad Terry didn't throw me the ball," he says laughing. "Had I dropped it, they would have hung me."[3]

In truth, Pearson never doubted his ability to catch the ball, something he had been doing from back in his childhood in Geneseo, Illinois. When Pearson entered high school there was so little interest in the football team that there was talk of ending the program. Four years later, the Maple Leafs had launched one of the greatest high school dynasties of all time.

Starting in Pearson's junior year, Geneseo was not only unbeatable, it was terrifying. The team racked up some frightening scores: 58–0 over Hall, 62–0 over Aledo, and 61–6 over Monmouth. In two years, the Maple Leafs shut out ten of eighteen opponents.

On offense, Pearson scored twenty touchdowns his senior year, Steve Penney added twenty-one to become a high school All-American, and the pair became known as the "Touchdown Twins." There were no state play-offs at the time, so Geneseo had to settle for back-to-back perfect seasons. "You think you are pretty damn good, but you'd like to test yourself," Pearson said later. "It would have meant something to see if we were that good. We thought so. We felt we were invincible."[4]

It eventually turned into a 52-game unbeaten streak, followed by a 22-game winning streak, and then another of 31 games. When the playoff era began, the Leafs won four titles and posted a winning record for 55 straight seasons.[5] All of those accomplishments are staggering, but even more incredible for a program that had been on its deathbed when Pearson began high school.

In truth, most of the credit goes not to Pearson, but to a mild-mannered man who looked more like a church deacon than a football coach. Bob Reade came out of Iowa and landed in Geneseo when the program was on its last legs following a winless season. He had a simple philosophy—a smash-mouth power running game combined with a hard-nosed defense—that was based more on mental toughness than Xs and Os. "We just believed in it," said Pearson. "After you start to win, you believe in it. He just ground it into our brains that this is the way you do it, and we did it. And we got better at it."[6]

Reade went 146–21–4 at Geneseo before leaving for Augustana College, where he created another dynasty. His teams there won four straight national titles and 60 games in a row to set a Division III record. Bob Reade eventually went into the College Football Hall of Fame and wrote a successful book on coaching at the college level. But he never forgot where it started in Geneseo, where the football field is now named in his honor. "Football was not the fashionable thing to do," he said about his arrival in 1962. "They had to forfeit all of their sophomore games the year before because they didn't have enough kids willing to play. But the effort those kids gave helped change things right away. I'm also proud of the fact the success has continued at Geneseo, long after I left. That just goes to show you how many good people have been involved through the years."[7]

One of those "good people" was trying to figure out where to play college ball in 1968. Pearson earned a coveted appointment to the Air Force Academy, but wanted to see if he could get other offers. He actually signed with Kansas State, but ended up at Northwestern, which was a lot closer to home. The Wildcats were not doormats in the Big 10 as they later became, and finished in second place in Pearson's junior and senior years. The team earned a top-twenty ranking and even knocked off powerful Ohio State in Columbus.

For those two seasons Pearson finished among the conference leaders in receiving and earned All-Big 10 honors, yet he was not selected in the annual NFL draft. His relatively small stature—not quite six feet tall and well under 200 pounds—scared away a lot of teams. The draft was seventeen rounds in those days, and teams selected 442 names without calling on Pearson. "If I was going to be drafted sixteen or seventeen, what's the point?" he asked. "I was going to be making the same money as the guys in the later rounds, which wasn't much because no one was making money. So I might as well be able to decide where I wanted to play."[8]

Pearson decided on the Steelers, in part because assistant coach Lionel Taylor had come to Northwestern to do some scouting work on him. Any free agent has dim prospects of making the team, and the Pittsburgh rookie draft class included Franco Harris, Gordon Gravelle, John McMakin, and Steve Furness. Still, Pearson came to camp believing in his chances. "When I got there and looked over the other rookies," he remembers, "I wasn't overly impressed with them. You have to take advantage of your opportunities and I got my chances. When they threw me the ball I caught it. I think there's a little bit of luck, too, but obviously I must have been doing something pretty well."[9] Pearson didn't have a great statistical preseason with only two catches in three games, but he showed enough, especially on special teams.

He stuck on a team that had talent at receiver—Ron Shanklin and Frank Lewis—but not much depth. Pearson spent all season on the practice squad, but knew that one injury would get him promoted to the active roster. It came in the last game of the season when Lewis broke a collarbone. "I never told Frank thank you for helping me out like that," he says with a chuckle. Al Young would replace Lewis in the starting lineup. "Al and Barry are fine receivers," said Chuck Noll. "They both run fine routes and have excellent hands. Neither has the kind of speed that Lewis has, but how many guys do? We'll just have to make a little adjustment."[10]

With the biggest game in Steeler history now looming, Barry Pearson was not only active, but going to play. "I knew I was going to be on some special teams, but beyond that you've got to be prepared because you never know. We didn't have a whole lot of receivers at the time, and if someone goes down, you gotta go."[11]

Pearson was mostly invisible in the game, except for that last, fateful play, which he carried in from the sidelines. The play came to be known as "66 Circle Option," although to this day Pearson disputes that. "Franco and I disagree on the name," he says. "I had it as 'Half Right, Split Opposite, 66 Out, Re-Out End,' where I do a twelve-yard pattern to get the first down and have the option to go in or out. Franco heard it as '66 Circle Option,' but I don't know who does the option on it, because it wasn't me.

"It really was just another way of doing the same thing, but he says one thing and I say another. But I ought to know because I brought the play in."[12]

Lined up in the left slot, opposite future Hall of Fame defensive back Willie Brown, Pearson wasn't looking for immortality on the play, just a first down. Both eluded him when Bradshaw had to run out of the pocket and fired a desperation pass to Frenchy Fuqua. Pearson never saw what happened in the collision between Fuqua and Jack Tatum, but he did watch Harris gallop into NFL history. "That play is the one that really elevated his status to the level it should have been," says Pearson. "He was a special player, so that was meant to be his moment."[13]

The following week in the AFC Championship against Miami, Al Young played in place of the injured Lewis and caught four passes, including a late touchdown that almost pulled out the game for Pittsburgh. While Pearson had no catches, he did have his moments the following season. Lewis got hurt again before the season opener, and Pearson responded with six catches in a win over the Lions that earned him a game ball. He finished the year with 23 receptions and three touchdowns, and scored another in a playoff loss to Oakland. And then it suddenly ended.

Concerned about the lack of depth at receiver, Pittsburgh hit the jackpot in the 1974 draft with future Hall of Famers Lynn Swann and John Stallworth. The writing was on the wall for Pearson, who was given his choice of three destinations in a trade—Chicago, New Orleans, or Kansas City. "The Bears had Bobby Douglass, who wasn't much of a passer, and the Saints were terrible," he said. "The Chiefs had been a solid organization up to that time."[14]

The Chiefs' team that had won a Super Bowl a few years before was now older and in decline, but Pearson still enjoyed his three years in Kansas City. It ended after the 1976 season with a knee injury that made it impossible for him to run without pain. Pearson coached for awhile, including a stint at Oklahoma State as Jimmy Johnson's receivers coach, but the demands made it impossible for him to spend any time with family. He became an executive in the food service business in Connecticut, and he remains there to this day in retirement.

Pearson's five-year NFL career included 86 catches for 1,312 yards, seven touchdowns, and a small, if anonymous, role in one of the most magical moments in league history. While others like Harris and Fuqua, and even some of the Raiders, have made the Immaculate Reception a focal point in their lives, Pearson has not. He has mostly left it behind as part of a different life from which he moved on. After Pearson left Pittsburgh, the Steelers went on to create one of the great dynasties in NFL history, winning four Super Bowls in six years. Pearson was the bystander, the footnote, just as he was for the Immaculate Reception itself.

"To me, being able to say that I was part of those teams that started the Steelers dynasty is truly amazing," he says, without a trace of bitterness. "I was able to play with some of the greatest names in NFL history and be part of the one of the greatest plays ever."[15]

"I've had a good life. I got to travel for business all over the place. I love doing what I did and wish I could have played longer, but that's the way it is. I guess I'm blessed to do it at the level I did and am still good physically. I feel pretty good that I got through it."[16]

CHAPTER 12

Miracle of All Miracles

And then, pandemonium.

"And it's caught out of the air!" yelled Fleming, his voice nearly drowned out by an increasing din in the stadium. "The ball is pulled in by Franco Harris! Harris is going for a touchdown for Pittsburgh! Franco Harris pulled in the football; I don't even know where he came from!"[1] Actually, Franco had come from the backfield. When Bradshaw started to scramble, Harris headed downfield to give him another passing option, something he had learned in his days at Penn State. Villapiano was assigned to Harris on the play "We're only going half speed," said Villapiano, "and I look back and when I saw Bradshaw throw, I accelerated to where the ball was going."[2]

So did Harris, who arrived at the Oakland 42-yard line and apparently plucked the ball out of the air right before it hit the ground. He raced down the left sideline past the Raiders' defensive backs, many of them with their arms in the air celebrating victory. That included Jack Tatum, who had started the entire sequence with his vicious hit on Frenchy Fuqua. "I didn't even know he had the ball," Tatum said of Harris. "I thought, 'He's sure in a hurry to get to the locker room.'"[3]

Instead, Harris was headed for the end zone, but he needed to brush aside one last desperate attempted tackle by safety Jimmy Warren. Warren was one of those who stopped to celebrate, and the seconds he lost may have cost him a chance at catching Harris. "I might have had him at the 10- or 12-yard line," said Warren, "but I grabbed him and his pads were wet. I just slipped off."[4] Like many of his teammates in a stunned Raider locker room, Warren had the look of a dazed hit-and-run victim. "I can't believe it," he kept saying. "It's a dream. Someone wake me when it's over."[5]

Just after the moment of impact between Jack Tatum (#31 in white) and Frenchy Fuqua (#33). Gerald Irons (#86) looks on while, at right, Phil Villapiano (#41) runs side by side with Franco Harris. The ball went to Harris who then took it through the startled Raiders to complete the Immaculate Reception. *Courtesy Pro Football Hall of Fame via AP Images.*

Up in the coaching boxes, some of the Pittsburgh assistants jumped up on a table as the play unfolded and began screaming, "Run Franco, run!" The mood was quite different in the Raiders' coaching box. "It was one of those times when you're not sure what you're looking at," said Oakland assistant Tom Flores. "Madden's going crazy, chasing officials around. The Pittsburgh crowd's going crazy. We're all thinking, 'What the hell was that?'"[6]

Just a few boxes down from the coaches, as Larry Fox watched Harris run through the end zone and into history, he ripped the original story from his portable typewriter. "Here," he barked at Ed Kiely, the Steelers' press liaison. "You can have this. It might be some good to you someday."[7]

At the home of Gina and Cad Harris, "Ave Maria" was still playing on the record player. To this day, their son Franco insists that the events were not coincidental. Likewise, Tony Stagno knows that finding his ivory hunchback, right as Harris caught the ball almost directly in front of him, was providential. "Al Vento finally reached over and found it and handed it to me," says Stagno. "The second he handed it to me the ball bounces off Tatum and here comes Franco, and all of a sudden he's running like hell for the goal line. Whether you want to believe in these things or not, I believe there's something to it."[8]

No one else could believe it either. As fans started pouring onto the field to join the celebrating Steelers, and Raiders milled around in a state of shock, the officials seemed unsure as to how to rule the play. Rules at the time disallowed a pass when it was batted from one offensive player to another, and it was certainly plausible that the ball ricocheted from Fuqua to Harris after the hit by Tatum. Madden claimed that the officials were so confused that no one signaled touchdown after Harris crossed the goal line.

More than five minutes passed by as referee Fred Swearingen conferred with umpire Pat Harder and back judge Brian Burk, and then called upstairs to Art McNally, the NFL supervisor of officials. "How do you rule?" McNally asked. "I called it double touching," said Swearingen. "Touchdown." McNally answered, "That's right."[9]

"Harder had the best view of the play," explained NFL executive Jim Kensil. "He went to Burk who agreed with Harder that Tatum and Fuqua both touched the ball."[10] Tatum, naturally, disagreed. "I hit him, but I don't believe I ever touched the ball. I think it bounced off the receiver."[11] Just as naturally, the officials' decision stood. "You talk about Christmas miracles," said Gowdy on NBC, "here's the miracle of all miracles."[12] Van Patrick echoed those thoughts on the national radio broadcast. "My, oh my, oh my," he gushed. "This place has gone completely berserk! [Harris] is being mobbed as the clock shows only five seconds left!"[13]

As the chaos continued, Art Rooney finally made his way from the elevator to the locker room. The Steelers' owner never did see the biggest play in franchise history, and arguably the most memorable play in NFL history. "I was standing by the elevator when one of the stadium guards came running at me yelling 'You won it! You won it!'" Rooney said later. "I asked him if he was kidding and he screamed, 'No, no! Listen to the crowd!'"[14]

After the field cleared and Pittsburgh knocked down a long pass from Stabler, the game ended, 13–7. "I was in a daze," said safety Mike Wagner. "I really questioned myself. 'Is this for real?' Then I saw everybody else was believing and I did too."[15] Noll led a prayer in the raucous Steeler locker room, while tackle John Brown seemed to sum up the feelings of players on both sides. "Tomorrow morning when I wake up and read the paper," he said, "I still won't believe it's real."[16]

The Raiders and their fans couldn't believe it was real either, and still don't. Down in Alabama, John Stallworth was convinced his team had been robbed. "I thought it was a bad call," he said. "The ball had to have touched the ground [or] it touched two offensive players so they should

Part of the confusion after the Immaculate Reception. As fans, players and coaches waited to hear if the touchdown would count, they overwhelmed the field and the local police force assigned for security. *Courtesy Detre Library and Archives, Sen. John Heinz History Center, Pittsburgh, Pennsylvania.*

have called it back." It was an appraisal that changed drastically two years later when Stallworth was drafted by the Steelers and led them to four Super Bowl wins in a Hall of Fame career. "I know it was a touchdown," he laughs today. "No question in my mind it was a touchdown."[17]

"You've got a fourth-down play," said John Madden. "You play 21 games for this moment, and then the ball bounces off the chest and into another player's arms and it's all over. That's the story of the game. What the hell do you say about that?"[18]

Plenty, if you're the Raiders. Oakland defensive back George Atkinson calls the play "The Immaculate Deception" because "the public was deceived, the officials were deceived, and we got deceived."[19] To this day, the Raiders believe that the play should not have counted, and that belief has spawned conspiracy theories as diverse and firmly believed as any connected to the Kennedy assassination. The theories roughly fall into four main groups:

• *The ball never touched Tatum, but bounced off of Fuqua, making it an illegal double touch.*

This is the most basic argument against the legality of the Immaculate Reception, but also the hardest to prove. The cameras that captured the play, both of NBC and NFL Films, were simply not sophisticated enough to conclusively show who touched the ball. Tatum went to his grave saying he simply smashed into Fuqua. "I hit him, but I do not believe I ever touched the ball," he said. "I think it bounced off the receiver."[20]

"The guy [Tatum] hit me and the ball bounced off my chest," Fuqua told a reporter in the Steelers' locker room.

"No, what you mean is the ball hit Tatum," corrected linebacker Andy Russell, listening nearby.

"Oh, yeah. That's right," Fuqua said. "Tatum hit the ball."[21]

Fuqua's initial comment never made it into print and since that time he has kept quiet, suggesting that he knows what happened but will let the mystery of the play live on. Shortly before Tatum passed away, he and Fuqua met at a speaking engagement, where Fuqua said, "I know what happened. Do you?" Tatum answered, "All I know is I was trying to take your damn head off."[22]

Much like the single-bullet or grassy knoll theories, this will remain a source of debate for decades. In 2004, a professor emeritus of physics at Carnegie Mellon University, John Fetkovich, conducted a series of tests in conjunction with the game films and concluded that the ball must have hit Tatum and therefore the officials made a right call, which is a view also shared by another physics professor, Tim Gay at the University of Nebraska.[23]

Many in the Rooney family firmly believed that the reception truly was Immaculate—a matter of divine intervention—the hand of God. The Rooneys were a strong Catholic family; Art Rooney had two sisters who were nuns and a brother who was a priest, and priest friends were always visible around practices and games. It was something of a friendly competition between Rooney and Penn State coach Joe Paterno, who believed the prayers of his mother helped the team pull out a miraculous win over Kansas in the 1969 Orange Bowl. After the Immaculate Reception, Paterno waved the white flag. "You can have Mom," he wired Rooney. "Send your sisters and brothers."[24]

"If Frenchy didn't touch the ball, and Tatum didn't touch the ball," said Chuck Noll, "well, the rule book doesn't cover the hand of the Lord."[25] Bradshaw and Harris concurred, with the quarterback calling it "a miracle sent from heaven." "I guess you could say it was a little bit of luck and God was with us," said Franco. "When you have a feeling that this could be the last play of the season and that you could blow it, then one more chance pulls it through for you."[26]

• *Franco Harris did not catch the rebound before it hit the ground but only trapped it.*

In addition to the problem of primitive camera technology, this theory is doubly hard to prove because no cameras were actually trained on Harris. They were all obviously focused on Tatum and Fuqua. In the NFL Films version of the play, the sideline camera does not follow the ricochet in time to pick up Harris, and the end zone camera is out of focus as Harris reaches for the ball, and then does not show the part of the ball closest to the ground. Similarly, the NBC sideline camera does not pick up Harris until he is already running with the ball. A camera behind the Steeler end zone offers the best vantage point, but it is more than 50 yards away from the action. When Harris reaches for the ball the camera shows it from behind, and the view is further obscured by one of the goal posts.

Thus, like the argument about which players actually touched the ball, this depends completely on the point of view of those on the field. "After the throw I turned and saw him scoop the ball, and it didn't hit the ground," said Steeler receiver Barry Pearson. "It was clean. I thought, 'He's going to score,' and he did. [But] thank goodness we didn't have instant replay."[27]

If anyone should know what happened, it's Harris. "I really can't answer that question," he says when asked if he trapped the ball, "I really can't. I wish I had an answer. There was so much pandemonium around me, I don't recollect all the stuff that was going on."[28] "More than likely," says Bradshaw, "because Franco doesn't speak, he probably trapped it on the ground."[29]

• *Officials missed a clipping penalty on the play that would have negated the touchdown.*

Phil Villapiano was still trailing Franco Harris as the ball bounced away from Tatum and Fuqua, but broke off after the deflection. When Harris got the ball, Villapiano was close enough to try for the tackle, but he did not see Pittsburgh tight end John McMakin. "McMakin!" Villapiano roars. "That guy dives at the back of my legs. Doesn't get me down, but I stumble. I think I could have made (the tackle) in the middle of the field. I had a really good angle."[30]

All video evidence seems to back up Villapiano's claims, with the NFL Films version clearly showing McMakin hitting Villapiano from behind. It is not a blatant clip, but certainly enough to warrant a penalty flag. In the confusion of the moment, none of the officials caught the clip as their eyes were riveted on Franco. "Franco missed his block on the play," says Villapiano, "so he comes jogging down the field—half speed. He's my man, so I'm jogging half speed with him. I saw Bradshaw throw, so I shot over to help make the tackle. Meanwhile, Franco, who had just drifted over ... the ball goes right to him. Had I been as lazy as Franco, that ball would have come to me waist-high."[31]

• *Despite evidence that the catch was illegal, NFL officials ruled it good anyway.*

It's one thing to miss a penalty like the McMakin clip, and those kinds of things happen all the time. But the accusation here goes much deeper and suggests that the NFL had a vested interest in Pittsburgh winning the game.

It started when Harris crossed the goal line. Madden contends that no official signaled touchdown, an interpretation contradicted by NBC's camera in the Steeler end zone which clearly shows back judge Burk raising his arms to indicate a score. However, the other officials did not immediately signal, but instead began conferring with one another. That's when Madden sought out Fred Swearingen, who was shortly on the phone with McNally. "My question was always, if he didn't know it was a touchdown when it happened," asked Madden, "how did you know if was a touchdown after he talked with the guy on the phone?"[32]

The intimation was that the officials looked at the replays of the game on television to make a decision, even though the use of instant replay to review calls was years away. "Franco's miracle left a question of doubt as to the legality of the play until TV reruns helped rule it a legal play," wrote Al Abrams of the *Pittsburgh Post-Gazette*. Abrams was in the press box and asked, "What would they have done before TV and replays? Why, the field officials' word rule and it would stick."[33] According to published reports in the *Oakland Tribune*, Steelers publicist Joe Gordon told reporters in the press box that the decision had been made by watching replays, although Gordon denied making the statement.[34]

It somewhat strains credulity to think that a definitive decision could have been made in the span of a just a few minutes based on grainy and inconclusive video evidence. "There was no decision from the press box and television replay was not used in making the decision," said Jim Kensil.

"The referee was simply clearing up a confusing situation and, at the same time, delaying the touchdown signal until order could be restored on the field."[35]

While McNally admitted looking at the replay, he says he did so only to confirm what Swearingen had already told him. "Don't tell me the officials are having a block on the rule," said McNally. "I looked at one shot on instant replay and in my mind, Tatum is coming up very strong and I felt the ball hit his chest."[36] According to McNally, Swearingen phoned him and said, "Two of my officials ruled that the ball was touched by opposing players. Two guys told me it was touched by Tatum and Fuqua." McNally then told him, "Everything is fine; go ahead and go [with your decision]."[37]

Art Rooney's son Dan was in the press box when the phone call came, handed the phone to McNally, and stood next to him throughout the conversation. While he could not hear Swearingen, Rooney could clearly hear McNally. "Well, you have to call what you saw," McNally said according to Rooney. "You have to make the call. Talk to your people and make the call!"[38]

Raiders executive assistant Al LoCasale said he got a much different version of the call from Marv Hubbard, who supposedly overheard Swearingen's end of the conversation. According to Hubbard and LoCasale, Swearingen may have talked to McNally, but he also called the police. "I'm the chief official of this ballgame," Swearingen reportedly said. "How many cops do you have to escort me off the field if I tell you what happened which is that the ball hit Pittsburgh and there's no touchdown?" "All I can give you is six police," came the reply. "Well in that case, six [points] for Pittsburgh!"[39] While such intentional malfeasance seems almost beyond belief, remember the incident Raiders tight end Bob Moore had with the Pittsburgh police the night before the game. Fans were pouring on to the field and the minimal police contingent was obviously overwhelmed.

Consider also the somewhat contentious relationship between Raiders owner Al Davis and the Steelers. Published reports suggested that Davis had on his payroll a Pittsburgh-area coach who had surreptitiously scouted the Steelers during training camp and the season. Davis supposedly reneged on a gentlemen's agreement for an exchange of game films, with the Steelers sending films of their last two games but Davis not returning the favor. Davis and the Raiders also had some local priests removed from their practice the week of the game, suggesting they were spies for Art Rooney. In fact, it was Rooney's favorite priest, Father John Duggan. "You're a priest, aren't you?" the Raiders told Duggan. "That makes you dangerous. Art Rooney has every priest in the country pulling for him."[40]

The relationship between Davis and the NFL was even stormier. It was Davis who tried to undercut the NFL before the 1966 merger by signing the league's big stars to AFL contracts, and in less than a year he would sue to force out of power his partners running the Raiders. Commissioner Pete Rozelle and the league seemingly had nothing but headaches from Davis, and certainly owed him no favors. From the other perspective, Davis viewed the Immaculate Reception as just another league screw job against the Raiders, and it only fueled his "us against the world" outlook that culminated the following decade when he sued Rozelle and the NFL when the league tried to block his move to Los Angeles.

As darkness settled on Pittsburgh, the city was in perhaps its most festive mood since the Pirates' dramatic World Series win over the Yankees a dozen years before. Parties broke out in neighborhoods all across the city as people everywhere jammed the streets, not to destroy or burn, but simply to celebrate. Legendary sportswriter Red Smith observed, "Not since Braddock was ambushed at Fort Duquesne had the town known a day like this."[41]

At one of the gatherings with some of his friends, Steeler fan Michael Ord came up with the name "Immaculate Reception." He told a woman named Sharon Lavosky, who liked it so much that she called the local television station to recommend it to Myron Cope. Nervous that it might offend some Catholics, Cope nonetheless used it on his WTAE-TV sportscast that night. "It was too good not to use he said."[42] Thus was launched one of the most iconic names in sports history.

Cope was standing on the sidelines watching the play, not in his customary position in the Steelers' radio booth. While he got a great look at the play, urging Franco on as he ran toward the goal line, he missed out on broadcasting immortality. "Don't think I wouldn't have had a few words to say about it," he said later.[43] Jack Fleming's call has been replayed hundreds, if not thousands of times on NFL Films, and for years Fleming received a residual before the rights were finally sold. "The Oakland announcer [Bill King] wasn't that excited by it and there wasn't enough audio from the television feed," said Fleming. "My total amazement was reflected in my voice."[44]

By the time of Cope's evening sports report, the Oakland Raiders were already back home trying to make sense of a season that ended in the most unlikely of circumstances. Long after his teammates had showered and dressed, Atkinson sat in front of his locker, still in full uniform. "We fight for four bleeping quarters," he said tearfully, "and this happens."[45] Their frustration would not end in the off-season or for years to come.

"Here it is years later," Madden said on the anniversary of the play, "and I'm acting like a little kid. It was the finality of it all. It was over. We had nothing. You wander around; you still don't know what happened."[46]

It was a dark day that sports fans in the Bay Area would never forget—and there was still more heartbreak to come.

Chapter 13

Now You Know
What It's Like to Lose

As the Cowboys and 49ers prepared for their playoff game at Candlestick Park, a murmuring began to build in the crowd. More than 61,000 fans, already excited for the kickoff, began to learn of the miracle in Pittsburgh. Many had listened to the game on portable radios, while a few even managed to see the ending on television. Eventually, the news trickled down to the field.

"We got the word on that in the tunnel getting ready to be introduced," said Staubach. "The word came back that the Steelers had won the game. We didn't see it, of course, but were told by people going by, 'Hey, you won't believe how the Steelers won.'"[1] By contrast, Skip Vanderbundt said the 49ers had no clue as to what happened. "Our concentration was focused on Dallas. All we knew was that it would be pretty cool if the 49ers won and the Raiders won, and we ended up playing each other."[2] Even though Vanderbundt and his teammates might not have known it yet, that particular dream had already died.

The coaches, too, were finishing their final preparations. This was to be the third straight year the teams had faced each other in the playoffs, and the last opportunity for the pupil to beat the teacher. "I know him like a book," Nolan said of Landry. "Sure, he'll have some changes. I'll have some too." Landry countered, "I'll have to make him think I'm going to change a whole lot. But I've got to change some."[3]

After a morning of rain and fog the sun had finally started to break through the clouds. The field was wet and somewhat slippery in spots with temperatures settling in the low 50s, and the slickness would play a factor at key points in the game. San Francisco won the toss and would defend the northeast end zone. In two previous playoff games with Dallas, the Niners had surrendered the first touchdown and never caught up. That would not be the problem this afternoon.

The Dallas strategy on the kickoff was simple—keep the ball away from Vic Washington. In only his second year in the NFL, Washington had established himself as one of the league's best and most versatile backs, although he almost never got an opportunity to show what he could do. Despite leading the nation in punt returns at the University of Wyoming, Washington, went undrafted because of concerns about his size (5'11") and durability. He headed to Canada, where in three seasons he led Ottawa to a Grey Cup title and was named player of the game with a record 79-yard touchdown run.

San Francisco linebacker Skip Vanderbundt returns an interception of Craig Morton as Walt Garrison tries to make the tackle. In two games against the Cowboys in 1972, Vanderbundt had three interceptions and two touchdown returns. Years later, Dallas quarterback Craig Morton would greet Vanderbundt at golf outings, calling him "my favorite receiver." *Courtesy Skip Vanderbundt.*

That earned him a ticket to San Francisco, where Dick Nolan called him "our best athlete."[4] Nolan tried him at defensive back, receiver, running back and kick returner before finally letting him return kicks and serve as a situation running back. In his 1971 rookie season, Washington accounted for more than 2,000 yards from scrimmage—811 rushing, 317 receiving and 858 in kick returns—and made the Pro Bowl. His 1972 numbers were less impressive, but he did have that 98-yard return for a score to open the game in Atlanta. "I really wanted to prove I could run in the major leagues," he said. "I did great in Canada, but let's face it—it's not the same. I had to prove I belonged with the best."[5]

Toni Fritsch's high kickoff came to Washington on the three-yard line, where he dropped it, picked it up and headed left. The 49er kick team started toppling Dallas defenders like dominoes, and by the time Washington reached his own forty he was pretty much in the clear. He cut back slightly as he neared the goal line but finished the 97-yard return almost untouched. Only seventeen seconds into the game San Francisco led, 7–0. "Vic Washington gives them an outside attack they didn't have before," said Tom Landry. "We didn't want to kickoff to [him] and look what happened."[6] Unruffled, Dallas then responded with a drive that included six straight runs by Calvin Hill and reached the Niner 20-yard line but could get no further. Fritsch kicked a 37-yard field goal and at the end of the first quarter San Francisco led, 7–3.

As the second quarter unfolded, a series of events conspired to put the Cowboys' season in serious jeopardy. The first went almost unnoticed, as defensive tackle Bob Lilly left the game and did not return. Despite time in the hospital during the week and forty shots in his back to get him ready, Lilly realized he just couldn't move well enough and removed himself from the game. "I could have played, but I wouldn't have been any good," he said. "I thought it was better for the team if Bill Gregory played."[7] Injuries had finally started to slow Lilly after an incredible thirteen-year career, and although he would play a full schedule the next season, he missed the 1973 NFC Championship, ending his streak of 196 consecutive games played.

John Brodie started the 49ers on a long drive that began on his own six-yard line and included a 56-yard completion to Gene Washington. On the Dallas 32, San Francisco tried to get tricky with a flea-flicker, but after taking a return handoff from John Isenbarger, Brodie's deep pass was intercepted by Charlie Waters at the one-yard line. Craig Morton gave the turnover back to San Francisco, fumbling when hit by defensive back Windlan Hall at the 15-yard line. San Francisco moved the ball inside the one, where on fourth down Larry Schreiber made the gamble to go for the touchdown pay off, pushing the pile into the end zone for a 14–3 lead.

Looking much like the team that had pratfalled in the season finale against the Giants instead of a Super Bowl contender, Dallas then handed the ball right back to the Niners. Three plays after the touchdown, Skip Vanderbundt, who had played so well in the Thanksgiving win at Texas Stadium, victimized Morton again, intercepting a pass at the Dallas 32. Once again, Brodie marched the team through a Lilly-less Dallas defense, and Schreiber again ran in from a yard out to make it 21–3. "That's about as bad as we've played, at least with the turnovers," Landry said later. He also admitted that at this point he was beginning to think "it just wasn't our day."[8]

In danger of suffering a repeat of the Thanksgiving blowout, Dallas finally responded. Calvin Hill had some tough runs to set up another Fritsch field goal, and then Morton started to connect with his own receivers. He hit Parks, and then found Alworth over the middle. Alworth caught the ball at the San Francisco 13, and when defender Jimmy Johnson slipped, he finished the 32-yard touchdown play to cut the halftime lead to 21–13.

Just as Lilly was beginning to wind down his career, so was the magnificent Alworth. For a decade his incredible athleticism and grace had defined the wide-open American Football League. "He made it look like a wide-open game," said owner Lamar Hunt of the Kansas City Chiefs, "because he always was wide open."[9] For seven straight seasons beginning in 1962 Alworth averaged 64 catches, ten touchdowns and 1,250 yards a year.

But things turned sour for Alworth in 1970. He borrowed money from the Chargers and then sued the team when it didn't come up with all the payments. Alworth then claimed that in retaliation, the offense froze him out of the game plan as his numbers dropped to only 35 catches and four touchdowns. When Alworth complained, San Diego owner Gene Klein responded, "He was lucky to be on the field at all."[10]

The Chargers solved the problem by shipping Alworth to Dallas before the 1971 season for three backups. San Diego coach Sid Gillman said nothing about the money issue, calling the trade "a difficult decision made in the best interests of the team. He was the greatest Charger and Mr. American Football League."[11]

Alworth joined Bob Hayes to give the Cowboys two Hall of Fame receivers, but despite catching a touchdown pass in Super Bowl VI and helping the Cowboys win the title, he was little more than a spare part. He caught only 34 passes and two touchdowns in the Super Bowl season, and in 1972 his numbers dropped to 15 catches and two scores. "In San Diego, I used to walk around the house mumbling, 'Watch it, catch it, tuck it, and run it,'" he said. "In Dallas, I growled at the cat, made faces in the mirror and kicked the trash can."[12]

The touchdown against San Francisco would be the last great highlight of a great career. The following week against Washington, Alworth would catch only one pass for 15 yards in his last NFL game. Believing he could play a few more seasons but frustrated by the lack of opportunity in the Cowboys' run-oriented offense, Alworth retired at the relatively young age of thirty-two. "Lance got to the point where he felt foolish," said his wife Marilynn. "He was just a sore thumb out there."[13]

When Roger Staubach relieved Craig Morton late in the third quarter of the playoff game, the 49er defense at first harassed him as much as it had Morton. Charlie Krueger (#70), Tommy Hart (#53) and a flying Skip Vanderbundt (#52) are all trying to get a piece of the Dallas quarterback. *Courtesy Skip Vanderbundt.*

On their first drive of the second half, Brodie hit Preston Riley with a 24-yarder, but kicker Bruce Gossett missed a 40-yard field goal attempt wide left. San Francisco was right back in business after Vanderbundt intercepted Morton again, stealing a pass that bounced through the hands of receiver Billy Parks. In a little over six quarters of play against Dallas, Vanderbundt had personally wrecked Morton for three interceptions, two fumble recoveries and two touchdowns. Years later, when the two met at speaking engagements or golf tournaments, Morton would refer to Vanderbundt as his leading receiver.

This time the mistake did not lead to points, but a punt pinned Dallas back on its five-yard line where Calvin Hill fumbled after a hit by Charlie Krueger. That was costly as Schreiber scored on his third one-yard touchdown run of the game and San Francisco seemed to be pulling away, 28–13.

With 1:50 left in the third quarter, Landry made the most fateful decision of the Cowboys' season. Three scores behind and with nothing to lose, he pulled the luckless Morton and sent Staubach into the game. "I felt I had to do something to change the mood of the game," Landry said. "We hadn't been doing much for three quarters and Roger has a way of turning things around."[14]

The situation was not all Morton's fault; he had thrown the one touchdown to Alworth and his receivers had dropped several passes. But more than anyone, Morton had to realize the significance of the moment. He had received much of the blame for the Dallas loss in Super Bowl V, a performance that opened the door for Staubach to become the starter. Now under the playoff spotlight again, he had faltered once more, finishing the day eight of 21 for but 96 yards and two interceptions, "sinking to the occasion" in the words of one sportswriter.[15] As Staubach warmed up on the sidelines Morton took the high road, walking over and giving his replacement a hug. "I have confidence in you," he said. "You can win."[16]

"I think that gave me as much confidence as anything that happened," Staubach said, "that Craig would feel like that and act like that after he'd been pulled. He's just a tremendous person."[17]

At first, the change made little difference, as Staubach was sacked, and then fumbled on a hit by Bob Hoskins on the last play of the third quarter. San Francisco recovered at the Dallas 31, giving the 49ers a chance to pound the last nail in the Cowboy coffin and shovel dirt on the grave. "They were laughing at us. Making fun of us during the game," said Waters. "They were really enjoying having the upper hand on us. They didn't think there was any way [we'd come back], because our offense was sputtering. We were doing absolutely nothing."[18]

The Niners played conservatively, setting Gossett up for a short 32-yard field goal, which he again shockingly missed wide left, bringing the first boos of the day from the Candlestick crowd. Dallas went nowhere on its next possession, but then got the ball back at its 20. Hill ran for 48 on a draw, and after a completed pass to Mike Montgomery, Cedric Hardman roughed Staubach to add 15 more yards. Fritsch kicked a field goal to narrow the margin to 28–16. With only nine minutes left in the game, fans in San Francisco weren't too worried and many of them started to head toward the exits. "Half of the stadium was empty," said Staubach "and their players, Dave Wilcox and those guys, were saying to us, 'Now you know what it's like to lose in the playoffs.'"[19]

Wilcox would eventually make the Hall of Fame as a linebacker. He also had a Hall of Fame mouth. "Dave talked to the other team all the time," said Vanderbundt. "He was an original as far as a bad-mouther was concerned. We used to laugh about it because he was so mild-mannered and quiet, until he stepped on the field and he became a different personality. He would get after anybody at any time. You didn't mess with him at all, and I'm talking teammates too."[20]

With a comfortable lead and time running out, the 49ers could be excused for rubbing it in. Perhaps they were thinking ahead to their next game, against either the Packers or Redskins, in the NFC Championship. Green Bay didn't really scare them that much. The Packers had a strong defense and running game, and sure they had beaten San Francisco earlier in the season, 34–24. But that game was in Green Bay in November, and now the Niners had all the momentum on their side. The Redskins were the class of the NFC, but the 49ers knew George Allen's style from his days as coach of the Rams, and they had beaten Washington in the first round of the playoffs the year before.

As the clock continued to tick away, and Wilcox jawed with anyone on the Cowboys who would listen, the other San Francisco players thought maybe, just maybe, this would be the year that their Super Bowl dreams came true.

CHAPTER 14

Rivalry—Part II

The Steelers–Raiders rivalry had its roots in the old NFL-AFL wars. The established NFL looked down on the younger league when it began play in 1960, ridiculing it as inferior, minor league, and "Mickey Mouse" football.[1] NFL supporters fully believed that even a weak team like the Steelers of the 1960s would have no trouble beating any of the AFL powers, including Oakland. That attitude was strengthened in Super Bowls I and II when the Packers easily handled the AFL champion Chiefs and Raiders.

The first signs that the AFL might be gaining on the NFL came in a series of exhibition games between 1967 and 1969 called the "Little Super Bowls." The preseason games obviously didn't count in the standings, but they were taken very seriously by both leagues—the AFL wanted to prove its worthiness while the NFL wanted to maintain its aura of superiority. "When I came into the NFL [in 1966]," said Redskins coach Otto Graham, "I said the top teams in the AFL could give any team in the NFL a battle. A couple of guys almost shot me for saying that."[2]

The first Little Super Bowl took place on August 5, 1967, when the Denver Broncos, one of the worst teams in the AFL, shocked the Detroit Lions, 13–7. Two weeks later, the Broncos beat another strong NFL team, the Minnesota Vikings, 13–9. The biggest eye-opener that preseason occurred in Kansas City, where the Chiefs took great delight in humbling the Bears, 66–24. The Chiefs had taken a lot of criticism after their Super Bowl I loss to Green Bay and remembered the words of Packers coach Vince Lombardi who said after the game that Kansas City wasn't as good as a lot of NFL teams. After the Chiefs ran up the score on Chicago, calling a timeout in the final minute to score another touchdown, receiver Chris Burford said, "I wonder what the world will say now. [Mr. Lombardi] said we aren't as good as other top teams in the National Football League—like the Bears. Now maybe people will get off our backs."[3]

The Steelers and Raiders did not play against each other in any of the Little Super Bowls, but there was a Bay Area confrontation between Oakland and San Francisco all three years. Before a record crowd in the Oakland Coliseum, the 49ers won the first meeting in 1967, 13–10. Oakland won the next two years, including a come-from-behind 42–28 win in the finale.

With Pittsburgh jumping to the new AFC in 1970, the Steelers were now in the same conference as the Raiders. Even so, the first meeting between the two teams on October 25, 1970, in Oakland had a tinge of the AFL-NFL rivalry. It also served as a coming-out party for the league's oldest pro.

In 1970, Oakland kicker and backup quarterback George Blanda was forty-three years old and had been playing professionally since 1949. He started with the Bears, but George Halas wanted him to quit quarterbacking and kick full-time. Blanda refused, and when he retired after the 1958 season, he figured his playing days were over.

The birth of the AFL gave Blanda new life and he set all kinds of passing records in leading the Houston Oilers to the first two league championships. When the Oilers figured he was washed up, Blanda went to Oakland in 1967, led the league in scoring with 116 points as a kicker and quarterback, and helped the Raiders make the Super Bowl. By 1970, he was the "grand old man" of the game—a good kicker, a savvy veteran, and someone who could come off the bench at quarterback and play effectively. By the end of the 1970 season, he would become a legend.

Daryle Lamonica was the unquestioned leader of the Raiders, a two-time AFL MVP, and he started against the Steelers on a sunny day at the Coliseum. Lamonica threw a first-quarter touchdown pass to Raymond Chester that gave Oakland a quick lead, but after the Steelers tied it, he appeared to injure his hand against the helmet of an onrushing defender. In came Blanda, who warmed up with a touchdown pass to Warren Wells on his first play from scrimmage and went on to throw two more scoring passes to Chester. For good measure, he also kicked a field goal in the Raiders' 31–14 win. Afterwards, his brother John teased him, "George, we've always said you're the third-best quarterback in the family, but the way you're developing we may have to move you up a notch."[4]

But George was just warming up. The Pittsburgh game marked the first of four straight games that Blanda came off the bench to rescue the Raiders from sure defeat with a win or a tie. In summary, his month after the Pittsburgh game looked like this:

- *November 1: Blanda kicked a 48-yard field goal as time expired to give Oakland an improbable 17–17 tie in Kansas City.*

- *November 8: Trailing the Browns by a touchdown in the fourth quarter, Blanda came off the bench to throw a scoring pass to Wells, and then kicked a 52-yard field goal with three seconds left to win it, 23–20. After the field goal, Raiders radio announcer Bill King gushed, "If you can hear me, this place has gone bananas! George Blanda has just been elected king of the world!"[5]*

- *November 15: As Broncos fans were celebrating what seemed like a sure win over Oakland, Blanda dashed their hopes with a fourth-quarter touchdown pass to Fred Biletnikoff that won the game, 24–19.*

- *November 22: In San Diego, Blanda kicked two field goals in the fourth quarter, including the game winner with just seconds left, in a 20–17 Raider win.*

- *December 6: After a loss to the Lions on Thanksgiving, Oakland pulled out a final miracle in New York against the Jets. On the last play of the game a desperation pass into the end zone bounced into the hands of Wells to tie the score. Lamonica threw the pass, but it was Blanda who kicked the winning point in a wild, 14–13 affair.*

Blanda's heroics made his must-see television, as ratings for the NFL spiked in games he played. He started screening his calls and lost track of the sacks of mail that poured in. "After five successive lightning bolts," he said, "I was beginning to think I lived in a fishbowl."[6]

The talk of the nation in newspapers, magazines and on late-night TV, Blanda became a hero to millions, especially America's geriatric set. "George Blanda has restored dignity and virility to every man over 40 years of age," wrote Jim Scott in *The Sporting News.* "Those of us with graying hair now feel that if a 43-year-old can win where the 20-year-olds can't, we can give up our slippered ease by the fireside."[7]

Before the season, Blanda half-jokingly said he would like to play until he was sixty-five, and after his 1970 season it seemed like he just might. He did last until 1975 when he finally retired at age forty-eight. Fittingly, his last points were a field goal in the AFC Championship game against Pittsburgh, a 16–10 loss. "Maybe I'm an oddball," he said, "but I really enjoy the game and I enjoy the practicing. Really, this has been my life."[8]

When Blanda and the Raiders visited Pittsburgh for a week three game in the 1974 season, Terry Bradshaw was no longer Pittsburgh's starting quarterback, but neither was backup Terry Hanratty. Frustrated with what he perceived as Bradshaw's lack of development, and always quick to pull a underperforming player, Chuck Noll instead turned to third-year pro Joe Gilliam, a former eleventh-round draft pick out of Tennessee State.

Gilliam grew up around football and his father was defensive coordinator of the Tennessee State team. He had a rocket arm, great mobility, and a quick mind. He also happened to be black.

Black quarterbacks were still exceedingly rare in the NFL in 1974, with only James Harris of the Rams seeing any significant playing time. With the Rams' offense struggling early in the season, coach Chuck Knox benched John Hadl in favor of Harris, who then went on to lead the team to three straight division titles. Despite such success, Harris was the only black starting quarterback in the league.

Until the arrival of Gilliam. His teammates called him "Jefferson Street Joe" in part for the area where he grew up, but more for his gunslinger mentality. "Joe doesn't like to hand off,"[9] laughed defensive tackle Joe Greene, as Gilliam filled that preseason with passes. More often than not they found their target, as in a 50–21 win over Chicago where Gilliam threw for three touchdowns and ran for another. His performance, aided by Terry Bradshaw's decision to sit out a week in support of a short-lived players' strike, led Noll to name him as the starter against Baltimore—the first black quarterback ever to start a season opener. "I've got a long way to go," Gilliam mused, "[but] I think I'm ready to play. I hope things continue to happen as they have."[10]

In that game against the Colts, he looked like the second coming of Johnny Unitas. Gilliam threw two touchdown passes, including a beautiful long strike to Lynn Swann, in leading the Steelers to a smashing, 30–0 win. "He did not fall on his face," marveled sportswriter Roy Blount, Jr. "Far from it. Two hours after the game, as the trash was being swept up in Pittsburgh's Three Rivers Stadium and football markings were being effaced so that more baseball could be played, Gilliam's bubbling spirit could still be sensed soaring above the field."[11] When Gilliam led the Steelers to 35 points the next week in Denver, *Sports Illustrated* put him on its cover and he seemed ready to become the face of the budding Steeler dynasty.

But at Three Rivers Stadium, the Raiders brought Jefferson Street Joe to an abrupt dead end. Gilliam played miserably, completing only eight of thirty-one passes with two interceptions. Bradshaw made a cameo appearance at the end, but the Steelers never did score and lost, 17–0. Publicly, Noll refused to blame Gilliam and when asked if he thought about pulling him out of the game said no, but he thought about replacing everyone else. "Everyone thinks the quarterback's going in there and carry the team all the time," he said. "Only if the supporting cast isn't worth a damn, neither is the quarterback."[12]

Privately, Noll was beginning to worry about Gilliam's confidence and how he was handling the pressure. Gilliam certainly heard the whispers around the city about his skin color. "I was totally shocked,'" Gilliam said. "I thought if you played well, you got to play. I guess I didn't understand the significance of being a black quarterback at the time."[13]

In some cases, the whispers weren't so quiet. "It became a race issue and things started to get nasty," said Steeler broadcaster Myron Cope. "I ran a talk show at the time and we took all kinds of calls from people upset because Joe was playing and he was black."[14] There were rumors that Gilliam was turning to drugs as a means of coping.

The Raider loss sent Gilliam's season and career spinning out of control. He started the next four games but seemed to lose his effectiveness and confidence each week, throwing only one touchdown pass over that span. When Pittsburgh hosted Atlanta in a Monday night game at the end of October, Bradshaw returned as the starter. After the Steelers' 24–17 win, Noll remained coy about the quarterback situation. "I really don't know," he said when asked about it. "The strange part is that we can go with any of the three quarterbacks and be pretty confident."[15]

Years later, Noll would admit that Gilliam's teammates couldn't trust him anymore because of the growing drug problem. He never got any significant playing time the rest of the season, despite leading the team to a 4–1–1 record, and he watched from the sidelines as Bradshaw quarterbacked the Steelers to the Super Bowl. Gilliam was cut following the 1975 season, bounced around some minor football leagues and even tried out for the USFL. Nothing seemed to work, and certainly nothing helped him recreate the magic of that six-week period in 1974.

The rest of the story has been well chronicled and even turned into a documentary. Gilliam's drug addiction got out of control, he pawned his two Super Bowl rings, and for a time he was living out of a cardboard box underneath a bridge. "To me," he said, "it was like the Ritz-Carlton."[16] He vowed to get his life straight, cleaned up and even opened up a youth football camp. With his life seemingly back on track, Gilliam died of a heart attack at age forty-nine in 2000. At his funeral, another black quarterback who had to overcome the pressures of racism paid him tribute.

"Joe made it all possible for every one of us black quarterbacks," said Doug Williams, who with the Redskins in 1987 became the first black quarterback to win a Super Bowl. "The struggles he went through eased the struggles we had to endure."[17]

As Gilliam found out in 1974, the Raiders–Steelers rivalry was not so much a game as it was a test of manhood. "They're a big, strong football team that just knocked our butts off," said Noll after that game. "They beat us physically and ultimately that's all that counts. They beat us in every department."[18] The beating the Raiders gave the Steelers on that day was symbolic of what the rivalry had become—a no-holds-barred, anything-goes bloodbath—that would dominate football in the rest of the decade. Even without their meeting in the 1972 playoffs, there's a very good chance a strong rivalry still would have developed. The Immaculate Reception simply gave it a kick start. "Pittsburgh will always be a rivalry for us because of what Franco did," said Oakland linebacker Gerald Irons.[19]

The first time the teams met after the Immaculate Reception was for a regular season game in November 1973 where the Raiders vowed revenge. "They kicked us in the teeth and stole our money," tackle Bob Brown said of the Immaculate Reception game. "That's been in the back of our minds."[20] But on a wet, sloppy field in Oakland, the Steeler defense did the kicking, knocking Ken Stabler from the game and tormenting his replacement Daryle Lamonica with four sacks and four interceptions. The 17–9 win was every bit as nasty as the Immaculate Reception game the year before. "He was grabbing me," Pittsburgh defensive tackle and former Raider Tom Keating said of Oakland guard Gene Upshaw. "I hit him in the back of the head once after a play; he punched me in the face. Nothing came of it."[21]

Later that year the Raiders did get their revenge with a 33–14 win over the Steelers in the first round of the AFC playoffs. Five years in a row the teams met in the playoffs and in a decade when the AFC dominated the league, the winner usually went on to win the Super Bowl. In 1974 and 1975, Pittsburgh beat Oakland in the AFC Championship, and then the Raiders finally turned the tables, advancing to the Super Bowl by beating the Steelers in 1976. Along the way, the games were marked by "greased jerseys, obscene footballs, a spying priest and a purposely frozen field."[22]

Forty years before "deflategate," Pittsburgh center Ray Mansfield claimed some of the footballs he was given in the 1973 playoff game were short of air, while others had obscenities written on them. The Steelers further accused Raiders players of greasing their jerseys to make them harder to tackle. Before the 1975 AFC Championship, the Raiders had a priest removed from one of their practices, claiming he was spying for his good friend Art Rooney. "They have too good a team to rely on that kind of stuff," said Steeler linebacker Andy Russell. "It's inconceivable to me that they would try dirty tricks like that, but I suppose it's possible."[23]

Eventually, the incidents turned from comical to violent. In the 1975 AFC Championship, Oakland defensive back George Atkinson leveled Lynn Swann with a vicious blow to the head that put the receiver out of the game with a concussion. The following year when the teams met in a regular season game in Oakland, Atkinson again slammed Swann's head to the ground, prompting Chuck Noll to complain about the "criminal element" the Raiders represented. "People like that should be kicked out of the game or out of football," he said. "It's a criminal act."[24] After viewing the game films, Pete Rozelle fined Atkinson $1,500 for the hit and Noll $750 for comments considered "detrimental to football."[25]

The rivalry then moved to the courtroom, as Atkinson filed a two-million-dollar slander lawsuit against Noll. When a district court in San Francisco ultimately exonerated Noll, Swann was ecstatic. "It's not only a vindication for the Steelers, it's a victory for football," he said. "Now you can go out there and play knowing there's a limit to the violence."[26]

After the 1976 AFC Championship game, the Steelers and Raiders have met only once in the playoffs, a first-round game after the 1983 season won by the Raiders, 38–10. The team was playing in Los Angeles at that point and went on to win its third Super Bowl by beating the Washington Redskins.

The stars of the '70s got older and retired, and by the 1980s the anger between the teams had cooled considerably. Still, for that magnificent five-year stretch the Raiders and Steelers defined football greatness. They won five Super Bowls between them, and the years they didn't win it the road to the championship invariably ran through Pittsburgh or Oakland. And it all started with the Immaculate Reception. "A ton of great memories remain from those great and gritty confrontations," Phil Musick wrote in the *Pittsburgh Press*, "when Good met Bad in a maelstrom of meanness. The two toughest, quickest, slickest, feistiest, funniest, meanest teams of the day locked in combat that produced high jinks as well as history and some of the most marvelous football every witnessed."[27]

While the intensity of the rivalry with Pittsburgh eventually cooled for the Raiders, their anger over the Immaculate Reception did not. From that point forward, the entire organization, fueled by the paranoia of Al Davis, was convinced that the NFL had it in for them. When the Raiders returned to Pittsburgh for the AFC Championship in 1975, a storm blanketed the field in ice at Three Rivers Stadium. Davis complained to Rozelle that the Steelers intentionally let the field freeze over to slow down Oakland's passing attack. "The tarp was accidentally torn," Art Rooney told Davis with a smile. "The damn thing was slashed," thundered Davis.[28]

His anger against Rozelle festered and finally boiled over when the league denied Davis permission to move the Raiders to Los Angeles. Davis sued, and when the first trial ended in a hung jury he accused the NFL of planting one of the jurors. Davis and the Raiders won the second trial, not only getting the right to move but also receiving $49 million in damages from the league. "In the past, I always considered Al like a charming rogue," said Rozelle. "In this instance, in my business judgment, he's gone to outlaw."[29]

Davis seemed to love the outlaw image, regularly bringing in castoffs from other teams regardless of their reputations or baggage. "The castoffs include eccentric personalities, hell-raisers, clubhouse lawyers, anti-authority types, even players thought to be outright, irredeemable head cases," observed one sportswriter.[30] These players also came to embrace the Raiders' anti-authoritarian attitude. Guard Gene Upshaw became head of the NFL Players Association and was the leader of a strike that wiped out almost the entire 1982 season. When Rozelle had to present the winning trophy to Davis after Super Bowl XV, no doubt biting his tongue the entire time, it was Upshaw who said, "I may not give Rozelle a chance to present the trophy. I may snatch it away from him. Rozelle sees me as the right arm of Al Davis, and if he can slap that arm, he will."[31]

Davis maintained his defiant attitude even after Rozelle died and the Raiders' fortunes declined in the 1990s. He moved the team back to Oakland, but after a Super Bowl loss in 2003, the team suffered through thirteen straight non-winning seasons. Davis had seven different coaches in the span, and was still plotting and scheming when he died at age eighty-two in 2011. In some ways, he wrote his own epitaph some thirty years earlier. "I don't want to be the most respected team in the league," he once said. "I want to be the most feared."[32]

Fittingly, the all-time series is about as even as it could get. Through the 2018 season the Raiders hold a slim 16–13 edge in regular season games, and the playoff series is tied 3–3. Whenever the teams meet these days, even forty years removed from their bloodbaths of the 1970s, the games are still physically brutal and emotionally charged. "We don't like each other," said Pittsburgh linebacker Jack Lambert of his battles with Oakland back in the day, "but we respect each other."[33]

Some things never change.

CHAPTER 15

If We Can Just Hang On...

Ed Beard was a tough linebacker and special teams captain for the 49ers who was known as "Biggie" by his teammates because of his ability to play beyond his smallish (6'1", 225 pounds) size. Beard was tough, steady, and had played in every game the previous three seasons. But late in the fourth quarter of the playoff game he collided with Dallas receiver Bob Hayes, wrecking a knee that would force him to retire at the end of season. Beard headed to the sidelines to watch the rest of the action, comforted by his team's seemingly safe 28–16 lead.

"Then," he said, "all hell broke loose."[1]

San Francisco tried to bleed the clock. "From the third quarter on," said Staubach, "they just tried to control the ball and not score at all."[2] The 49ers ran Schreiber twice and punted, and when they held Dallas again, Schreiber carried three more times. The NFL's fourth-ranked offense seemed perfectly content to take the air out of the ball. "We didn't go conservative at the end," Dick Nolan insisted after the game. "We knew they weren't going to back down. We knew they would keep coming."[3]

The strategy did not produce a first down, but ran the clock to the two-minute warning where Dallas took over on its own 45 after a short punt. On the Mutual Radio Network game broadcast, Al Wester turned to his partner Monty Stickles. "One fifty-three on the clock, Monty," he said. "Are they home free?" "Not really," Stickles replied. "There's still enough time. You saw what happened earlier today between the Oakland Raiders and the Steelers."[4]

Like Art Rooney and Myron Cope in Pittsburgh, a group of Dallas sportswriters, including columnists Frank Luksa of the *Ft. Worth Star-Telegram* and Bob St. John of the *Dallas Morning News*, left the press box early. They decided to watch the last few minutes of the game from the field before heading to get interviews from the Cowboys' locker room, which they assumed would be like a morgue. At this point, the stadium elevator decided to malfunction, stranding the group for several minutes. They were unconcerned, figuring they wouldn't miss anything important.

Suddenly, Staubach and the Cowboys caught fire. He passed twice to Walt Garrison for 16 yards, and then hit Parks for 19 more. Now on the San Francisco 20, Parks beat Bruce Taylor to the post and caught the touchdown that made it 28–23 with just 1:30 remaining. It was the game of a lifetime for the young receiver as Parks caught seven passes for 136 yards and the score. At age 24, and with Hayes and Alworth on the down sides of their careers, he seemed to have a bright future in Dallas.

Called "Harpo" because of his frizzy hair and resemblance to the famous Marx Brothers comedian, Parks was as enigmatic as he was talented. "It bothered Billy that football was so important," said Staubach. "He resisted the notion that football was meaningful, and to him, it wasn't."[5] Once he refused to play, claiming a sore knee, when in reality he was simply upset that his friend and teammate Tody Smith had been deactivated that week. Rabidly anti-war in the Vietnam War era, Parks threatened to sit out another game when Melvin Laird, then the Secretary of Defense, came to visit. "And he was serious," said Staubach. "Billy beat to his own drummer. When Billy was out there, he played hard, but football wasn't his deal. He could take it or leave it."[6]

Coming to Dallas in the Duane Thomas trade, he held out and went home to decide if he wanted to play for the Cowboys. During the season Parks caught only 18 passes and one touchdown, and then at the end of the year demanded a trade back to his native California, either with the Raiders or Rams. "I don't think he's made up his mind whether he wants to play football," said Dallas assistant coach Mike Ditka. "He isn't committed to the involvement the game demands."[7]

That kind of attitude wasn't going to cut it for Tom Landry, so in May 1973 the Cowboys sent Parks and his pal defensive end Tody Smith to Houston. Parks had a couple of decent seasons with the Oilers but caught only one pass his final year in 1975. In the trade, Dallas received draft picks that turned into Ed "Too Tall" Jones and quarterback Danny White, so in that sense it can be said that Parks gave the Cowboys long-term value. In the short term, his touchdown gave a pulse to the faint Dallas comeback hopes.

By this time the press elevator was working again and the Dallas writers, sensing something was up, rushed for the field. But they were stopped by a security guard who would not let them pass until the game was over.

A Roger Rally Leaves SF in Tears

Staubach 'Hearts' Dallas to Win

New Slot for Laugh-In
Ron St. John would have started this wide smile before the winning touchdown pass from Roger Staubach ever arrived.

Franco Rescues Steelers

Bearcat Brown   **Travis Roach**
A Close Look at Cotton Bowl Foes, Page 2B

The Game Ball
Franco Harris, right, throws down ball that beat Oakland as Steeler teammate Ron Shanklin offers a jubilant hug.

The front page of the *Dallas Morning News* sports section on December 24, 1972, tried to capture the madness of Immaculate Saturday. The story by Cowboys beat writer Bob St. John won an award from the Pro Football Writers Association, even though he never saw the dramatic ending. *© 1972, the Dallas Morning News, Inc. Reprinted with permission.*

After briefly considering rushing the guard the storming the field, the group stood in frustration, unable to get a good view of what was going on.

With only one time out and 1:30 remaining, Dallas could not kick deep and hope to stop the clock and get the ball back. Its only chance was an onside kick, and San Francisco countered by sending in its "hands" team on the return, putting backs and receivers on the front line to better handle the kick. One of those players was Preston Riley.

As Toni Fritsch approached the ball for the kick, he made an unusual move, bringing his right foot behind his forward left foot, much like a player might use his arm to make a behind-the-back pass in basketball. While no one watching had likely seen the move before, it was not unknown to the Cowboys. "He used to try all these tricky ways of kicking the ball," said Charlie Waters, "and he used to do this thing where he'd run up to the ball and run past it. And he'd kick it behind his back."[8]

A former auto mechanic and soccer player from Austria, Fritsch gained fame in his homeland as a right winger on the Austrian national team. He was found by Cowboys scouts and given a tryout at Vienna Stadium, where he made 29 of 30 field goals from forty yards out. "I have only three, maybe four good years left in soccer," Fritsch said after signing a Dallas contract at age 26. "This udder business I can kick till I am old man."[9]

Fritsch's struggles with English, along with his quirky personality, made him a popular teammate. One night at training camp, his teammates sent Fritsch on a late-night mission to get pizza. Rushing back to beat curfew and avoid a fine, Toni was stopped by the police. Unfortunately, he did not have his driver's license.

"Kowboy keeker," Fritsch tried to explain. "Es Kowboy fam-us keeker."

The cop looked at the pudgy, balding Fritsch and laughed.

"Sure," he said, "and I'm Bob Lilly."[10] Off Toni went to jail, where the team had to bail him out.

In Fritsch's first game in 1971, he lined up to attempt a game-winning kick against St. Louis. The Cardinals, and especially defensive end Larry Stallings, began taunting him.

"Hey, you little shithead, you're going to blow it!" Stallings yelled. "You're gonna choke, you midget bastard."

Linebacker Dave Edwards, lining up as a blocker, began to laugh. "Save your breath," Edwards shot back. "He can't understand a word of English." After Fritsch nailed the kick to win the game, writers asked him if he had heard Stallings.

"Yes, I hear," he said. "And I tell him, 'You got a big ass and nothing here,'" as Fritsch tapped his temple with a finger.[11]

He also had amazing kicking dexterity. During a lull in practice, the other kickers—Mike Clark and punter Ron Widby—killed time by trying to kick Fritsch's soccer ball into a waste basket on one bounce. After several unsuccessful attempts, they let Fritsch try and he flicked the ball with his foot into the basket on the fly. "One day he got his interpreter to bet Walt Garrison that he could not only make every field goal he kicked, but that he could land the football on the horizontal crossbar on every kick," Charlie Waters remembered. "After 12 kicks, starting at 20 yards and moving back 48 yards, Toni had successfully landed the ball on the crossbar on all 12, and he collected a hundred dollars from Walt."[12]

Aided in part by surprise and the somewhat slippery turf, the onside kick careened to Riley who moved forward to cover it. But the ball bounced off Riley, thanks in part to a hit by Dallas linebacker Ralph Coleman, and into the arms of Mel Renfro, who recovered at midfield with 1:25 to play. "All I saw was the football on the ground," he said. "I grabbed it and hung on for dear life."[13]

In a game filled with big plays, this was the biggest, as Dallas would have had no chance to win had San Francisco recovered. "The onside kick was the big play," Staubach confirmed. "We recover that and it's a new ball-game."[14] The irrepressible Fritsch simply shrugged when asked about the kick. "The other team," he said, "they don't know which way comes the ball."[15]

As Dallas players exulted on the sidelines, the Niners defense trudged back on the field. They had been talking over some changes in scheme and strategy with assistant coach Paul Wiggin but barely had time to discuss much less implement them. Despite the momentum change, they still had the lead. "If we can just hang on," thought Vanderbundt, "we can win this thing. We're on our heels because of this change in emotion, but we never felt like we were going to lose. We've got to shut them off. We've just got to hold on."[16]

Listening to their radios to catch the end of the game, many Niner fans who had left the stadium just a few moments before now decided to turn around and head back. Those who got back in saw a horrifying sight. Staubach dropped back, scrambled for 21 yards and bobbled the ball, but held on at the San Francisco 29. He then hit Parks for 19 yards on a sideline pattern that put the ball on the ten-yard line with less than a minute to play. Even though Parks got out of bounds, Dallas used its last time out. "There must be 61,500 fans who have their hearts jammed in their throats right now," Wester told radio listeners.[17]

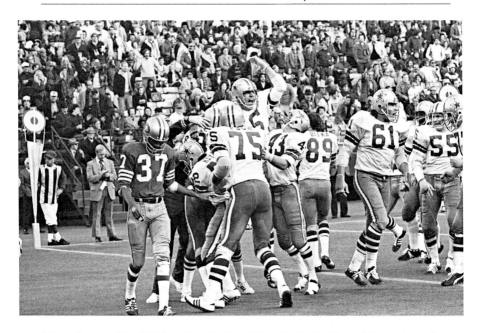

Three hours after Pittsburgh pulled out its miracle, Dallas celebrated another. The Cowboys exult after the game-winning touchdown pass to Ron Sellers, who is mobbed by teammates, including Jethro Pugh (#75), Bob Hayes (#22) and Cliff Harris (#43). San Francisco fans and players, especially Jimmy Johnson (#37), were in disbelief. *Courtesy Bettman Collection/Getty Images.*

After the catch, receiver Ron Sellers, largely a non-factor in the game with only one reception, had a suggestion. "We were in the huddle and I just blurted out to Roger, 'I've got a curl across the middle; throw it to me,' and he called the play," said Sellers. "I had run the curl all day and they hadn't thrown it to me one time, and I had been open. That's the reason I told him I was open." Sellers added that no one else came forward with the idea; it was just a result of his "big mouth."[18]

Landry had sent in "83 pass," another sideline to Parks, and Staubach admitted he wanted to go that direction because Parks had the hot hand. But the 49ers came with a blitz, leaving Sellers one-on-one with Windlan Hall. Staubach looked to Parks, but read the blitz and quickly came back to Sellers who had gotten inside position on Hall. Photos taken of the moment show a huge grin creasing Sellers' face as Staubach's perfect pass settled into his arms. "I just looked that ball into my hands all the way as the coach says," he laughed.[19] Somehow, Dallas led 30–28 with only 52 seconds to play.

Pandemonium broke out on the Dallas sidelines, even though the game was not yet over. The Cowboys, a team noted for cool demeanor and computer-like efficiency, were jumping all over each other. Some, like defensive end Larry Cole, were rolling on the ground, unable to restrain the emotion. Billy Truax raised his hands toward the heavens in prayer. "It was bedlam on the sidelines," said Waters. "It was total ecstasy. We were rolling around and diving on each other like a bunch of children. One of the great, high happy moments in sports."[20]

Not so for the 49ers, who still had those 52 seconds to try and salvage the wreckage. Two completions brought the ball near midfield and Gossett began warming up on the sidelines for a possible game-winning attempt. Riley, who played a solid game aside from the onside kick, caught a 24-yard pass to get inside the Dallas 40, but a holding penalty wiped out the gain and moved the ball all the way back to the San Francisco 30 with just eleven seconds to play. A Brodie desperation throw was intercepted by Waters, and after a kneel-down Dallas had stolen the game, 30–28. Dallas players almost danced off the field, while the 49ers stood around as if waiting for another play that would never come, boos cascading down on them from the remaining fans in the stadium. "I felt so sorry for those guys when the game was over," said Dallas guard Blaine Nye. "I couldn't even look at them."[21]

The Dallas writers were equally stunned. Luksa, St. John and their group had missed one of the most exciting finishes in NFL playoff history. They got the details from other writers and then headed to the locker room to ask questions about an ending they never saw. "I put all the drama I could [into my story]," said St. John. "When I got back to Dallas people were phoning and complimenting me. It was judged the best game story that year by the Pro Football Writers Association. That not only taught me something about myself but also about contests."[22]

St. John was recognized for his story, but some sort of award should go to Jerry Magee of the *San Diego Union-Tribune*. Magee wrote sports in San Diego for more than fifty years, primarily covering the American Football League, and he may have the best line of all summing up the afternoon. "Dallas scored 14 points with less than two minutes to play to beat San Francisco 30–28 Sunday," he wrote, "in the most miraculous play-off finish staged in the NFL in the last three hours."[23]

"The real turning point was our guys not quitting," Landry told reporters in the exuberant Cowboys' locker room. "San Francisco couldn't believe they lost, which I can understand. It looked like they had it won. It's just unreal to have that many big plays in the last two minutes."[24] Staubach faced reporters with no shirt on, the long red scar on his right shoulder a visible reminder of a surgery that now seemed like such a long time ago. "This locker room is more excited than the Super Bowl locker room last year,"[25] he said, a feeling that Landry seconded. "I've never experienced anything this exciting," said the coach, who called it the greatest comeback in his thirteen years in Dallas. "In the Super Bowl, we knew [victory] was coming. This time, we didn't have time to control our emotions."[26]

The emotions on the San Francisco side were understandably different. Reportedly, Vic Washington sat in front of his cubicle throwing up, while Riley, who caught four passes for 41 yards, smoked nearby, tears streaming down his face.[27] Several teammates came up to tell him it wasn't all his fault. Cas Banaszek had the holding call that wiped out Riley's gain, and Gossett missed two crucial field goal attempts. Despite a strong first half, Hall let Sellers slip inside him for the winning score. A change in any one of those plays could have made the difference.

Dick Nolan was badly shaken as he faced the media. "I've never had anything like this happen before," he said.[28] Landry could empathize with his friend and former assistant, having experienced the tormenting playoff losses to the Packers and Browns. "I'm sure Dick felt the same way we felt in the ice game in Green Bay," he said. "It's ungodly. A coach can't feel worse than that."[29]

"We were crushed," said Vanderbundt. "The locker room was dead silent. Dick Nolan was beyond words. I don't even know if he spoke to the team because he was so distraught. I felt bad for that man. I love the guy; he's the reason I stayed in the league for ten years. He so badly wanted to turn the page on Dallas."[30]

"They made a helluva comeback," said Beard. "Maybe everything was going too good for us."[31] Many were struck by the obvious comparison to the dramatic finish in the Minnesota game the previous week. This time, San Francisco was on the wrong end of the thunderbolt. "History really doesn't repeat itself that much," said Staubach, "but I guess in this case the analogy is a good one."[32]

The final statistics falsely suggested that Dallas outplayed the 49ers. The Cowboys outgained San Francisco in total yards, 402 to 255, and held the 49ers to 105 yards rushing on 37 carries. Dallas shot itself in the foot most of the afternoon with five turnovers and five sacks. Calvin Hill added 125 yards, most of it coming on that draw play toward the end, but also had two costly fumbles. Washington had the best day rushing for San Francisco with 56 yards on just ten carries.

In reality, San Francisco controlled play from Vic Washington's opening kickoff return up until the final two minutes. The 49ers forced Dallas into an afternoon of mistakes and capitalized on almost every one—the notable exceptions being the two missed field goals by Gossett. The misses, which seemed inconsequential at the time, and an overly conservative offense in the fourth quarter, opened the door just wide enough for the Cowboys to slip through.

The obvious difference in the game was Staubach, who finished 12 of 20 for 174 yards and two touchdowns, most of it accomplished in the last three minutes. Landry made a specific point to defend Morton after the game, saying, "We had bad field position and the only chance we had was to put Roger in there. He had a hard time keying his defense at first, but he got better. Morton wasn't that bad, it's just that the turnovers were killing us."[33] It was a twisted bit of logic considering that Morton directly contributed two interceptions and a fumble, and no one was really buying it, especially the 49ers. "If Craig Morton had stayed in the game," said receiver Gene Washington, "we win."[34]

The following day, the Redskins beat Green Bay, 16–3, so the Cowboys packed their bags and headed to the NFC Championship in Washington. The teams had split their season series, each winning at home, so the Redskins appeared to have the advantage. But the Cowboys and Roger Staubach had just pulled off one miracle and certainly no one discounted the possibility of another. That is, if Staubach would even play. The unexpected comeback against the 49ers would force Tom Landry to once again decide between Staubach and Morton at quarterback, and as it had the year before, the choice determined the Cowboys' season.

The seasons for the Raiders and 49ers had already been determined and there was perhaps more gloom to come. In the days leading up to Immaculate Saturday a mathematician named Reuben Greenspan had made a dire prediction. Greenspan believed that earthquakes were tied to lunar and solar eclipses, and noting a solar eclipse on January 4, said that a major quake would hit on that date in San Francisco. He even predicted the time and size—9:00 a.m. and 7.4 on the Richter scale.

It was not hard to think of Greenspan as a crackpot—he lived as a recluse in Arizona—and most people didn't take the prediction too seriously. "That's nonsense," said Bruce Bolt of the seismographic station at the University of California in Berkeley. "No one has been able to find a key in predicting the exact time when an earthquake of a given size will occur."[35] San Francisco mayor Joseph Alioto good-naturedly invited Greenspan for a dinner that night that included "seven courses of crow."[36]

Others were not so confident. There were increases in purchases of earthquake insurance and several local residents decided to head out of town just to be sure. "I've been running the theory through a computer and getting pretty good results," said Dr. William Kautz of the Stanford Research Institute.[37] Kautz also noted that Greenspan had correctly predicted several quakes, including one the year before in Los Angeles, a record of success that earned him the nickname the "earthquake prophet."

Of course, no earthquake took place, which forced Greenspan to admit that he had gotten his calculations wrong. He missed hitting the big San Francisco earthquake by more than 16 years, as a 1989 quake devastated the area, killing 67 people and causing more than $5 billion in damages. It struck right before Game Three of an all–Bay Area World Series between the San Francisco Giants and Oakland A's.

As night settled in the Bay on the night of December 23, 1972, fans of the Raiders and 49ers might not have minded if Greenspan's prediction had come true. They had already witnessed two disasters; how much worse could a third one be?

CHAPTER 16

Do the Guys Still Blame Me?

We beat the Vikings and the 'Skins, but the Cowboys did us in. We might just have won it all, but Preston Riley dropped the ball.—"We Are the 49ers" by the Niner Knuckleheads

The word "goat" gets thrown around a lot in sports. In a modern sense, it has become an acronym meaning "the greatest of all time," and to be called a GOAT (capitalization required) is about the highest compliment a player can receive. For his multiple Super Bowl rings and MVP awards, Patriots quarterback Tom Brady has often been called the GOAT. "People who hate the Patriots may try to argue about this," wrote Mike Freeman in 2018, "[but] it's pretty clear that Brady is the GOAT."[1]

But the lower-case "goat" has a much longer history that traces an origin all the way back to the Bible. In Leviticus, the priest could make an offering of a goat, "but the goat on which the lot for the scapegoat fell shall be presented alive before the Lord to make atonement upon it, to send it into the wilderness as a scapegoat."[2] Thus, the goat was the athlete who had to take all the blame, usually for an egregious mistake. When Roy Riegels ran the wrong way with a fumble and cost the University of California the 1929 Rose Bowl, newspaper accounts said that because Riegels was only a junior, "the goat of the coast game can prove his worth next season."[3]

In the wreckage of the 49ers playoff loss on Immaculate Saturday, as so often happens in difficult and unexpected defeats, there was a need to try to fix blame and find a scapegoat. If something, or someone, could just be held accountable, then it might make it easier to explain the inexplicable. San Francisco linebacker Skip Vanderbundt lightheartedly put the blame on the 49er wives. With the score 28–13 late in the third quarter, "our wives were in the stands deciding what to wear to the Super Bowl before the game was over," Vanderbundt said with a laugh. "I blame [my wife] because she jinxed us. The fat lady hadn't sung yet; she hadn't even warmed up yet."[4]

A more logical target was Roger Staubach, who came off the bench and rallied the Cowboys to three straight scores and the victory. To this day, the San Francisco players are convinced that if Craig Morton had stayed in the game there would have been no comeback. "No knock on Craig," says Vanderbundt, "but Staubach had so much more mobility. If Craig Morton is still in the game, we win. Absolutely, Staubach was the difference."[5]

Other fingers pointed at quarterback John Brodie, who many said got too conservative and sat on the lead in the fourth quarter. Bruce Gossett missed two very makeable field goals, just one of which would have made the difference. The 49ers defensive backfield, which included a future Hall of Famer and two All-Pro players, got torched over the course of the last few minutes of the game.

But those names are just footnotes. The main headline was, and seemingly always will be, Preston Riley.

Riley was a speedy wide receiver out of Vicksburg, Mississippi, who played college ball at what was then Memphis State University—a receiver on a team that primarily ran the ball. A ninth-round draft choice, he played sparingly in his first two seasons—1970 and 1971—catching only ten passes and no touchdowns, but he seemed to blossom in 1972. Dick Nolan wanted more speed at receiver and by the end of the year put Riley in the starting lineup ahead of sure-handed but slower Dick Witcher.

Riley's 1972 numbers were still modest, only eleven catches and one score, but he was gaining the coaches' confidence on special teams and in crucial situations. He was on the field against Dallas for both the onside kick and in the final minute when San Francisco nearly pulled off its own miracle comeback. If not for a holding call, Riley's reception and carry into Dallas territory with just seconds left might have set up Bruce Gossett for a winning field goal attempt.

"No one on the team blames Preston," said Vanderbundt. "Cas [Banaszek] got called for holding on that play and he blames himself. Windlan Hall got beat by Sellers on the play that won the game; he can blame himself. Gossett missed a field goal so I guess he can blame himself. Hey, the other team gets paid to play too. They just made the plays. Many guys came up to him afterwards and said, 'Hey, it happens. Don't worry about it. You can't go back and change it.'"[6]

"They ought to get off of poor Preston," said Niners defensive end Cedric Hardman. "He just made the last of a lot of errors that day. I did more to lose that game than he did."[7]

But the fans and the media would not get off. Riley heard the criticism, and brooded over the mistake, replaying it in his mind to the point that it adversely affected his play. "All we had to do was get the ball and run out the clock," said Lou Spadia, 49ers president at the time. "The ball went right through Preston Riley's legs. Preston Riley didn't say a word. He dressed, left the clubhouse and was never seen or heard from again."[8]

San Francisco helped in that regard, trading Riley to the woeful Saints in the off-season, a move what was tantamount to banishment to Siberia. Hoping for a fresh start in New Orleans, Riley instead found he could not escape his past. In a 1973 season preview, it was noted that "the starter [for San Francisco] most of last year was Preston Riley, who became the goat of the playoff loss to Dallas when he fumbled an onside kickoff in the closing minutes."[9] Riley played one game in 1973 for the Saints, caught no passes, and dropped out of the league at the relatively young age of 26.

Riley's tragedy lived far beyond his short 49ers career. Dwight Clark, who made "The Catch" to beat Dallas in the 1982 NFC Championship game, remembers the Super Bowl that followed two weeks later. The 49ers were leading Cincinnati 26–21 toward the end of the game, and Clark was on the field to defend against an obvious onsides kick. "All I could think of was that unfortunate onside kick against Dallas when they fumbled it," said Clark. "Running across the field that's all I could think about."[10] The kick came to Clark who held on to preserve the 49ers' first Super Bowl title.

Forty-three years later, Riley's nightmare would be repeated by Brandon Bostick of the Green Bay Packers. In the 2015 NFC Championship, needing just an onside recovery to advance to the Super Bowl, Bostick fumbled. Seattle recovered, scored and then won the game in overtime. Bostick was released after the season, but not before receiving death threats from fans on social media. "I never, ever felt that pain before," he says, "just realizing how close we were to playing in the Super Bowl. I don't even know how to describe what I felt like. I don't know if you can describe what it is to feel like nothing, like you're worthless. There are no words I can put toward the feeling."[11]

Sports psychologists have only recently begun to appreciate the emotional gravity of such moments. Bill Buckner let a ground ball go through his legs that contributed to the Red Sox World Series loss in 1986. Excoriated by Boston fans, Buckner learned to live with his mistake, even to the point of being able to laugh at it. Donnie Moore, by contrast, gave up a famous home run that same season (to the Red Sox, no less) that helped lose the pennant for the California Angels. Tormented by other physical and psychological issues, Moore committed suicide three years later. "I think insanity set in," said Mike Pinter, Moore's agent. "He could not live with himself after the home run. That home run killed him."[12]

Caught somewhere in-between is Preston Riley, for whom time has not healed all wounds. He can't forget, in part, because fans and the media won't let him forget. His name became a black mark in the Bay Area; a running punch line that turned his life into a joke. More than thirty years after the bobble, San Francisco sportswriter Ray Ratto observed, "49er fans remember the Preston Riley fumble game more than they do that 17–14 win at Minnesota two years earlier."[13]

The Preston Riley game. Not the Roger Staubach game or the Bruce Gossett game. It's a name not quite as famous as the Immaculate Reception, but one with just as long a memory. When Jose Cruz, Jr., made a bonehead play that cost the San Francisco Giants a baseball playoff game in 2003, one newspaper commenter observed, "Jose Cruz Jr., welcome to the Bay Area Sports Pariah Hall of Shame. Have a seat over there next to Preston Riley."[14]

No wonder Preston Riley has dropped out of the spotlight, or at least is not trying to get back into it. There are some addresses and phone numbers for him as he bounced around North Carolina, Tennessee, and his native Mississippi. He currently lives in Ridgeland, just outside the capital of Jackson, and only about 50 miles from his hometown of Vicksburg. Riley is pretty much incommunicado for those seeking to dig up his NFL past, including even his own former teammates. "I really don't think that much about it anymore," he said in a rare interview in 1982. "I'm still hanging in there."[15]

When the Boston Red Sox won three World Series titles in the 2000s, for many fans it helped erase the stigma attached to Buckner's error. Buckner was welcomed back like a long-lost member of the family, returning to Fenway Park on Opening Day 2008 to throw out the first pitch, and he and received a standing ovation that brought tears to his eyes. "I really had to forgive," he said, "not the fans of Boston, per se, but I would have to say in my heart I had to forgive the media. For what they put me and my family through. So, you know, I've done that and I'm over that."[16] Said Red Sox player Kevin Youkilis, "I've probably never almost been in tears for somebody else on the baseball field. There's not too many people that can do what he did today and face thousands of people that booed him, threatened his life. For a man to step out there on the field, it shows how much of a man he is."[16]

Maybe it's time for Preston Riley. "The Catch" made by Dwight Clark to beat the Cowboys in the 1982 NFC Championship game went a long way in helping fans get over Riley's fumble. So too did five Super Bowl titles in the next thirteen years. Maybe it's now time to bring back Preston Riley to a 49ers game and let bygones be bygones. Journalist Herb Caen, who covered San Francisco for sixty years and may have known more about the Bay Area than anyone, wrote shortly before his death, "Preston Riley, wherever you are, all is forgiven."[17]

Preston Riley is in some ways the real legacy of the 49ers playoff loss to Dallas. There is heartbreak, of course, for all the members of that team in letting a potential Super Bowl get away. But most of them have moved on in one way or another. From the defense, Jimmy Johnson and Dave Wilcox made the Pro Football Hall of Fame. Brodie played professional golf for a while before turning to broadcasting. Receiver Gene Washington became an official in the NFL office and for a time served as the league's director of football operations.

Skip Vanderbundt sells and leases commercial real estate in Sacramento, often closing multi-million dollar deals. He sets his own schedule and lives close enough to children and grandchildren to visit them frequently. In light of such things, the lack of a Super Bowl championship, or even the 1972 playoff loss, have not defined his life.

The same cannot be said for Preston Riley.

"The last I heard from him I got a call one night at my house in Sacramento," says Vanderbundt. "It's Preston Riley calling from Tennessee and I had not talked to him in twenty years. He calls up and he's absolutely drunk as a skunk. He says, 'Skip, do the guys still blame me?' And I had to look down from the phone. I said, 'Preston, what are you talking about? We never blamed you. There were so many mistakes made by all of us.' The fact that he called me, still blaming himself twenty years later, is sad."[18]

CHAPTER 17

Victory Postponed

While Pittsburgh's upcoming AFC Championship game with unbeaten Miami dominated talk in the city, it was by no means the only news. In the last week of December, former president Harry Truman died at the age of eighty-eight after a short illness. The same day of the Immaculate Reception, an earthquake—not foreseen by Reuben Greenspan or anyone else—devastated Nicaragua, killing some 6,000 people, injuring 20,000 more, and leaving a quarter of a million homeless. Relief efforts were already underway, and Pittsburgh Pirates star outfielder Roberto Clemente, a Puerto Rican native who had just three months before collected his 3,000th hit, announced he would fly to Managua to give help. "He did not just lend his name to the fund-raising activities the way some famous personalities do," said friend and television producer Luis Vigoraux. "He took over the entire thing, arranging for collection points, publicity and the transportation to Nicaragua."[1]

The Steelers practiced under unusually warm temperatures for December, and by game time Sunday it was still a balmy 58 degrees and sunny. Despite a perfect 15–0 record, the Dolphins did not have home-field advantage as the NFL rotated that privilege among division winners at the time. On Tuesday, Miami coach Don Shula announced that Earl Morrall would once again start at quarterback for Bob Griese as he had done since the fifth week of the season when Griese had broken an ankle against San Diego. "Earl will start in Pittsburgh," Shula said. "Each week Griese is getting more and more time to heal and get back in the groove."[2]

There had been talk that Griese might start against the Steelers given he was now almost fully healed. Shula was tempted to bring him in the second half of the team's lackluster playoff opener when Cleveland led

14–13 in the fourth quarter. But Morrall engineered a game-winning 80-yard drive capped by Jim Kiick's decisive touchdown run with just minutes to play. Shula said that Griese would be available to come off the bench if needed. There was some mild panic in Pittsburgh when Terry Bradshaw spent a night in the hospital with the flu, and Chuck Noll briefly flirted with the idea of starting backup Terry Hanratty, but Bradshaw seemed ready to go by the end of the week.

Another quarterback controversy dominated preparations for the Dallas–Washington matchup for the NFC Championship, the third meeting between the teams that season. As usual, it involved Roger Staubach and Craig Morton, and as usual Tom Landry was having trouble deciding between the two. Morton had led the Cowboys all year, but Staubach's heroics in the San Francisco game suggested he might be ready to retake command of the team. By Wednesday, Landry had still not named a starter. "We'll go with the quarterback who we think can win for us," he said predictably.[3]

By now, it seemed like everyone had an opinion. Dick Nolan of the 49ers guessed Staubach would start, while the Dallas players felt Morton would be the better option. "I don't think Roger was sharp enough to go an entire game," said linebacker Lee Roy Jordan. "Roger was rusty."[4] Even the Redskins weighed in with some psychological warfare. Defensive tackle Diron Talbert said he hoped Staubach started because he thought Roger wouldn't be ready to play. To complicate matters, Staubach also came down with the flu and didn't practice most of the week.

Despite all that, Landry went with Staubach, just as had in his momentous decision the year before. Wanting to keep the Redskins guessing as long as possible, Landry didn't announce his choice until Thursday, adding he thought the team could win with either quarterback. "I really thought I deserved to start," said Staubach, "though if Coach Landry had started Craig, I wouldn't have been upset."[5] Bob Lilly would also try to play after resting his bad back the entire week. As the wild card team, Dallas would play at Washington in the late Sunday afternoon game, while Pittsburgh hosted Miami at noon. "Boy, wouldn't it be great to come up with another thriller like the one which raided the Raiders," said Bradshaw. "But one like that of last Saturday comes along once in a lifetime, I guess."[6]

Fans in Three Rivers Stadium Sunday were not only greeted with warmer weather, but also with a bit more security. It had been something of an embarrassment to the NFL the previous week when fans poured on to the field after the Franco Harris touchdown, holding up play for several minutes. "The fans in Pittsburgh just aren't used to being in the playoffs," said NFL executive Val Pinchbeck, Jr. "They got a little carried away with it. We don't want any more incidents or confusion."[7]

Pinchbeck and other NFL officials met with the Steelers and local police several times, and on Wednesday he announced that the NFL would take over security for the game. "The one last Saturday at Three Rivers wasn't as bad as pictured," scoffed local columnist Al Abrams. "The field mob scene was a detonation from a fuse which has been burning for 40 years. It didn't take long to get the crowd behind the lines once they learned Harris's odd touchdown was official."[8] Abrams's paper, the *Post-Gazette*, fanned the flames of potential security issues by disclosing that the Dolphins would be staying at the William Penn hotel downtown.

Even with all that planning, neither the NFL nor local security could stop Franco's Italian Army. In addition to their traditional routine, they managed to hire a plane to drop thousands of leaflets over the Dolphins' sideline that called for Miami's surrender to "ethnically superior forces."[9]

For a team in only its third playoff game in franchise history, the Steelers showed little fear of the unbeaten Dolphins. They intercepted Morrall on the first drive of the game, and then launched a drive of their own—seven minutes, 11 plays, all on the ground, down to the Miami two. On third down, Bradshaw rolled left where he fumbled after a vicious hit by safety Jake Scott. The ball bounced into the end zone where it was recovered by Pittsburgh tackle Gerry Mullins for a 7–0 lead. Once again it looked like the fates were smiling on the Steelers. Twice in the first half they recovered their own fumbles, and one they didn't get—a Franco Harris fumble deep in Pittsburgh territory—was ruled down by contact.

Unfortunately, the hit on Bradshaw left the quarterback woozy and he limped off the field, not to return until the second half. "Bradshaw was weak to start with," said Noll, referencing his bout with the flu, "then he had a pinched nerve in his neck which affected his right arm and he had trouble remembering things."[10] In came Hanratty, and his rust showed immediately. Hanratty would finish the day five of ten for only 57 yards.

The Pittsburgh defense was still stifling Miami and forced a punt from midfield in the second quarter. Punter Larry Seiple noticed that no one was rushing on his right side, so he took off and ran 37 yards to the Steeler 12-yard line. Larry Csonka finished the drive catching a touchdown pass from Morrall to tie the game. "We didn't force enough on the punt and Seiple just put the ball under his arm and ran," said Noll of the biggest play of the game. "He was a very alert punter."[11]

After Pittsburgh regained the lead in the third quarter with a Gerela field goal, Shula decided to bring in Griese for Morrall, a move that paid off right away when Griese hit a streaking Paul Warfield with a 52-yard completion. Miami got a huge break when a Jack Ham interception was negated by an offside call, and Kiick ran two yards to put the Dolphins back on top, 14–10. "We're not playing as well now as we did earlier in the season," a prescient Mercury Morris said before the game. "Fortunately, we've been able to come up with the big play at the right time."[12]

The Dolphins blocked a long Gerela field goal and then methodically marched to their last touchdown on another run by Kiick. Pittsburgh hopes flickered when Bradshaw returned in the fourth quarter and cut the lead to 21–17 on a great one-handed touchdown catch by rookie Al Young. The Steeler defense held, and the capacity crowd started thinking of a second Immaculate Reception, but Bradshaw threw two interceptions in the last three minutes, and Pittsburgh's season was over, 21–17. Miami moved to 16–0 and on to the Super Bowl.

Even so, there was not a sense of defeat in the stadium, only feelings of thanks and appreciation. Pittsburgh fans had seen their team go farther than they ever hoped possible, and it was obvious that in the coming years this young team was only going to get better. The crowd stood and applauded as the weary Steelers trudged to their locker room. "We didn't lose," said Tony Stagno, still commanding Franco's Italian Army. "Remember that. We just ran out of time. We've postponed victory until next year."[13]

In the locker room it was believed that Bradshaw had suffered a pinched nerve in his neck, but it was becoming more obvious that it was something closer to a concussion. Bradshaw admitted that he had a hard time remembering plays.

"I was aware of what was going on at halftime, but I had trouble thinking," he told reporters.

"You mean," a writer said, "you had trouble with your concentration?"

"Yeah, that's it," Bradshaw replied. "It was my concentration."[14]

As one final depressing postscript to the season, a day after the game the plane carrying Roberto Clemente and several relief workers crashed shortly after takeoff from San Juan. His death shocked the sporting world, and especially the city of Pittsburgh, where he had led the Pirates to two World Series championships. Clemente was eulogized all across the U.S. and Latin America, and ultimately parks, statues and memorials were created in his honor. Major League Baseball waived the mandatory waiting period so he could enter the Hall of Fame. "It's just as well the Steelers didn't beat the Miami Dolphins on Sunday," wrote Pat Livingston in the *Pittsburgh Press.* "In light of developments that night in the skies above

Puerto Rico, nobody would have cherished the memories of the city's football celebration."[15]

The second half of the conference championship doubleheader opened in Washington under cloudy skies and a slight drizzle of rain. After fumbling away their first possession deep in Dallas territory, Washington embarked on a drive that consumed 18 plays and 9:15 on the clock. Curt Knight, who had suffered through a miserable regular season missing 16 of 30 attempts, hit the first of four field goals on the day, and Washington led, 3–0.

Defensively, the Redskins shut down the Cowboys' running game, limiting Calvin Hill to 22 yards and Walt Garrison to 15. The leading rusher on the day was Roger Staubach, who scrambled for 59 yards, but was also sacked three times. Ron Sellers and Billy Parks, who had starred in the comeback over San Francisco, were held to three combined catches and no touchdowns. "I don't think Billy Parks paid a whole lot of attention on what he was supposed to do," said Staubach. "For some reason he didn't have the same enthusiasm for that game he did in San Francisco the week before."[16]

It was a fitting culmination to a frustrating season for the Dallas receiving corps. Before a game against Detroit in October, Landry had benched future Hall of Famers Lance Alworth and Bob Hayes in favor of Sellers and Parks. "I don't know why it's me being picked on," said Hayes, who had also been benched during the 1970 season. "I feel as if it's an injustice to me, but I'll do my part and hang in there."[17] While Alworth retired after the season, and Parks headed to Houston in a trade, Hayes hung around for two more inconsequential years with the Cowboys. In 1975, the former "World's Fastest Human" finished out his career with the 49ers, catching just six passes and no touchdowns.

Surprisingly, Sellers was also gone after just one season in Dallas. At midseason Landry observed, "Our pass offense showed more confidence with [him] in there. Sellers has made the big play for us all season and he needs to be on the field."[18] But Sellers had a body (6'4", 180 pounds) and the skills (he led his high school to a state basketball title) much more suited to basketball than football. "If I hadn't been so thin I probably would have gone to college on a basketball scholarship," he said. "But people kept telling me I was too light to play football; that I'd get killed. It made me mad and I decided to show everybody."[19]

Sellers showed everyone for four-plus NFL seasons, but apparently the critics were right—his body *wasn't* made for the constant pounding of football. Injury concerns prompted Landry to send him to Miami in the offseason in exchange for receiver Otto Stowe. Sellers lasted only part of one season with the Dolphins and caught but two passes for no touchdowns, and the following year was waived out of the league. It was an ignominious end at age 26 for the man who made the Pro Bowl in his rookie season and caught one of the most dramatic passes in Cowboys history.

Washington's receivers fared much better, especially Charley Taylor. The Redskins' plan was to isolate Taylor as much as possible on Charlie Waters, a natural free safety who had moved to cornerback when the Cowboys benched Herb Adderley. But Waters simply didn't have the speed to keep up with wide receivers in man coverage, and in this game he became easy pickings. Taylor beat Waters for 52 yards and then a 15-yard score, increasing the margin to 10–0.[20] Toni Fritsch kicked a field goal to cut the lead to 10–3, but he also missed a 23-yarder as time expired to slow the Dallas momentum at halftime.

Not that it mattered. Early in the fourth quarter with Waters injured and out of the game, Taylor burned his replacement Mark Washington on a 45-yard score. Taylor finished the day with seven catches, 146 yards and two touchdowns, while quarterback Billy Kilmer was nearly perfect—14 for 18, 194 yards and two scores. After Taylor's touchdown it was simply Knight kicking field goals and the Washington defense putting the clamps on Staubach in an easy 26–3 victory.

Much like the Steelers, the Redskins had suffered through decades of losing and had not won an NFL title since 1943. Now, they were headed to their first Super Bowl. "A lot of people wrote us off as too old, too slow and too heavy," said Redskins coach George Allen. "Nobody wanted them. I just want to say they're a great group."[21] Allen visited with President Richard Nixon at the White House Rose Garden on Monday. Nixon, who had a presidential retreat in Key Biscayne and had won two Republican nominations in Miami, nonetheless rooted for Washington as his hometown team. He must have been somewhat disappointed when Miami capped a perfect season by beating the Redskins, 14–7, in Super Bowl VII.

Most of the conversation in the losing Dallas locker room centered on the selection of Staubach over Morton as the starting quarterback, but almost everyone agreed that the Redskins had so thoroughly outplayed Dallas that the argument was moot. "We were moving the football last week," mused Landry, "but we were stopping ourselves with fumbles and interceptions. I don't know if Craig could have gotten something going."[22]

The Redskins were happy to try and fan the embers of the controversy, and as usual, it was Diron Talbert doing the talking. "They just had the wrong man in there," he said after the game. "Landry made a bad decision. Morton was the guy who got them there."[23] That raised the ire of the normally placid Staubach. "I think that when you win a football game you savor it, and you don't talk about it," he said. "That's just bush league talk. I guess there is some bitterness; he's not crazy about me, and I'm not crazy about him."[24]

Staubach eventually came to realize that Talbert's criticism was part of George Allen's psychological warfare against the Cowboys, but that didn't make it any easier to take. He called it the only feud he ever had in the NFL, and the bitterness remained even years later. "I have a fetish about not name-calling other athletes," he said. "The things the press and other people say about you are upsetting, but when your peers start bad-mouthing that's something else. To do it when you're down.... I have no respect for that."[25]

Talbert and Staubach kept their feud going the rest of the decade, with Talbert predicting a knockout of Staubach before a Thanksgiving game in 1974. Talbert got his wish, but obscure backup Clint Longley came in and rallied Dallas to a dramatic 24–23 win. "Next time they'll have to kill me," said Staubach of his not finishing the game. "I'm not one to mix words, but I saw what they said."[26] When Dallas came to Washington the following season riding the success of the resurrected shotgun formation, Talbert needled Staubach, "The only reason they put him in the shotgun is to give him time to read defenses. He's been in the league seven years and still doesn't know how to read very well."[27]

"Some of the quarterbacks on other teams are best friends of mine," Talbert continued. "But me and [Staubach] just haven't hit if off right. That's certainly fine with me."[28]

CHAPTER 18

You're Supposed to Be Tough

For many of the 1972 San Francisco players, July 30, 2011, was a stark reminder that there are more important things in life than the outcome of a football game. It was also a reminder that the game they had loved and played so well could be deadly violent.

On that day the players, most of them now in the late 60s, gathered to celebrate the life of teammate Forrest Blue. Blue had died after battling dementia for years, dementia ostensibly brought on by the repeated concussions he suffered playing offensive center during an eleven-year NFL career. Blue was big, smart and agile; a first-round draft pick in 1969 out of Auburn University, he made the NFL Pro Bowl team four straight years starting in 1971. "It took me awhile to realize what a special person he was," said his former wife Anne. "He was bright and smart, he was handsome; he was athletic. He was the whole package."[1]

Blue lived life to the fullest, whether it was skydiving more than fifty times or body surfing in Argentina. He played the same way on the football field, right at the center of the action, anchoring a line that became perhaps the best in the game. Blue, Len Rohde, Cas Banaszek, Woody Peoples and Randy Beisler protected John Brodie, and while stars like Brodie and receiver Gene Washington got the credit, it was the ascendance of the offensive line that marked the rebirth of 49er football.

But it all came with a price. "On the offensive line, literally every play you're blocking somebody," said Rohde, "so as a result you're getting contact on your head every play."[2] "That's when head slaps and helmet-to-helmet hits were legal," said 49er teammate Skip Vanderbundt. "You'd get dinged. You'd get one once or twice a season really bad. And you'd remember them; that you couldn't get up and staggered off the field the wrong way."[3]

As with so many football players, the symptoms did not appear until well after Blue retired. He had many successful years as a general contractor in California, but slowly his personality began to change. He struggled with depression, memory loss, hallucinations and finally dementia, and lived out his final years in an assisted living facility. Daughter Brittany Blue said he became paranoid, claiming that people were using his contracting license to perform illegal work at the care facility, and he often talked of "little people that lived in the walls."[4] Blue was the classic case of what was later called CTE, chronic traumatic encephalopathy—in other words, crippling brain damage from too many concussions.

Vanderbundt, who roomed with Blue for five seasons, was there at the memorial service, although Blue's body was not. Except for the brain, which was sent to Boston University as part of an ongoing study of CTE in NFL players, he was cremated and the ashes scattered in San Francisco Bay. The service itself was not religious, but was mainly a time for family, friends and teammates to get together and think of the older, happier times.

But those times have faded for so many, especially the players. It's not so much time that had dimmed the mind, but the combat itself. One of the sad, lasting legacies of Immaculate Saturday is that while fans can still treasure the moments, many of those who created the memories cannot.

Besides Blue, a host of other players involved in those playoff games suffered long-term consequences. Ken Stabler, the young, hard-charging and hard-living Raider quarterback who almost won the Immaculate Reception game with his late touchdown run, died in 2015 at the age of 69. While the cause of death was colon cancer, an autopsy revealed that Stabler had "moderately severe" CTE, which in the last years of his life caused ringing in his head so severe that he broke a bridge in his mouth from gritting his teeth. He also suffered loss of direction and sensitivity to noise. "On some days, when he wasn't feeling extremely bad, things were kind of normal," said his longtime partner, Kim Bush. "But on other days it was intense. I think Kenny's head rattled for about 10 years."[5]

The only way to determine CTE is posthumously, and a 2016 study by Boston University of 94 brains donated by former NFL players, including the one belonging to Forrest Blue, found evidence of the disease in 90 cases. That's a staggering number, and one that has many older players wondering if they will be next on the list. Raider linebacker Gerald Irons has showed increasing signs, as has teammate and defensive back George Atkinson. Atkinson, who once had contests with fellow defensive back

Jack Tatum to see who could get the most "knockouts" of opposing players, now has irritability, depression and memory loss. "The only way you didn't get your bell rung was not making contact," he said.[6]

Contact seems to be common denominator, but certainly not the only factor.

Of the cases studied, seven involved quarterbacks, including Earl Morrall, who in 1972 helped the Miami Dolphins win the Super Bowl. After his death in 2014 at the age of 79, Morrall was found to have Stage-4 CTE. And yet, Roger Staubach, who estimates that he had around 20 concussions in his career, including six that completely knocked him out, showed no signs of dementia or CTE as he approached his late 70s.

Staubach may have been one of the few players from Immaculate Saturday to understand the dangers related to concussions, and it was that concern that eventually caused him to retire even though he could have played several more seasons. In his final NFL game, a 1979 playoff loss to the Rams, Staubach was driven to the ground by linebacker Jack "Hacksaw" Reynolds, and admitted that the hit left him groggy and confused. When the Cowboys got the ball late in the game trailing by two points, the quarterback who had engineered the dramatic comeback over the 49ers in 1972, and then completed the Hail Mary to beat Minnesota in 1975, was in no shape to bring the Cowboys back. "I was messed up," Staubach said. "All we needed was a field goal, and had I been healthy I think I could have done something like run for a first down. I'm not saying we would have won, but it was certainly a factor."[7]

After the game, Staubach consulted with Dr. Fred Plum, a pioneer in neurological treatment and concussions. Plum told Staubach that he had suffered a dangerous number of concussions and that the next one could cause serious problems. Based on the advice of Plum and the entreaties of his wife, Staubach retired after that 1979 season. "I am still healthy and functional," he said in 2018, "but I do worry about it."[8]

Despite his history with concussions, Staubach did not join the list of nearly 5,000 former NFL players who sued the league in 2011. The lawsuit contended that for years the NFL was aware of the dangers of concussions but hid that information from its players. The suit was settled in 2013 for $765 million, but the judge overseeing the case was concerned that the amount was insufficient to cover the cost of adequate treatment. In 2015, Judge Anita Brody removed the $765 million cap and the final total was put at one billion dollars. When finally approved in 2016, it meant that 20,000 retired NFL players would receive payments for medical treatments for the next 65 years. "Despite the difficult health situations retired players face today, and that many more will unfortunately face in the future," said players' attorney Christopher Seeger, "they can take comfort in the fact that this settlement's significant and immediate benefits will finally become available to them and last for decades to come."[9]

As part of the settlement, the NFL did not admit fault, consistent with its stubborn approach to the problem. When the first reports of concussion issues began to surface in the early 1990s, NFL officials and doctors brushed them aside. "Concussions are part of the profession," said Elliot Pellman, team doctor for the Jets and later the chair of the league's traumatic brain injury committee. "[They are] an occupational risk."[10]

No wonder NFL players didn't take the dangers seriously. Gary Plummer, a linebacker who played 12 years for the Chargers and 49ers in the 1990s, had come to believe that concussions only happened when a player got knocked out. When he learned that there were actually three grades of concussions, ranging from mild to severe, he was stunned. By that standard, Plummer guesses he may have had 2,000 concussions in his career. "As a middle linebacker, if I didn't have five to 10 of those a game, I didn't play that week."[11]

When Dr. Bennet Omalu first made the link between CTE and NFL concussions after the death of Pittsburgh lineman Mike Webster in 2002, NFL doctors immediately attacked the findings. "These statements are based on a complete misunderstanding of the relevant medical literature on chronic traumatic encephalopathy ... [and] demonstrate the flaws in Omalu's assertions."[12] The NFL did not publicly acknowledge a link between concussions and CTE until 2009, which the league confirmed in testimony before Congress in 2016.

For his part, Omalu, who wrote a book and became the subject of a movie called *Concussion*, has remained steadfast. "I don't attack the NFL," he said. "The NFL is a corporation. What do corporations do? They try to make money by selling a product or service. The NFL is not in the business of healthcare."[13]

But increasingly, the NFL has had to make healthcare its business, given the growing attrition rate of its on-field product. New rules and new equipment have been designed to lessen the dangers. Players who suffer big hits now go into concussion protocol, which mandates their removal from play until medically cleared to return, and in some cases that could mean weeks or even months. The NFL tweaks the protocol every season and imposes stiff fines for teams that rush players back to the field too quickly. "Our protocols have worked overwhelmingly in a positive manner," said Dr. Allen Sills, the NFL's chief medical officer in 2017, "but that doesn't mean we're satisfied. No protocol covers every situation, and no medical test is 100 percent perfect."[14]

And no standard of testing, equipment or rule change can overcome the simple laws of physics. Every year, the players are bigger, faster, and seem to hit harder. All those bodies moving around in a small space drastically increase the chances for injury. "It's a brutal game," says Staubach, "so it's still going to be a game that's not perfect. It's a physical deal. You know, force equals mass times acceleration. That's the only thing I remember from my engineering days."[15]

While the force, mass and acceleration were much smaller in 1972, there's another factor left out of the equation—toughness. In a game that seems to be ever changing, it is the one constant that has been in the league from the beginning. Gary Plummer attended that concussion seminar reluctantly at the request of his agent, Leigh Steinberg. "It was very progressive of Leigh, but of course I didn't know it at the time. As linebackers we were like, 'This isn't for us. This is for those pussies on the other side of the ball.'"[16]

That credo was very much a part of the NFL on Immaculate Saturday. "You're supposed to be tough and invincible," said Cowboys offensive tackle Rayfield Wright, who was named lineman of the year in 1972. "If something's wrong with you, you try to hide it. Which is exactly what I did."[17]

Wright believes he may have received a concussion on his first-ever play in the NFL against legendary defensive end Deacon Jones of the Rams. A blow to the side of the head sent Wright spinning backwards and down to the ground. After taking a few moments to clear his head, he got up and kept playing—a pattern he repeated throughout his 13-year career. It was a toughness that sent him to the Hall of Fame, but eventually led to dementia, headaches and memory loss. "I'm scared," he admitted. "I don't want this to happen. You don't want people to look at you any differently. You don't want people to know."[18]

Now, of course, everyone knows. They know the plight of Wright, Atkinson, Stabler and so many others, including Forrest Blue. "Forrest was a unique individual," said Vanderbundt. "He was one of those guys who burned the candle at both ends. He was always going, always doing things. It was just so sad that he died at such a young age. [But], physiologically maybe some guys can take a punch and some can't. It's just part of their DNA."[19]

There were a lot of conflicting emotions at Blue's memorial service, mainly a combination of love, anger and fear. Love for a friend and team-mate that meant so much, anger for the circumstances that caused his death, and fear not only of the unknown, but also of the idea that they could be reuniting again soon under similar tragic circumstances.

"I think that's what America is experiencing now," said Omalu. "America is in love with football but is struggling with its truth. But just like the man in love, give him time."[20]

CHAPTER 19

Keep It Immaculate

"People often ask me how I threw, what was considered by many, the most famous pass of all time—the Immaculate Reception. I tell them, it was very much like at my bachelor party, where I just closed my eyes and heaved."[1]—Terry Bradshaw

Immaculate Saturday represented a commencement in both understandings of the word. The dictionary definition, from Latin, means to begin or start. Commencement has also come to be known as an ending, at least as it applies to a school graduation.

In the short run, the 1972 seasons of the Oakland Raiders and San Francisco 49ers both came to an end. For Oakland, it was the beginning of a period that saw them win four straight AFC West titles, only to lose in the playoffs each year. Three times the Raiders lost to the Steelers and three times they lost to the eventual Super Bowl champions, as Oakland replaced Dallas as "the Team That Couldn't Win the Big One." "I don't know what we have to do to win this thing," lamented guard Gene Upshaw after a third playoff loss to Pittsburgh. "It's just an empty feeling. It's escaped us again."[2]

It was likely a more painful finish for the Niners as the loss marked the end of their three-year run as division champions and Super Bowl contenders. The team wasn't necessarily old; it's just that the younger players coming in—Windlan Hall, Ralph McGill, and Bruce Taylor—would not match the careers of the old vets on their way out—John Brodie, Jimmy Johnson and Charlie Krueger. Unlike Dallas, Pittsburgh and Oakland, San Francisco did not adequately restock itself in the draft. The team slid to 5–9 in 1973, followed by seasons of 6–8 and another 5–9. Attendance declined each season, and on the day after Christmas 1975, Dick Nolan was fired after eight years. "I know the reasons, but I'll not comment on them," Nolan said of his dismissal. "I don't want to hurt people."[3]

More than anything it was his inability to beat Dallas that cost Nolan his job and ended the 49ers short stay on top. "Dick Nolan against Tom Landry was like Tom Landry against Vince Lombardi," said Nolan, slipping into the third person. "Landry couldn't get past Lombardi, and I didn't get past Landry. But I'm still proud of what we did. We just didn't have enough experience to get over the hill."[4] For three straight years his 49ers met the Cowboys in the playoffs, and three times they went home losers. The most crushing loss was the one on Immaculate Saturday—a defeat that seemed to confirm to the players that while they had come close to crossing the threshold of greatness, they would never get there. "We just didn't finish the game," said receiver Gene Washington, "and I still think it might have been psychological. It was the Cowboys and we didn't know quite how to put away the Cowboys when we had to do it."[5]

The Niners wandered in mediocrity for awhile, especially under the helm of general manager Joe Thomas. "We had to decide whether to go all the way in making changes or just part way," he said during the disastrous 2–14 season in 1978. "We went all the way."[6] The makeover included a trade that sent five draft picks for an over-the-hill O.J. Simpson. Thomas left, Bill Walsh came in, and nine years after Immaculate Saturday the 49ers got a measure of revenge, beating Dallas in the NFC Championship, 28–27. In a reversal of the earlier game, San Francisco scored late to win on a touchdown pass from Joe Montana to Dwight Clark that came to be known as "The Catch." In a bit of irony, it was considered the game that ended the Dallas dynasty while launching one for the 49ers.

By that time, Dick Nolan had already been hired and fired in three years as coach of the New Orleans Saints. The man who twice led the 49ers a game from the Super Bowl ended his NFL head coaching career losing 12 straight in New Orleans and watching fans come to games with paper bags on their heads. Nolan reunited briefly with Tom Landry as a special assistant in the 1980s; he died in 2007 from Alzheimer's disease. Bill Walsh and owner Eddie DeBartolo get most of the credit for turning the 49ers into a dynasty, but it was Dick Nolan who laid the groundwork. Sportswriter Art Spander, who covered Bay Area sports for five decades, said simply, "Dick Nolan turned the Niners into winners."[7]

The game also effectively ended the Cowboys career of quarterback Craig Morton. When Landry pulled him out and Staubach engineered the comeback, it became obvious who the main man in Dallas was going to be. Even so, Landry made a pretense of opening up the quarterback competition again during the 1973 training camp. "Right now, after what took place last year, I don't know what will happen," said Morton. "Coach Landry says the job is up for grabs. All I can do is try and do the job I did last year."[8] "I'm counting on getting my job back," Staubach said before camp started. "I'm going in with the attitude that I'll start. I'm sure Craig has the same attitude too."[9]

Landry made the predictable decision and for a third straight year picked Staubach, who went on to lead the league in passing while Morton threw only 32 passes all season. The only question was whether Morton would be content as Staubach's backup, which Landry correctly guessed he would not. "Sometimes it is unfortunate to have to make such a decision," Landry said. "Craig is disappointed; he would like to be traded to another club. I told him I would see what I could do."[10]

The trade came in the 1974 season and turned into a bonanza for Dallas. The Cowboys sent Morton to the Giants in return for a number-one draft pick that turned into Hall of Fame defensive tackle Randy White. Morton languished in New York for parts of three seasons before getting a new lease on life in Denver. At the age of 34, Morton led the Broncos during their transcendent "Orange Crush" season of 1977, getting the team to the Super Bowl for the first time in franchise history. Ironically, the Broncos met Dallas and Roger Staubach in Super Bowl XII, with Staubach returning the embrace Morton had given him on Immaculate Saturday, hugging his former rival at the coin toss. Presented with a unique opportunity for redemption, Morton instead threw four interceptions, suffered four sacks and was embarrassingly pulled in the third quarter of a 27–10 loss. Sadly, he completed as many passes to the Dallas defense as he did his own receivers, leading sportswriter Don Pierson to observe cuttingly, "Craig Morton always did want to pass the Dallas Cowboys to a Super Bowl victory."[11]

While one career died in San Francisco on Immaculate Saturday, another reputation was born. It was the first of the 23 times Roger Staubach rallied the Cowboys to win when trailing in the fourth quarter. He became the Jolly Roger who would not give up the ship, and "Captain Comeback" for his seeming uncanny ability to remain cool in the face of desperate hopelessness. "It was the beginning time for the great comebacks that Roger is so well known for throughout his career," said safety Charlie Waters. "When we won that game against San Francisco, from that moment on, we always believed that we could win the ballgame."[12]

San Francisco was the first miracle, but it might not have been the best. Four years later in a playoff game in Minnesota, the Cowboys trailed the Vikings with less than a minute to play. "I hate to admit it," said Landry, "but I didn't think we had any chance to win the game."[13] Staubach threw up a wing and a prayer—what he later called a "Hail Mary" pass—that Drew Pearson caught for the game winning touchdown. "The stadium was stunned," said Staubach. "I've never been in a stadium that was so quiet. I think that particular play was the single biggest play I've ever been a part of."[14]

Fittingly, the last regular season game Staubach played in 1979 he pulled another rabbit out of the hat, this time throwing two touchdowns in the final two minutes to beat Washington, 35–34. Seven years had passed since Immaculate Saturday—the receivers changed, the defenders changed, the circumstances changed; only Staubach remained the same. "I think the biggest thing about Roger is that he never quit," Cowboys defensive end Bob Lilly said. "It didn't matter how much the Cowboys were down."[15]

While Immaculate Saturday kick-started an NFL legend, it also launched a dynasty. The game confirmed what the Steelers themselves already knew—that they were young, getting better and headed for a championship. "The Immaculate Reception was the end of people saying, 'Same old Steelers,'" said Franco Harris. "And it was a time when we showed things weren't going to be the same around here anymore."[16]

Pittsburgh needed a couple of more pieces to the puzzle, which came in a 1974 draft considered the greatest of all time. It produced four Hall of Famers—Lynn Swann, Jack Lambert, John Stallworth and Mike Webster—and led to four Super Bowl titles in six years. "No official designation has been bestowed upon the Steelers' 1974 draft class as the greatest in NFL history," notes the Steelers' organization. "Then again, no such official designation seems necessary."[17]

Pittsburgh became the "Team of the 70s," just as Green Bay had dominated the league the decade before, and while it didn't win every championship, it competed consistently at the highest level. What's more, the players *knew* they could win and enjoyed the pressure of being on top. "There's just something about the Steelers," said Cowboys running back Tony Dorsett. "Maybe it's their presence. They know how to beat you."[18]

Sadly, as the Steeler dynasty got older and stronger, it no longer seemed to need Franco's Italian Army. The group seemed young and hip in 1972, but as the team kept winning and Franco became a bigger name, the demands became too great. Tony Stagno resigned his commission and the Army had no commander. "It was a great gimmick for a couple of years," said Harris. "It's just that people started to think he was my agent or something. They'd call Tony's bakery and ask if I could speak at some banquet. Tony would tell them he had no say about what I did. They would cancel their bakery orders and slam down the phone."[19]

By the late '70s, Myron Cope's "Terrible Towel" had become the unofficial fashion statement in Pittsburgh. The fresh-faced youngsters of 1972—Harris, Bradshaw, Joe Greene—to whom winning seemed so new and surprising, became grizzled veterans accustomed to championships. The Army seemed like a quaint relic of a simpler time, a feeling its members recapture every so often. Stagno died in 1999, but Vento lives on, and now and again he and his son will sit down to lunch with Franco Harris over some prosciutto and wine to talk about the old days. "They were having so much fun," says Franco of the Army. "It was pretty fun for me, too."[20]

Perhaps the Cowboys suffered most from the Steeler dynasty, losing two close Super Bowls between the teams. They jockeyed back and forth for supremacy throughout the decade, but the Steelers came out on top. In Super Bowl X, the rough-and-tumble Steelers weren't penalized a single time, despite Mel Blount beating up receiver Golden Richards to the point that he had to leave the game. Also uncalled was Jack Lambert's roughing of Cliff Harris after a missed Pittsburgh field goal, a moment credited with turning around the game in the Steelers' favor.

In Super Bowl XIII, Dallas seemed to have the momentum when a controversial pass interference penalty on Benny Barnes—called by Fred Swearingen, the referee on the field for the Immaculate Reception—tilted the game back in Pittsburgh's favor and the Steelers won, 35–31. It was small consolation to Dallas that the NFL later agreed it was a bad call. "After viewing films of the play, we are of the opinion that there should have been no penalty called," wrote NFL Commissioner Pete Rozelle.[21] Landry called it "the kiss of death"[22] regarding the game, and in a sense, for the Cowboys' hopes for a dynasty. "That was the most disappointing game I ever played in," said Staubach, "because we had this great team. Breaks were going to determine the outcome. No one dominated the other."[23]

The Steelers viewed the Cowboys like an irritating little brother. The little brother could make some noise at times and demand attention, but in the end, the big brother would have to administer a smackdown. "Joe Greene knew they could intimidate us," said Dorsett. "He'd say, 'Tony, you can't beat us by tricking us,' and I knew he was right."[24] Dallas general manager Tex Schramm added, "It just seems that when the Steelers play the Cowboys, the Steelers win because they are more physical. Maybe they are."[25]

In his study on birth order, Austrian psychiatrist Alfred Adler noted that the oldest child is "often given responsibility and expected to set an example." The second child is competitive because "there is always someone ahead." In the case of twins, "one is usually the stronger" while the other "may have identity problems."[26]

All of these characteristics seem to apply to Immaculate Saturday. The "older twin," the Pittsburgh–Oakland game, has become the stronger of the two to the point that the Dallas–San Francisco game has been almost completely overshadowed. This is somewhat understandable from several perspectives. The game was in San Francisco and certainly the 49ers don't want to remember it in any way. From the Dallas side, both Ron Sellers and Billy Parks who figured so prominently in the comeback, were both gone by the start of the next season and are considered footnotes in Cowboys history.

The game itself was also later overshadowed by the comeback that came to define the Cowboys of the 1970s—Roger Staubach's "Hail Mary" touchdown to beat the Vikings in the 1975 playoffs. When the Cowboys opened new headquarters in suburban Frisco, Texas, in 2016, the Hail Mary play was memorialized with statues of Staubach and receiver Drew Pearson. The Hail Mary game was nowhere near as exciting as the comeback against San Francisco, yet it was included in a DVD set of the Cowboys' ten-greatest games released in 2008. The 49er game was omitted entirely.[27]

In various fan votes for the Greatest Play of All Time, the Hail Mary pass usually gets some sort of mention. Invariably, the Immaculate Reception ranks one, two or three. On the 40th anniversary of the Harris catch in 2012, it was noted, "There have been roughly 1,500,000 plays in NFL history spread over more than 14,600 games, starting all the way back in 1920. There never has been a play like the Immaculate Reception."[28]

There were major observances of the 25th, 30th and 40th anniversaries of the Immaculate Reception, and on the 40th anniversary players from both the Steelers and Raiders were invited back to Pittsburgh for a special celebration. The festivities included the unveiling of an Immaculate Reception monument at Heinz Field, which joined life-sized statues of Harris and the catch at the Pittsburgh airport and at the Western Pennsylvania Sports Museum. As Harris dedicated the new monument he told the assembled crowd, "Isn't this beautiful, guys? That play really represents our teams of the '70s."[29]

Does it really? The Steelers won four Super Bowls during the 1970s, but didn't even make the Super Bowl in the Immaculate Reception season. A more fitting play to represent the Pittsburgh dynasty might be one of

Lynn Swann's great Super Bowl catches or Terry Bradshaw throwing a touchdown pass to beat the Cowboys in Super Bowl despite getting concussed by Larry Cole.

Perhaps the Immaculate Reception stays alive because it represents promise—a fresh-faced franchise looking forward with optimism and enthusiasm, instead of a grizzled one looking wistfully backwards. The sadness of hindsight is that all those championships came at a price. Backup quarterback Joe Gilliam fell into drug addiction and died before he reached 50. Hall of Fame center Mike Webster's early death at 50 first alerted the nation to the dangers of repeated concussions and chronic brain injuries. None of those storm clouds were on the horizon in 1972, and the Immaculate Reception seemed to promise nothing but blue skies ahead. The play is the pair of bronzed baby shoes in the parents' closet, symbolizing a time when anything seemed possible.

Maybe that's why the surviving Steelers are working so hard to keep the memories alive. Franco Harris has virtually turned the event into a one-man cottage industry. He copyrighted the term "Franco's Immaculate Reception," and shortly after the 40th anniversary weekend, he began selling personalized Franco Harris footballs with the signatures of the players who attended.

On December 23 every year, Franco makes a phone call to former backfield mate John "Frenchy" Fuqua. "Frenchy!" he says. "Wake up. Happy anniversary!"[30] With Jack Tatum now gone, Fuqua is the only living person who knows what transpired when he reached for Bradshaw's desperation pass. While an entire nation of football fans has analyzed, investigated, and looked at videotape of the play from every conceivable angle, trying to figure out just what actually happened, Fuqua is content with history's version. He is besieged with speaking opportunities and says that he has received offers of up to $250,000 to tell what he knows. But while he suggests he knows the truth, Frenchy sees himself as the keeper of the flame, and he is determined not to let the mystery die.

"You ought to come clean and tell the truth," Bradshaw once told him. "You know damn well you touched [the ball]."[31]

Fuqua will only give a knowing smile.

"I was kidding with [Art Rooney] after that game," he says. "I said, 'Chief, should I tell what happened?' He told me, 'Frenchy, keep it Immaculate. If you know what happened, that's good enough.'"

"Will I tell before I die? I doubt it very seriously."[32]

Franco also makes another call on December 23. Around 4:07 p.m.—close enough to the exact time that he scored the Immaculate touchdown—

Harris calls Raider linebacker Phil Villapiano to remind him of their shared place in history. Villapiano has developed a wonderful sense of humor about it, and on one occasion he and Harris enthralled diners at a Pittsburgh Italian restaurant with a detailed recreation of the play.

But beneath the surface—under the jokes and kidding that have become a Raider defense mechanism—is a proud man who would love another chance to rewrite the ending to the most famous play in football.

"I told Franco the last tackle I ever make in my life is I'm going to come off the airplane with about 12 Heinekens in me and ram that statue [at the airport]," says Villapiano. "I'm going to drive it over the top and we're going to both go down on to that dinosaur that's down below. It will go right through my body and his body, too."[33]

You can hear the emotion in Villapiano's voice, almost as if nearly fifty years have melted away and he's back on the field at Three Rivers Stadium, knocked to the ground by John McMakin, futilely watching Franco Harris run into history.

"[Franco] tells me I'm losing it," he continues. "No, that's what I want to do. I want to make the last tackle of my life at the airport. I'm going to take him over the top."[34]

Chapter 20

Postgame

What If

A popular project of the NFL Network and NFL Films, *Top 10* is a series of programs that ranks various league players, games and records. In 2017, the series debuted a program called *Top 10: What Ifs*, which looked at how the league would be different if certain scenarios had played out differently. For example, what would have happened if there had been no NFL-AFL merger, or what would have happened to the Steelers if they had not cut a young Johnny Unitas? What would have happened to the Colts?

One of those interesting questions, ranked number two on the list, asked what would have happened if Pittsburgh had not pulled off the Immaculate Reception. What if the officials had overruled the touchdown, if Franco Harris had not caught the rebound, or if Harris had been tackled and the clock had run out? "This game sets the tone for how the entire 1970s is played all the way through," says NFL writer Jason Cole.[1]

Various NFL writers and contributors came up with three interesting hypotheses:

• *The Steelers dynasty would not have happened, and the team would have won only one Super Bowl instead of four.*

"If it doesn't happen," said former Steelers quarterback Charlie Batch, "then I don't think the dynasty happens."[2] "If the Immaculate Reception doesn't count," seconded NFL writer Pete Prisco, "then you don't have the Steelers' dynasty, right?"[3] Many others have followed along these lines, suggesting that the play "represents the franchise turning point."[4]

But this is an extremely difficult argument to make and obscures the fact that the Immaculate Reception did not immediately lead to a Super Bowl win for Pittsburgh. In fact, it took two more years for the Steelers to win their first championship, and it was the success of that 1974 draft rather than the Immaculate Reception that pushed them over the top. The Immaculate Reception may be one of the signature plays in NFL history, but it did not threaten to slow down or derail the Steeler dynasty.

Even after the AFC Championship loss to Miami, the Steelers knew they were good and would only get better. "I don't know how they can be 16–0," said Dwight White of the Dolphins after the game. "They didn't impress me as being that good. But we are, and we are going all the way next season. Say, I'm ready to go to camp right now."[5]

Had the Immaculate Reception turned out in the Raiders' favor, there's no reason to believe it would have changed the Steelers' fortunes the rest of the decade.

• *The Raiders go on to win the Super Bowl, ruining Miami's perfect season.*

The premise here is that if the Raiders beat the Steelers in the playoffs, there's a pretty good chance they go on to spoil the Dolphins' unbeaten season and then win the Super Bowl.

This one is not quite so farfetched. Oakland obviously had a good team and certainly would have given the Dolphins a great game. Plus, the AFC Championship game would have been played in Oakland because of the NFL's rotating playoff schedule (the same reason Miami had to play in Pittsburgh despite a better record during the regular season).

It's worth noting that at the time, Miami had never won in Oakland—ten straight losses overall—and in fact, would not win a game there until 1997. That includes playoff losses in 1970 and 1974, the latter coming in the famous "Sea of Hands" game when the Raiders scored on a miracle play in the final minute. Even when the Raiders hosted the game in Berkeley in 1973, using the University of California's home field, they ended Miami's eighteen-game winning streak. Before a record home crowd of 74,121, Oakland won, 12–7.

Consider also that the unbeaten Dolphins were not exactly manhandling teams. They had to rally in the fourth quarter to escape the Browns in the first round of the playoffs, 20–14, and then beat the Steelers by four and the Redskins in the Super Bowl by seven. During the regular season, they played only two teams with winning records and barely escaped the Vikings (16–14), Bills (23–23), and Jets (28–24). The Dolphins themselves would admit that their 1973 Super Bowl champion, even with two losses, was a better team overall. "Certainly, it's more memorable to be perfect," said guard Ed Newman, "but the players will tell you they thought the '73 team was better."[6]

• *John Madden wins the Super Bowl, goes on to win two more, and thus does not retire prematurely.*

The conjecture is that if Madden goes on to win a Super Bowl in 1972, he's more likely to stick around for Super Bowl wins in 1976 and 1980,[7] but that's a hard argument to make. Madden retired following the 1978 season at the relatively young age of 42, not because of a lack of championships, but because his intense style of coaching burned him out and led to an ulcer. "I only knew one way to do this job," Madden said when he announced his retirement, "and that was to give it everything I had. I just don't have it anymore."[8] If anything, winning a championship so soon might have convinced Madden to get out even earlier than he did, given the pressure Al Davis put on the entire organization to keep winning.

Madden was unconventional in many senses, such as taking a bus to games instead of flying during his long tenure as a broadcaster, and there is no indication he would have stayed in coaching simply to pile up championships. When he retired, Madden said he would never coach again, and unlike so many who make that promise, he kept it. During his career, he won 103 games and lost only 32, and of the men who coached in the NFL for at least ten years, his .759 is the highest winning percentage of all time.

Two important predictions were not made on the *Top 10* program. The combination of thousands of fans swarming the field and a minimal police presence could have resulted in a very dangerous, even deadly, situation. Had officials reversed the call and disallowed the Immaculate Reception, it's not hard to envision a scenario in which a riot breaks out. Even in 1972, newspapers reported an average of about twenty sports-related riots a year, most of them at football games.[9] Earlier in the year, back in February, a riot had broken out at a University of Minnesota basketball game. After players exchanged punches, fans rushed the court in what *Sports Illustrated* called "an ugly, cowardly display of violence."[10]

All the same ingredients were in place at Three Rivers Stadium—an angry crowd, fueled by alcohol, and with almost no way to hold them back. "There was no way they were going to call it any other way with all those people on the field," said Madden. "Somebody would have been killed."[11] That might have included the officials, especially head referee Fred Swearingen. "Swearingen had a problem," said Raiders linebacker Phil Villapiano.

"I think, if he would have ever reversed that call, that man might have died. And all the other officials too."[12] Added Oakland tight end Raymond Chester, "If you could have packaged all that anger and frustration, it probably would have been nuclear."[13]

If some kind of disturbance had taken place on the field, there's also a possibility it may have hastened the advent of instant replay. The NFL actually began testing instant replay in 1976, and by 1978 used it on a limited scale for some preseason games. "We still need a minimum of twelve cameras to get all the angles on every play," said Nick Skorich, then the assistant supervisor officials, of the preseason trial. "Electronically, I don't think we're there yet."[14] By 1985 the technology had improved enough to try again, once more during preseason games, and the league formally approved instant replay for regular season games in 1986.

Even with the more primitive technology of 1972, it's hard to envision a situation in which a Pittsburgh loss would not have prompted some sort of call for instant replay. While Oakland certainly had plenty to be sore about, no call was overturned and the referee's decision was simply upheld. Had the decision been reversed, taking a sure win away from Pittsburgh on the Steelers' home field, thrown in with a potentially riotous crowd, an inflamed situation would have turned incendiary. The NFL might have been willing to overlook the technological drawbacks of replay if it could help prevent the repeat of a fiasco.

If there are any doubts of that, consider what Browns owner Art Modell said when the league was considering replay in 1985. "[Owners] didn't want a playoff game decided by a bad call," he noted, "and so they tried to push it through right there."[15] If that was the thought in 1985, it certainly could have applied in 1972.

The bottom line, however, is that all of the conjecture is pointless. In 1972, there was no replay, no recourse for the Raiders, and no turning back for the Steelers. "That play, if you're a Steeler fan, you believe in it," Fuqua says. "If you're a sinner, like them damn Raiders, you'll never accept it. So it's almost like the Bible, a myth to some and a faith to others."[16]

News of the Non-Immaculate

Not all the sports news on December 23, 1972, was about the NFL playoffs. A selection of headlines from around the country from the weekend of Immaculate Saturday:

• *Morris Officially Gets His "1,000"*

Dolphins running back Mercury Morris got an early Christmas present when the NFL gave him the nine yards he needed to reach the 1,000 yard rushing mark. Morris thought he ended the season with 991 yards rushing, but in reviewing films of the Dolphins' October game with Buffalo, the league said that a nine-yard loss credited to Morris was actually a fumble by quarterback Earl Morrall. Dolphins coach Don Shula gave Morris the good news. "First, I didn't believe Shula," said Morris. "I thought he was goofing on me."[17] Morris finished the year with exactly 1,000 yards, and combined with Larry Csonka's 1,117 yards, it made the Dolphins the only team in NFL history with two thousand-yard rushers in the same season.

• *The Falcons' Dave Hampton Hits 1,000-Yard Goal Then Loses It*

Unlike Morris, Atlanta running back Dave Hampton probably felt like the Grinch stole his Christmas. Hampton reached the coveted 1,000-yard rushing mark in the last game of the season against Kansas City. The game was stopped and Hampton received the game ball and a standing ovation from the home crowd. Unfortunately, on the next drive Hampton lost six yards on a pitchout to fall back to 994 yards and he never got the chance to carry the ball again. Atlanta lost the game, 17–14, and Hampton lost his record. The following season, he finished three yards short of a thousand. "Right now, it's the most disappointing thing that ever happened to me," he said after the game. "I was so close, but so far away, and there was nothing to do about it."[18]

• *Weeb's Decision Entirely His Own*

After a successful coaching career that saw him become the only man to win titles in both the AFL and NFL, Weeb Ewbank of the New York Jets announced that he would retire after the 1973 season. He coached Johnny Unitas to two championships with the Colts, and then a decade later led the Jets and Joe Namath to a win over Unitas in the Super Bowl. In the very last game as coach, Buffalo's O.J. Simpson broke the all-time single season rushing record in a 34–14 Bills victory.

"If I can contribute in some way, I'll stay around," Ewbank said after the announcement. "If I retired from football completely, I'd go crazy. It's been my whole life."[19] Ewbank did stay on as vice president and general manager, but when the team lost seven of its first eight games in 1974, he resigned. Ewbank died in 1998 at the age of ninety-one.

• *Football Still Big with Mrs. Lombardi*

The Packers impending playoff game with Washington was their first in five years and the first since the death of legendary coach Vince Lombardi. Lombardi had coached both teams, serving only one year in Washington before his death from cancer in 1970. "I'm an officer of the Redskins," said his widow Marie Lombardi. "It's more of an honorary position than anything else, but I still have that feeling. I'm a Redskins fan first and I'll root for them all the way."[20]

That Marie Lombardi would watch the game, much less attend it, was something of a change for her. She felt that the pressure and tension of coaching had shortened her husband's life. "My first reaction after he died was that I was very angry at football," she said. "I felt football had taken too much out of Vince. But the Redskins were wonderful to me and I don't have that feeling anymore. I like football again and go to all the games."[21]

• *Ealey's Success with 'Cats May Change NFL's Attitude*

Quarterback Chuck Ealey took the Canadian Football League by storm in his 1972 rookie season. Ealey won CFL Rookie of the Year, was named to the All-Star team, and earned MVP honors in the Grey Cup after leading Hamilton to the championship. He accomplished all these things mainly because the NFL was still reluctant to give black quarterbacks a chance. "A black has never been given a real chance at quarterback in the NFL," wrote Dink Carroll in the *Montreal Gazette*. "They are signed by NFL clubs ... but are quickly converted to defensive halfbacks and flankers when they turn professional."[22] After an All-American senior season at the University of Toledo, Ealey told NFL teams he would not change positions and he then went undrafted. He played seven seasons in the CFL before an injury ended his career, but he helped pave the way for other black quarterbacks such as Warren Moon.

• *Woody Stages Ho-Ho-Ho Act*

Usually volatile Ohio State football coach Woody Hayes was in a jovial mood as his team prepared for its Rose Bowl showdown with USC. Taking a break from their California workouts, the Buckeyes toured Disneyland and mugged it up for photographers with Mickey Mouse. "Why don't we have our two biggest men lifting him up?"[23] Woody suggested to the cameramen, so lineman John Hicks and fullback Champ Henson put Mickey on their shoulders.

A week later, right before kickoff of the Rose Bowl, Hayes would have a far less agreeable encounter with photographer Art Rogers of the *Los Angeles Times*. Rogers filed battery charges against Hayes, saying the coach shoved him, causing double vision and swollen eyes. "That ought to take care of you, you son of a bitch," Hayes reportedly yelled when Rogers intruded on a pregame huddle.[24] When asked about it in a press conference after the game, Hayes exploded and slammed his microphone to the ground. "Oh, for Jesus Christ's sake, forget it," he yelled, before storming out. "That's the end of this interview. He [Rogers] wasn't hurt."[25] To top off Woody's bad day, USC destroyed the Buckeyes, 42–17. Ohio State issued an apology and Rogers eventually dropped the charges.

• *Freshmen Added Depth to 1972 Football Season*

Despite the loss in the Rose Bowl, it was still a banner year for Ohio State's Archie Griffin. Thanks to a rule change by the NCAA, freshman were now immediately eligible to play. Griffin led the Buckeyes in rushing, broke a school record with 239 yards against North Carolina in only his second game, and proved that freshmen could contribute right away. "The freshman eligibility rule," observed Fred McMane of United Press International, "at first scorned by many major college coaches, became widely accepted by mid-season."[26]

• *Pitt Acts to Solve Major Problem*

As usual, there were plenty of college coaches on the move after the season. Iowa State's Johnny Majors left to take over a moribund program at the University of Pittsburgh. The once-proud Panthers finished 1–10 in 1972, the ninth straight year the program failed to have a winning record. "It's not like winning or losing," Majors said on taking the job. "It's like winning or death—and we don't want to die here."[27] Majors didn't die, and in just four seasons had a national championship and a Heisman Trophy winner in Tony Dorsett. Earle Bruce left the University of Tampa to take over for Majors at Iowa State, and Hayden Fry took over at North Texas after getting fired by Southern Methodist. Bruce and Fry would later go on to great success in the Big 10—Bruce at Ohio State and Fry at Iowa.

• *UCLA Batters Pitt for 50th Straight Win*

The University of Pittsburgh was also in the news on the basketball court as the Panthers became yet another victim of John Wooden's dynasty at UCLA. The Bruins beat Pitt, 89–73, to inch closer to the NCAA record streak of 60 straight games set by the University of San Francisco during the Bill Russell era. UCLA would go on to win the national title again, its seventh straight, and would not lose until January 1974 when Notre Dame ended the Bruins' winning streak at 88.

Wooden had returned to the bench after minor heart trouble forced him to miss a game for the first time in his twenty-five years at UCLA. In a commentary of how opponents viewed the unbeatable Bruins back in those days, Pitt coach Buzz Ridl said of the sixteen-point loss, "I'm glad it wasn't a rout."[28]

• *NBC Protests Olympics TV*

Frustrated at what it perceived was a rigged system, NBC lashed out at the recent deal signed between the Olympics and rival ABC to televise the 1976 Summer games from Montreal. NBC charged that "through secret and non-competitive procedures" it was impossible for any network to outbid ABC for the U.S. television rights. "The ability of any other party to obtain U.S. television rights has been nullified in advance and the bidding procedure has been made a sham."[29]

NBC got its revenge in 1988, outbidding ABC for rights to the Summer and Winter games, and the network has televised every Olympics since then.

• *Shorter Tells It Like It Is*

Olympic marathon champ Frank Shorter said the U.S. was falling behind rival countries in track and field, specifically the sprints. The Russians and Finns dominated the running events at the recent Olympics in Munich, due in great deal to how those countries subsidized their athletes. Shorter also blamed the groups running U.S. track, including the Amateur Athletic Union and the U.S. Olympic Committee, for not keeping up with modern training techniques. "Some of the administrators are truly incompetent," Shorter said. "They can all fly away as far as I'm concerned."[30] The newly-formed International Track Association would help, but Shorter added that he was "not optimistic."

• *AL Fights for Change*

American League baseball owners held a secret meeting in New York to set in motion one of the biggest rule changes in major league history—a designated hitter who would bat regularly for the pitcher during the course of the game. Concerned with lower batting averages, dominant pitching, and declining attendance, AL owners had tried twice before to implement a DH, only to be turned down both times by the Playing Rules Committee. The frustration "has added fuel to the AL's resentment, and determination to force [Major League Commissioner Bowie] Kuhn into the hassle," according to the *Cleveland Plain-Dealer*.[31] The DH was formally approved a month later on a three-year trial, but was so popular that it became a permanent fixture in the American League. The other main topic at the meetings—interleague games during the regular season—would not become a reality until 1997.

- *"Gabby Hartnett," Former Cub Catcher Dies at 72*

The Hall of Fame catcher died December 20 on his 72nd birthday. In a nineteen-year career, Hartnett batted .297 and hit 236 home runs, the most famous of which came in 1938. With the score tied 5–5 in the ninth inning of a crucial game with Pittsburgh late in the season, umpires warned the teams that if the Cubs didn't score the game would be called on account of darkness and replayed in its entirety. Harnett hit a "homer in the gloaming" in the gathering twilight of Wrigley Field, giving the Cubs the win and eventually the National League pennant.[32]

- *Hockey Star Given Order of Canada*

Boston Bruins star forward Phil Esposito was among 67 Canadians recognized for their outstanding achievements and service to the country. Three months earlier, Esposito had helped a team of Canadian all-stars beat the Soviet national team in an exhibition that came to be known as the Summit Series. Paul Henderson's dramatic goal in the eighth and final game helped Canada win the series four games to three with one tie.

But it was Esposito's speech after game four that really turned things around. A 5–3 loss in Vancouver put Canada behind in the series with four games upcoming in Moscow. The team was booed off the ice and Esposito responded in a fiery post-game television interview. "Esposito blasted fans who booed the Canadian players. In the Soviet Union, he was the on-ice leader who helped the team come back to win the series [which] was watched by the largest television audience in Canadian history."[33]

"All of us guys are really disheartened and disillusioned, and we're disappointed," said Esposito in the interview, the sweat and frustration obvious on his face. "We cannot believe the booing we've got in our own building. I cannot believe it. We're trying; we're doing the best we can. We did this because we love our country, and for no other reason. We came because we love Canada."[34]

"The Americans have their great speeches from Gettysburg and Kennedy's 'Ask not what your country can do for you' speech," said sportswriter Roy MacGregor of the *Toronto Globe and Mail*. "Our greatest speech was by a sweaty hockey player in a rink in Vancouver."[35]

• *Poor Attendance Problem for New Hockey Circuit*

Halfway through its inaugural season, the fledgling World Hockey Association was having the problems associated with any new league, including low attendance and ownership issues. The Ottawa Nationals averaged less than 2,500 fans per game, and the team was getting outdrawn by the local junior hockey club. But there were surprising success stories in Hartford and Quebec, and other fans were coming out to see former NHL stars Bobby Hull and Gordie Howe, lured to the new league with big money contracts. "Relatively speaking, we're probably three to five years ahead of where the American Football League and American Basketball Association were at this point," said WHA president Gary Davidson.[36] Those challengers eventually forced a merger with the established leagues, and so did the WHA. In 1979, the NHL absorbed four WHA franchises— the Edmonton Oilers, Quebec Nordiques, Winnipeg Jets, and New England Whalers.

• *Billie Jean King Emotional Queen*

Sports Illustrated made history twice in naming its annual Sportsman of the Year. For the first time, two people shared the award, and in another first, one of the honorees was a woman. Billie Jean King captured three Grand Slam singles titles in 1972 to become *SI*'s first female winner. "I'm glad to see this breakthrough," said King, who added that, "they've been asking me since I was 21 when I planned to retire and become a housewife. I probably will play several more years."[37] King was named along with UCLA basketball coach John Wooden, who in the spring won his sixth straight NCAA title.

• *Sports Executive Raps Apathy*

In a criticism even more appropriate today than it was back then, a Canadian physical fitness executive criticized her countrymen for laziness and apathy. Janet Marchand, athletic director of the Canadian Amateur Basketball Association, called Canadians "lazy sheep" that needed a kick in the behind. "We have a society where 85 percent of the men sit in front of the idiot box and watch the Green Bay Packers or Winnipeg Blue Bombers when they could take the kids down the block to the neighborhood school gym. And the kids sit and watch too while junk is being injected into their brains … their young bodies are not developing."[38]

Summing Up

On October 13, 1985, Saul Finkelstein, a resident of the Squirrel Hill section of Pittsburgh made a solitary pilgrimage to a section of brick wall on the University of Pittsburgh campus. Finkelstein sat down at a wall across from Schenley Plaza next to a marker that read "457 feet." He pulled out a cassette recorder and began playing a tape of one of the most famous games in baseball history—the seventh game of the 1960 World Series. In the bottom of the ninth, the Pirates' Bill Mazeroski hit a dramatic home run to beat the imperious New York Yankees. The section of wall was all that remained from Forbes Field where the game was played.

Finkelstein came that day to mark the 25th anniversary of Mazeroski's homer and returned every October 13 until his death to repeat the ceremony. Soon, other Pirate fans joined in and a "Game 7 Gang" was born. By the time of the 50th anniversary in 2010, the crowd had swelled to more than 1,500 to observe what came to be known as "Mazeroski Day." Mazeroski himself was there in 2000, marveling at what he had wrought. "This is something," he said as the crowd stood at 12:59 p.m. for the National Anthem and then passed around hot dogs and popcorn to listen to the game. "I never thought there would be something like this going on 40 years later."[39]

As we have seen (in Chapter 19), the same kind of emotional attachment exists with the Immaculate Reception, which also has anniversary celebrations, devoted players and fans, and dedicated statues. Likewise, there is a statue dedicated to Roger Staubach and Drew Pearson at the Cowboys' team headquarters ("The Star") in suburban Frisco.

But what about a more recent event like the Steelers' dramatic win over Arizona in Super Bowl XLIII? Pittsburgh clinched the Super Bowl win when Santonio Holmes caught the winning touchdown pass with 35 seconds left. Will there one day be a statue of Holmes and quarterback Ben Roethlisberger? Will Dallas fans one day gather to listen to a replay of Tony Romo throwing a last-minute touchdown pass to beat Detroit in a 2014 playoff game?

Of course, all of that remains to be seen, however unlikely.

The Immaculate Reception and Franco's Italian Army share the same kind of emotional impact as the Mazeroski homer. They touched something deeply in a group of fans—something akin to civic pride—that bonded them together. They were nascent, organic experiences that simply evolved out of the culture in which they were born.

The Immaculate Reception and Staubach's first miracle in San Francisco also engendered a "did I just see that?" feeling of pride. It's a feeling that comes along only on rare occasions in life and under special circumstances, such as when an exasperated parent watches in disbelief as a child finally rides that bicycle—no training wheels!—without falling down.

That's the "I was there!" camaraderie of the Immaculate Reception and to a lesser extent the Cowboys at Candlestick Park. By the time of Holmes and Roethlisberger the feeling in Pittsburgh was more like, "Been there, done that," and with Dallas and Romo it was, "Aren't we *ever* going to win another Super Bowl?" Pittsburgh fans were happy to be sure, but it was more of a "Great, we won again," take a selfie-at-the-stadium, now-let's-trash-the-other-fans-on- social-media vibe. The training wheels had been off for a long time and the kid was grown up now with a family of his own.

When the NFL debuted its "100th Season" promotion during Super Bowl LIII, a commercial during the game brought back many of the game's great players for a bit of fantasy. Dressed in tuxedos at a lavish party, stars like Joe Montana, Deion Sanders, and Barry Sanders suddenly began to chase a football around the ballroom. At one point, Terry Bradshaw picked up the ball and threw it across the room. Several players reached for it and the ball was tipped.

Right before it hit the ground, Franco Harris snatched the ball and began to run. As Franco dodges would-be tacklers and broken dishes, Joe Greene looks on approvingly from his seat, smiles, and simply says, "Yes!"

Such is the power of December 23, 1972. Such is the power of memory and myth. Such is the power of Immaculate Saturday.

"We're always told we can't turn back the clock," says Herb Soltman of the Game 7 Gang. "Nonsense. We can and we should."[40]

Chapter Notes

Acknowledgments

1. Peter Golenbock, *Cowboys Have Always Been My Heroes* (New York: Warner Books, 1997), p. 553.

Preface

1. Bill Barnwell, "Inside 16 Crucial Plays from the NFL Conference Championship Games," *ESPN*, 21 January 2019. http://www.espn.com/nfl/story/_/id/25813279/inside-16-crucial-plays-2018-nfl-conference-championship-games.

2. The Dolphins beat the Chiefs, 27–24, in double overtime, still the longest NFL game ever played.

3. Lance Davis, "The 5 Most Expensive NFL Stadiums to Attend," bankrate.com, 1 February 2016. https://www.bankrate.com/personal-finance/smart-money/the-5-most-expensive-nfl-stadiums-to-see-a-game/#slide=1.

4. Shanna McCarriston, "Super Bowl 53 Ticket Prices in 2019 as Compared to History," *The Sporting News*, 2 February 2019. http://www.sportingnews.com/us/nfl/news/super-bowl-53-ticket-prices-2019-compared-to-history/174xcq78jo83s114sg0f3zcb33.

Chapter 1

1. "SI's 25 Lost Treasures," *Sports Illustrated*, 11 July 2005, p. 114.

2. Dan Gigler, "Immaculate Reception Football Means a Lot to its Caretaker," *Pittsburgh Post-Gazette*, 18 November 2012. http://www.post-gazette.com/hp_mobile/2012/11/18/Immaculate-Reception-football-means-a-lot-to-its-caretaker/stories/201211180146.

3. Chris Togneri, "'Immaculate' Football Holds Special Meaning for West Mifflin Father who Scooped it Up," *Pittsburgh Tribune-Review*, 20 June 2015. http://triblive.com/news/projects/ourstories/8541621-74/baker-ball-sam.

4. Gigler, "Immaculate Reception Football Means a Lot to its Caretaker."

5. Bob Karlovitz, "'Sports Detectives' Investigates Immaculate Reception Ball," *Pittsburgh Tribune-Review*, 20 April 2016. http://triblive.com/aande/moreaande/10296559-74/barrows-says-baker.

6. Gigler, "Immaculate Reception Football Means a Lot to its Caretaker."

7. *Ibid.*

8. Dave Crawley, "Man Who Scooped Up Immaculate Reception Football Tells Story," *KDKA-TV*, 21 December 2012. http://pittsburgh.cbslocal.com/2012/12/21/man-who-scooped-up-immaculate-reception-football-tells-story/.

9. Micah Peters, "5 Takeaways From the Most Exciting Day of College Basketball Ever," *USA Today*, 19 March 2015. http://ftw.usatoday.com/2015/03/5-takeaways-most-exciting-day-of-college-basketball-ever.

10. Mark Newman, "One Year Later, Recalling Baseball's Best Night Ever," MLB.

com, 28 September 2012. http://m.mlb. com/news/article/39125938//.

11. Tyler Kepner, "The Wildest Game in Modern History," *New York Times*, 16 May 2009. http://bats.blogs.nytimes.com/2009/05/16/the-wildest-game-in-modern-history/.

12. Gary Myers, "Top 10 Greatest Plays in NFL History: From the Immaculate Reception to John Elway's Helicopter Ride," *New York Daily News*, 9 September 2015. From: http://www.nydailynews.com/sports/football/top-10-greatest-plays-nfl-history-article-1.2354371.

13. Gene Collier, "Steelers' Immaculate Reception: 40 Years Later, It Still Thrills Us," *Pittsburgh Post-Gazette*, 23 December 2012. http://www.post-gazette.com/sports/steelers/2012/12/23/Steelers-Immaculate-Reception-40-years-later-it-thrills-us-still/stories/201212230196.

14. Duke Ritenhouse, "49ers' Historic 'Catch' Anniversary is Sunday," *Reno Gazette-Journal*, 9 January 2016. http://www.rgj.com/story/sports/2016/01/09/ers-historic-catch-anniversary-sunday/78576594/.

15. Mark Ribowsky, *The Last Cowboy: A Life of Tom Landry* (New York: Liveright, 2014), p. 517.

16. Although there is some dispute about that; for more information, see Chapter 11.

17. Vito Stellino, "NFL Confidential: Rules at the Time Made Immaculate Reception Legendary," *Florida Times-Union*, 22 December 2012. http://jacksonville.com/sports/premium-sports/2012-12-22/story/nfl-confidential-rules-time-made-immaculate-reception.

18. Gigler, "Immaculate Reception Football Means a Lot to its Caretaker."

19. Alfie Potts Harmer, "Top 15 Most Expensive Pieces of Sports Memorabilia Ever Sold," *The Sportster*, 24 January 2016. http://www.thesportster.com/entertainment/top-15-most-expensive-pieces-of-sports-memorabilia-ever-sold/.

20. Togneri, "'Immaculate' Football Holds Special Meaning."

21. Gigler, "Immaculate Reception Football Means a Lot to its Caretaker."

22. Togneri, "'Immaculate' Football Holds Special Meaning."

23. *Ibid.*

24. Gigler, "Immaculate Reception Football Means a Lot to its Caretaker."

Chapter 2

1. Bruce Tomaso, "NFL Network Presents—'Tom Landry, A Football Life,'" *Dallas Morning News*, 2 November 2011. http://thescoopblog.dallasnews.com/2011/11/nfl-network-presents-tom-landr.html/.

2. Kalyn Kahler, "From Staubach to Dak: An Oral History of the Cowboys' Quarterbacks," *Sports Illustrated*, 1 November, 2017. https://www.si.com/2017/11/01/dallas-cowboys-quarterbacks-oral-history-roger-staubach-troy-aikman-tony-romo-dak-prescott.

3. "Is Tom Landry a Computer?" *Gettysburg (PA) Times*, 14 January 1971, p. 15.

4. Kahler, "From Staubach to Dak: An Oral History of the Cowboys' Quarterbacks."

5. Mark Ribowsky, *The Last Cowboy: A Life of Tom Landry* (New York: Liveright, 2013), p. 248.

6. Steve Perkins, *Winning the Big One* (New York: Grosset & Dunlap, 1972), p. 4.

7. *Ibid.*, p. 5.

8. Dan Daly, *The National Forgotten League* (Lincoln: University of Nebraska Press, 2012), p. 356.

9. Tex Maule, "The Purple Gang Rubs Out L.A.," *Sports Illustrated*, 5 January 1970, p. 17.

10. Jim Murray, "Who Needs Emotion? Not Landry and His Cowboys," *St. Petersburg Times*, 16 August 1972, p. 3C.

11. Pete Dougherty, "Herb Adderley Lived Both Sides of Rivalry," *USA Today*, 9 April 2016. https://www.packersnews.com/story/sports/nfl/packers/dougherty/2016/04/09/herb-adderley-lived-both-sides-rivalry/82832962/.

12. *75 Seasons* (Atlanta: Turner Publishing, 1994), p. 161.

13. Roger Staubach and Frank Luksa, *Time Enough to Win* (Waco: Word Books, 1980), pp. 33–34.

14. Kahler, "From Staubach to Dak: An Oral History of the Cowboys' Quarterbacks."

15. Perkins, *Winning the Big One*, pp. 123–124.

16. "Landry Undecided About Quarterback," *Wilmington (NC) Star-News*, 27 July 1973, p. 8C.

17. Perkins, *Winning the Big One*, p. 159.

18. Dan Daly, *The National Forgotten League* (Lincoln: University of Nebraska Press, 2012), p. 360.

19. "Proud Roger Proves He's a Tough Guy," *Sarasota Herald-Tribune*, 18 January 1972, p. 2C.

20. "Landry Has 2 Problems: Morton, Thomas," *Sarasota Herald-Tribune*, 18 January 1972, p. 2C.

21. "Morabito Rites Set," *Pittsburgh Post-Gazette*, 29 October 1957, p. 20.

22. *75 Seasons*, p. 115.

23. Ron Fimrite, "Mind You, This Time it's Not All Over," *Sports Illustrated*, 25 January 1982, p. 33.

24. *75 Seasons*, p. 187.

25. Daly, *The National Forgotten League*, p. 179.

26. Ron Kroichick, "Coach Established 49ers as a Winner," *San Francisco Chronicle*, 12 November 2007. http://www.sfgate.com/sports/article/Coach-established-49ers-as-a-winner-3235040.php.

27. Personal communication, 31 October 2017.

28. "Multiple Sets Raises Scoring," *Kingsport (TN) Daily News*, 21 November 1972, p. 6.

29. Peter Golenbock, *Cowboys Have Always Been My Heroes* (New York: Warner Books, 1997), p. 456.

30. Tex Maule, "The Cowboys Take it on the Lam," *Sports Illustrated*, 10 January 1972, p. 12.

31. Perkins, *Winning the Big One*, p. 203.

32. "Brodie Didn't See George Andrie," *Newburgh (NY) Evening News*, 3 January 1972, p. 7B.

Chapter 3

1. Ben Shpigel, "Vikings Shock Saints on Stefon Diggs's Last-Second Touchdown," *New York Times*, 14 January 2018. https://www.nytimes.com/2018/01/14/sports/vikings-stefon-diggs-saints.html.

2. *Ibid.*

3. Personal communication, 16 January 2018.

4. *Ibid.*

5. *Ibid.*

6. *Ibid.*

7. Kalyn Kahler, "From Staubach to Dak: An Oral History of the Cowboys' Quarterbacks," *Sports Illustrated*, 1 November 2017. https://www.si.com/2017/11/01/dallas-cowboys-quarterbacks-oral-history-roger-staubach-troy-aikman-tony-romo-dak-prescott.

8. *Ibid.*

9. Perkins, *Winning the Big One*, p. 23.

10. *Ibid.*

11. Zac Crain, "Tony Dorsett is Losing His Mind," *D Magazine*, February 2014. https://www.dmagazine.com/publications/d-magazine/2014/february/dallas-cowboys-tony-dorsett-is-losing-his-min./

12. For more on concussions and their connection to Immaculate Saturday, see Chapter 18.

13. Peter Golenbock, *Cowboys Have Always Been My Heroes* (New York: Warner Books, 1997), p. 615.

14. Personal communication, 16 January 2018.

Chapter 4

1. Roy McHugh, "Smoke Rings," 28 January 1970, *Pittsburgh Press*, p. 60.

2. Rob Ruck, Maggie Jones Patterson and Michael P. Weber, *Rooney: A Sporting Life* (Lincoln: University of Nebraska Press, 2010), p. 272.

3. Bryn Swarz, "Heart of a Champion: The 40 Toughest Players in NFL History," *Bleacher Report*, 3 December 2008. http://bleacherreport.com/articles/88750-heart-of-a-champion-the-40-toughest-players-in-nfl-history.

4. Dan Daly, *The National Forgotten League* (Lincoln: University of Nebraska Press, 2012), p.175.

5. "Kiesling's Description of Steelers: Amateurs Pretending to be Pros," *Pittsburgh Post-Gazette*, 24 October 1956, p. 22.

6. Johnette Howard, "Immaculate Reception Memories," *ESPN*, 23 December 2012. http://espn.go.com/nfl/story/_/id/8774529/remembering-immaculate-reception.

7. Ruck, Patterson and Weber, *Rooney: A Sporting Life*, p. 378.

8. Tom Rose, "NFL Draft," *Washington (PA) Observer-Reporter*, 6 April 1982, p. D1.

9. "American Central," *Sports Illustrated*, 18 September 1972, p. 66.

10. "'Same Old Steelers' Tag May be Dispelled in '72," *Rome (GA) News-Tribune*, 20 August 1972, p. 4C.

11. *Ibid.*

12. Malcolm Moran, "Raiders Have Come a Long Way Since 1960," *Wilmington (NC) Star-News*, 18 January 1981, p. 7D.

13. Tom LaMarre, *Oakland Raiders: Colorful Tales of the Silver and Black* (New York: Globe Pequot, 2003), p. 146.

14. Kevin Cook, "Rowdy and Rough," *ESPN*, 13 August 2012. http://www.espn.com/nfl/story/_/id/8203175/nfl-1970s-football-was-rowdy-rough.

15. Will Grimsley, "Raiders Make Bad-Guy Image Work For Them," *Bowling Green (KY) Daily News*, 17 January 1984, p. 1B.

16. Robert F. Jones, "Lamonica's Movable Feast: He Was the Main Dish," *Sports Illustrated*, 12 January 1970, p. 39.

17. "American West," *Sports Illustrated*, 18 September 1972, p. 69.

18. Mike Vaccaro, "Csonka Says Coughlin Just Like Dolphins Coach Shula," *New York Post*, 31 January 2012. http://nypost.com/2012/01/31/csonka-says-coughlin-just-like-dolphins-coach-shula/.

19. Charles Feeney, "Early Steeler Defeats Cut Rooney Deeply," *Pittsburgh Post-Gazette*, 22 December 1972, p. 15.

Chapter 5

1. After retirement in 1967, Tubbs stayed with the Cowboys organization another 22 years as a linebackers coach.

2. Tex Maule, "The Cowboys Ride High on Defense," *Sports Illustrated*, 9 September 1963, p. 47.

3. Martin Hendricks, "McHan Once Held the Packers' Starting Job Over Starr," *Milwaukee Journal-Sentinel*, 18 March 2015. http://archive.jsonline.com/sports/packers/mchan-once-held-the-packers-starting-job-over-starr-b99459968z1-296680551.html/.

4. *Ibid.*

5. Peter Golenbock, *Landry's Boys: An Oral History of a Team and an Era* (New York: Triumph, 2005), p. 127.

6. Gary Cartwright, "Turn Out the Lights," *Texas Monthly*, August 1997. https://www.texasmonthly.com/the-culture/turn-out-the-lights/.

7. Tom Mertens, "Obituary: Gabbo Gavric, 1938–2010," *Soccer America*, 15 March 2010. https://www.socceramerica.com/publications/article/37216/obituary-gabbo-gavric-1938–2010.html.

8. "Mass Firing Starts Colt Housecleaning," *Fredericksburg (VA) Free Lance-Star*, 21 December 1972, p. 8.

9. "Johnny U.'s Last Play as a Colt—An Interception," *Montreal Gazette*, 18 December 1972, p. 29.

10. Dave Brady, "Simpson Goes to 49ers for 5 Draft Picks," *Washington Post*, 25 March 1978. https://www.washingtonpost.com/archive/sports/1978/03/25/simpson-goes-to-49ers-for-5-draft-picks/2e74e1d1-4de0-47a7-b844-ac31887a3052/?utm_term=.15ff7312d526.

11. Jerry McDonald, "49er Flashback: 1979 Team was Dreadful Despite Walsh, Montana, O.J. and Al Cowlings," *San Jose Mercury News*, 28 October 2016. http://www.mercurynews.com/2016/10/28/49ers-in-1979-an-0-7-start-with-walsh-montana-o-j-and-al-cowlings/.

12. Michael Silver, "Candlestick Moments: Iconic San Francisco 49ers Reminisce," NFL.com, 19 December 2013. http://www.nfl.com/news/story/0ap2000000300929/article/candlestick-park-moments-iconic-san-francisco-49ers-reminisce.

13. Michael Silver, "A Tale of Two Cities," NFL.com, December 2015. http://www.nfl.com/twocities.

14. *Ibid.*

15. T.J. Simers, "Johnson Puts It All On the Line," *Los Angeles Times*, 22 January 1994. http://articles.latimes.com/1994-01-22/sports/sp-14222_1_cowboy-coach-jimmy-johnson.

16. Silver, "Tale of Two Cities," 2015.

17. *Ibid.*

18. T.J. Simers, "Dallas Dynasty Shows First Signs of Crumbling," *Los Angeles Times*, 16 January 1995. http://articles.la

times.com/1995-01-16/sports/sp-20568_1_nfc-championship-game.

19. "Teague: Hit Came From Cowboys' Frustration, Anger," *Associated Press*, 26 September 2000. From: http://lubbock online.com/stories/092600/pro_09260 0089.shtml#.WgNwPVWnGM8.

20. "Terrell Owens Defends Infamous Celebration on Cowboys' Star," *Fox Sports*, 10 February 2016. https://www.foxsports.com/nfl/story/dallas-cowboys-terrell-owens-celebration-star-san-francisco-49ers-defense-021016.

21. Mike Schumann, "Mike Schumann Honors Teammate, Friend, Dwight Clark After Emotional Reunion," *KGO-TV*, 23 October 2007. http://abc7news.com/sports/mike-shumann-honors-teammate-friend-dwight-clark-after-emotional-reunion/2560032/.

22. Silver, "Tale of Two Cities."

Chapter 6

1. Dave Anderson, "Franco's 'Destiny' Survived Draft, Noll-Art Jr," *Pittsburgh Post-Gazette*, 16 January 1975, p. 11.

2. Jack Sell, "Franco Harris Finally Becomes a Steeler." *Pittsburgh Post-Gazette*, 26 July 1972, p. 23.

3. "Injuries Have Hampered Career of Terry Beasley," *Florence (AL) Times*, 22 September 1974, p. 20.

4. Personal communication, 31 October 2017.

5. Peter Golenbock, *Cowboys Have Always Been My Heroes* (New York: Warner Books, 1997), p. 446.

6. Gary Cartwright, "The Lonely Blues of Duane Thomas," *Texas Monthly*, February 1973. http://www.texasmonthly.com/the-culture/the-lonely-blues-of-duane-thomas/.

7. Perkins, *Winning the Big One*, p. 88.

8. Golenbock, *Cowboys Have Always Been My Heroes*, pp. 500–501.

9. Cartwright, "The Lonely Blues of Duane Thomas."

10. "Duane Thomas Deal Canceled by Dallas," *Daytona Beach Sunday News Journal*, 5 August 1971, p. 29.

11. Cartwright, "The Lonely Blues of Duane Thomas."

12. Golenbock, *Cowboys Have Always Been My Heroes*, p. 405.

13. "Roger Scrambling More, But Landry is Not Upset," *Bangor (ME) Daily News*, 5 January 1972, p. 13.

14. The annual charity game matched the defending NFL champions against a team of college all-star seniors. It was played in Chicago from 1934 until 1976, when it died for lack of interest. The final game between Pittsburgh and the college stars was called in the third quarter because of a torrential downpour at Soldier Field.

15. Ron Fimrite, "When the Stars Cross," *Sports Illustrated*, 7 August 1972, p. 16.

16. Golenbock, *Cowboys Have Always Been My Heroes*, p. 509.

17. "Cowboys Exhibition Win Over Rams Proves Costly as Staubach is Injured," *Washington (PA) Observer-Reporter*, 14 August 1972, p. C6.

18. "National East," *Sports Illustrated*, 18 September 1972, p. 52.

19. "Sellers Sold On Cowboys," *Reading (PA) Eagle*, 21 September 1972, p. 57.

20. *Ibid.*

21. George Blanda and Jack Olsen, "That Impossible Season," *Sports Illustrated*, 2 August 1971, p. 34.

22. Milton Richman, "Sports Parade," *Hendersonville (NC) Times-News*, 7 December 1970, p. 10.

23. *Ibid.*

24. Jeff Samuels, "Raider Offense 'Stabler' with Ken at QB," *Pittsburgh Press,* 9 November 1973, p. 36.

25. "It's NFL Playoff Time Again," *Sarasota Journal*, 22 December 1972, 1-D.

26. Jimmy Miller, "Coach's Defense Rivals Steelers," *Pittsburgh Post-Gazette*, 18 September 1972, p. 20.

27. Dan Daly, *The National Forgotten League* (Lincoln: University of Nebraska Press, 2012), p. 359.

28. "Lamonica Gets a Delayed Call from Madden," *Pittsburgh Press*, 18 September 1972, p. 26.

29. Phil Musick, "Could '72 Be Year of the Steelers?" *Pittsburgh Press*, 18 September 1972, p. 25.

30. *Ibid.*

31. Golenbock, *Cowboys Have Always Been My Heroes*, p. 512.

32. Kalyn Kahler, "From Staubach to Dak: An Oral History of the Cowboys' Quarterbacks," *Sports Illustrated*, 1 November 2017. https://www.si.com/2017/11/01/dallas-cowboys-quarterbacks-oral-history-roger-staubach-troy-aikman-tony-romo-dak-prescott.

33. Perkins, *Winning the Big One*, p. 85.

34. *Ibid.*, p. 84.

35. Milton Richman, "Staubach Wished Morton Success," *Lexington (NC) Dispatch*, 25 September 1972, p. 10.

36. Phil Musick, "Opportunity Knocks and Steelers Fail to Answer," *Pittsburgh Press*, 9 October 1972, p. 25.

37. *Ibid.*

38. *Ibid.*

39. Phil Musick, "Bad Day All Around for Steelers," *Pittsburgh Press*, 9 October 1972, p. 28.

Chapter 7

1. Mark Roth, "Earlier Immigrants Reshaped the Region, Then Blended In," *Pittsburgh Post-Gazette*, 19 May 2014. http://www.post-gazette.com/local/city/2014/05/19/Pittsburghs-new-immigrants-Earlier-immigrants-reshaped-region-then-blended-in/stories/201405180230.

2. *Ibid.*

3. Rob Ruck, Maggie Jones Patterson and Michael P. Weber, *Rooney: A Sporting Life* (Lincoln: University of Nebraska Press, 2010), p. 47.

4. Gary Rotstein, "Ethnic Neighborhoods Becoming Thing of Past," *Pittsburgh Post-Gazette*, 25 May 2003. http://old.post-gazette.com/localnews/20030525ethnicreg3p3.asp.

5. "A Flavor of Larimer Avenue," *Paesani di Pittsburgh*, 2005. http://paesanidipittsburgh. omeka.net/exhibits/show/capturedmemories/herbamen/flavoroflarimeravenue.

6. "Franco's Italian Army." https://www.watchyourbacknyc.com/blogs/news/run-piasano-run-franco-harris-and-his-italian-army.

7. Ira Berkow, "Franco: The Man and His Army," *Gadsden (AL) Times*, 26 December 1972, p. 12.

8. Don Kowet, *Franco Harris* (New York: Coward, McCann & Geoghegan, 1977), pp. 77–78.

9. "Franco Harris on Franco's Italian Army, the Immaculate Reception, and growing up in a multicultural family," *Italian American Experience*, 2 October 2016. http://italianamericanexperience.com/franco-harris-on-francos-italian-army-the-immaculate-reception-and-growing-up-in-a-multicultural-family/.

10. "Franco's Italian Army is Unbiased," *Sarasota Herald Tribune*, 29 November 1972, p. 1E.

11. Nicholas P. Ciotola, "Spignesi, Sinatra, and the Pittsburgh Steelers: Franco's Italian Army as an Expression of Ethnic Identity, 1972–1977," *Journal of Sport History* 27, no. 2 (2000), p. 277.

12. Hubert Mizell, "The Hero of the Apes," *St. Petersburg Times*, 10 January 1975, p. C1.

13. "Strategists Mapping Plans," *Spartanburg (SC) Herald*, 15 December 1972, p. C3.

14. Ron Reid, "Black and Gold Soul With Italian Legs," *Sports Illustrated*, 11 December 1972, p. 37.

15. "Cadence in Cleveland," *Paesani di Pittsburgh*, 2005. http://paesanidipittsburgh.omeka.net/exhibits/show/capturedmemories/francositalianarmy/cadenceincleveland.

16. Thomas P. Benic, "Cheers, Chants, Songs Spur Steeler Triumph," *Pittsburgh Post-Gazette*, 4 December 1972, p. A1–A2.

17. Jimmy Miller, "Steelers Rerun Might One," *Pittsburgh Post-Gazette*, 4 December 1972, p. 27.

18. Ruck, Patterson and Weber, *Rooney: A Sporting Life* 2010, p. 106.

19. Pat Livingston, "Cowboys May Be Trying to Psyche Redskins," *Pittsburgh Press*, 17 December 1972, p. D3.

20. Ed Bouchette, "Cope Helped Draft Sinatra Into 'Army," *Pittsburgh Post-Gazette*, 21 May 1998, p. A2.

21. *Ibid.*

22. "Franco Harris on Franco's Italian Army, the Immaculate Reception, and growing up in a multicultural family," *Italian American Experience*, 2 October 2016. http://italianamericanexperience.com/franco-harris-on-francos-italian-army-

the-immaculate-reception-and-growing-up-in-a-multicultural-family/.

23. Ruck, Patterson and Weber, *Rooney: A Sporting Life*, 2010, p. 406.

24. "Wait Worth It, Declares Owner of Steelers," *Spokane Daily Chronicle*, 18 December 1972, p. 25.

25. Ed Bouchette, "Cope Helped Draft Sinatra Into 'Army," *Pittsburgh Post-Gazette*, 21 May 1998, p. A12.

26. "Frenzied Fans Welcome Steelers Home," *Washington (PA) Observer-Reporter*, 19 December 1972, p. A-8.

27. *Ibid.*

Chapter 8

1. "Meredith Returns to 'Monday Night,'" *Lexington (NC) Dispatch*, 5 August 1977, p. 14.

2. "Brodie Hurt Worse Than First Reported," *Owosso (MI) Argus-Press*, 26 October 1972, p. 16.

3. Ron Reid, "Battle Royal of Leftovers," *Sports Illustrated*, 4 December 1972, p. 24.

4. "San Francisco's Spurrier Gets Offensive Honors," *Spartanburg (SC) Herald-Journal*, 22 November 1972, p. B4.

5. Personal communication, 31 October 2017.

6. "Frisco Presents Gift to Redskins," *Lawrence (KS) World*, 24 November 1972, p. 17.

7. "Defense Award to Vanderbundt," *Meridian (CT) Morning Record*, 29 November 1972, p. 11.

8. Personal communication, 31 October 2017.

9. Reid, "Battle Royal of Leftovers," p. 22.

10. Perkins, *Winning the Big One*, p. 203.

11. Personal communication, 31 October 2017.

12. Tex Maule, "Old Brodie Went Witcher-Way," *Sports Illustrated*, 25 December 1972, p. 11.

13. Dennis Georgatos, *Game of My Life: San Francisco 49ers* (New York: Sports Publishing, 2007).

14. "Forgotten Men Won it For 49ers," *Montreal Gazette*, 18 December 1972, p. 29.

15. *Ibid.*

16. "Why Did Viks Go For Tie? They Sought Winning Record," *Eugene (OR) Register-Guard*, 17 December 1972, p. 2D.

17. Tex Maule, "Champion Blahs in Big D," *Sports Illustrated*, 18 December 1972, p. 22.

18. "Illegal Blocking Claim Irks Dallas' Alworth," *Victoria (TX) Advocate*, 13 December 1972, p. 2B.

19. "Inconsistency Cost Him a Job," *Beaver County (PA) Times*, 14 September 1972, p. B2.

20. Georgatos, *Game of My Life*, 2007.

21. "Douglass Steals Spotlight From Raiders," *Toledo Blade*, 18 December 1972, p. 29.

22. "Soft Schedule? Not So, Says Miami's Shula?" *St. Petersburg Times*, 18 December 1972, p. 3C.

23. Tex Maule, "Old Brodie Went Witcher-Way," *Sports Illustrated*, 25 December 1972, p. 13.

24. "Soft Schedule?" p. 3C.

25. Milt Richman, "Law of Averages to Catch Up With Dolphins, *Boca Raton News*, 22 December 1972, p. 12.

26. Maule, "Old Brodie Went Witcher-Way," p. 13.

27. Al Abrams, "Sidelights on Sports," *Pittsburgh Post-Gazette*, 20 December 1972, p. 22.

Chapter 9

1. "2 Plane-Crash Victims Found After 70 Days," *Toledo Blade*, 22 December 1972, p. 1.

2. The driving force behind the lawsuit was Washington attorney Robin Ficker, who was a passionate sports fan in the D.C. area. For a dozen years he had courtside seats right behind the opposing team's bench at Washington Bullets home games and became the most notorious heckler in NBA history. One night, he so got under the skin of Utah Jazz coach Frank Layden that Layden went after him and had to be restrained by security.

3. Scott Allen, "Many Local Fans Couldn't Watch the Last Redskins-Packers Playoff Game in 1972," *Washington Post*, 6 January 2016. https://www.washingtonpost.com/news/dc-sports-bog/wp/2016/01/06/many-local-fans-couldnt-watch-the-last-redskins-packers-playoff-game-in-1972/.

4. "Nixon Slaps at Blackout," *St. Petersburg Times*, 22 December 1972, p. 1B.

5. Harvey Frommer, *When It Was Just a Game: Remembering the First Super Bowl* (Lanham, MD: Taylor Trade, 2015), p. 140.

6. The NFL policy was amended in 1973 to lift blackouts for games sold out 72 hours in advance. In 2015, the league voted to suspend its blackout policy for the entire season. Rozelle's prediction of the league "eating itself" has not yet come true, even though there are now games on Sundays, Mondays and Thursdays.

7. "'Saddle Sores' Plague Cowboys," *Bonham (TX) Daily Favorite*, 21 December 1972, p. 6.

8. Perkins, *Winning the Big One*, p. 163.

9. Golenbock, *Cowboys Have Always Been My Heroes*, p. 237.

10. "Lilly Says He'll Be Ready," *Bonham (TX) Daily Favorite*, 22 December 1972, p. 8.

11. "We're Still the Champs—Landry," *Sarasota Tribune*, 23 December 1972, C4.

12. "Cowboys Begin Uphill Climb Against 49ers," *St. Petersburg Independent*, 23 December 1972, p. 2-C.

13. *Ibid.*

14. "We're Still the Champs—Landry," *Sarasota Tribune*, 23 December 1972, C4.

15. "Cowboys Regrouping with Vows of Victory," *Victoria (TX) Advocate*, 19 December 1972, p. 1B.

16. *Ibid.*

17. "At Long Last Steelers First," *Toledo Blade*, 18, December 1972, p. 26.

18. Al Abrams, "Sidelights on Sports," *Pittsburgh Post-Gazette*, 20 December 1972, p. 22.

19. Charley Feeney, "Playing Games," *Pittsburgh Post-Gazette*, 22 December 1972, p. 15.

20. "Brodie's Return Excellent," *St. Petersburg Times*, 20 December 1972, p. 1C.

21. "We're Still the Champs—Landry," *Sarasota Tribune*, 23 December 1972, C4.

22. "Brodie Gets First Call," *St. Petersburg Independent*, 22 December 1972, p. 1-C.

23. Ron Fimrite, "Mind You, This Time It's Not Over," *Sports Illustrated*, 25 January 1982, p. 35.

24. Wells Twombly, "Kezar: The Wonderful Dump," *The Sporting News*, 9 January 1971, p. 12.

25. Personal communication, 31 October 2017.

26. Cowboys Cautious on Footing," *Victoria (TX) Advocate*, 21 December 1972, p. 3B.

27. Eric Prewett, "Lamonica Declares Balance of Running, Passing Needed," *Washington (PA) Observer-Reporter*, 20 December 1972, p. D-5.

28. "It's NFL Playoff Time Again," *Sarasota Journal*, 22 December 1972, p. 1-D.

29. Steelers' White Fits Name of 'Mad Dog,'" *St. Joseph (MO) Gazette*, 22 December 1972, p. 1B.

30. Gary Mihoces, "It's 'Steeler-Mania' For Fun and Profit," *Lexington (NC) Observer-Reporter*, 21 December 1972, p. C-6.

31. "Steeler Pep Rally Ready," *Lawrence (KS) Journal-World*, 22 December 1972, p. 15.

32. "Oakland End Says Police Beat Him Up," *Eugene (OR) Register-Guard*, 24 December 1972, p. 3B.

33. "Franco's Italian Army." https://www.watchyourbacknyc.com/blogs/news/run-piasano-run-franco-harris-and-his-italian-army.

34. Robert Markus, "Raider May File Lawsuit Against Pittsburgh Police," *Chicago Tribune*, 24 December 1972, Section 3, p. 5.

35. Dave McConnell, "Police Give Version of Fracas at Steeler Rally," *Pittsburgh Post-Gazette*, 28 December 1972, p. 13.

36. "Ex-Raider Bob Moore's Suit Dismissed," *Washington (PA) Observer-Reporter*, 6 October 1977, p. C3.

Chapter 10

1. "'Lucky' Steelers Win," *St. Petersburg Times*, 25 December 1972, p. 4-C.

2. Gary Mihoces, "It's 'Steeler-Mania' For Fun and Profit," *Lexington (NC) Observer-Reporter*, 21 December 1972, p. C-6.

3. Rob Ruck, Maggie Jones Patterson and Michael P. Weber, *Rooney: A Sporting Life* (Lincoln: University of Nebraska Press, 2010), p. 411.

4. *Ibid.*

5. Joe Carnicelli, "Greene: Didn't Think This Day Would Ever Come," *Windsor (ON) Star*, 22 December 1972, p. 23.

6. Jack Sell, "Guy Names Art Missed 'Work of Art,'" *Pittsburgh Post-Gazette*, 25 December 1972, p. 78.

7. Ira Berkow, "Sports of the Times: Frenchy is Alive and Still Doing Swell," *New York Times*, 20 August 1981, p. 14.

8. "A Dolphin Tunes Out Steelers," *Pittsburgh Post-Gazette*, 26 December 1972, p. 16.

9. Derek Burns, "Phil Villapiano's Plan to Tackle Franco, the Immaculate Reception," *Talk of Fame Sports Network*, 19 December 2016. http://www.talkoffamenetwork.com/phil-villapianos-plan-tackle-franco-immaculate-reception/.

10. Kevin Cook, "Rowdy and Rough," *ESPN*, 13 August 2012. http://www.espn.com/nfl/story/_/id/8203175/nfl-1970s-football-was-rowdy-rough.

11. "Steelers Get Early Christmas 'Gift,'" *Chicago Tribune*, 24 December 1972, Section 3, Page 5.

12. Cook, "Rowdy and Rough."

13. Al Abrams, "Sidelights on Sports," *Pittsburgh Post-Gazette*, 25 December 1972, p. 78.

14. Gene Collier, "Steelers' Immaculate Reception: 40 Years Later, It Still Thrills Us," *Pittsburgh Post-Gazette*, 23 December 2012. http://www.post-gazette.com/sports/steelers/2012/12/23/Steelers-Immaculate-Reception-40-years-later-it-thrills-us-still/stories/201212230196.

15. Rob Ruck, Maggie Jones Patterson and Michael P. Weber, *Rooney: A Sporting Life* (Lincoln: University of Nebraska Press, 2010), p. 412.

16. "Oakland Raiders vs. Pittsburgh Steelers," *Mutual Broadcasting Network*, 23 December 1972.

17. "Franco Harris on Franco's Italian Army, the Immaculate Reception, and growing up in a multicultural family," *Italian American Experience*, 2 October 2016. http://italianamericanexperience.com/franco-harris-on-francos-italian-army-the-immaculate-reception-and-growing-up-in-a-multicultural-family/.

18. "Franco's Italian Army." https://www.watchyourbacknyc.com/blogs/news/run-piasano-run-franco-harris-and-his-italian-army.

19. "An 'Immaculate' Memory, steelers.com, 23 December 2018. https://www.steelers.com/news/an-immaculate-memory.

20. Derek Burns, "Phil Villapiano's Plan to Tackle Franco, the Immaculate Reception," *Talk of Fame Sports Network*, 19 December 2016. http://www.talkoffamenetwork.com/phil-villapianos-plan-tackle-franco-immaculate-reception/.

21. The name came from the practice developed by former Cleveland Browns owner Arthur McBride who owned taxi companies as part of his financial empire. When coach Paul Brown wanted to stash a player without putting him on the active roster, McBride would put the player on the payroll of the taxi company.

22. Personal communication, 28 November 2017.

23. Paul Zeise, "Steelers Receiver Barry Pearson Came Away From 'The Play' With a Great Story to Tell," *Pittsburgh Post-Gazette*, 14 October 2012. http://www.post-gazette.com/sports/steelers/2012/10/14/Steelers-receiver-Barry-Pearson-came-away-from-The-Play-with-a-great-story-to-tell/stories/201210140211.

24. Cook, "Rowdy and Rough."

25. Tom Rose, "Immaculate Reception: 'Absolutely Unbelievable,'" *Greene Co. (PA) Observer-Reporter*, 19 December 1999, p. B7.

26. "Oakland Raiders vs. Pittsburgh Steelers," *NBC*, 23 December 1972.

27. "Oakland Raiders vs. Pittsburgh Steelers, *Pittsburgh Steelers Radio Network*, 23 December 1972.

28. "Oakland Raiders vs. Pittsburgh Steelers," *Mutual Broadcasting Network*, 23 December 1972.

Chapter 11

1. *75 Seasons, the Complete Story of the National Football League, 1920–1994* (Atlanta: Turner Publishing, 1994), p. 42.

2. *Ibid.*, p. 43.

3. Paul Zeise, "Steelers Receiver Barry Pearson Came Away From 'The Play' With a Great Story to Tell," *Pittsburgh Post-Gazette*, 14 October 2012. http://www.post-gazette.com/sports/steelers/2012/10/14/Steelers-receiver-Barry-Pearson-

came-away-from-The-Play-with-a-great-story-to-tell/stories/201210140211.

4. Taylor Bell, *Dusty, Deek, and Mr. Do-Right: High School Football in Illinois* (Champaign: University of Illinois Press, 2010), p. 90.

5. The string was finally broken in 2018 when Geneseo went just 4–5, but the Maple Leafs still have an overall record of 675–309–19.

6. Personal communication, 28 November 2017.

7. Steve Tappa, "Geneseo Will Honor Coaching Legend Bob Reade Friday," *Quad Cities Dispatch-Argus*, 5 September 2008. http://www.qconline.com/sports/high_school_sports/geneseo-will-honor-coaching-legend-bob-reade-friday/article_f7a3979e-6ee8-5f69-b72d-76f1b9061b76.html.

8. Personal communication, 28 November 2017.

9. *Ibid.*

10. "2 Playoff 'Unprovens,'" *St. Joseph (MO) Gazette*, 21 December 1972, p. 2B.

11. Personal communication, 28 November 2017.

12. *Ibid.*

13. Zeise, "Steelers Receiver."

14. Personal communication, 28 November 2017.

15. "Barry Pearson, Steelers Wide Receiver, 1972–1973," *Pittsburgh Sports Daily Bulletin*, 6 December 2011. https://pittsburghsportsdailybulletin.wordpress.com/2011/12/06/barry-pearson-steelers-wide-receiver-1972-1973/.

16. Personal communication, 28 November 2017.

Chapter 12

1. "Oakland Raiders vs. Pittsburgh Steelers," *Pittsburgh Steelers Radio Network*, 23 December 1972.

2. Hank Gola, "Immaculate Reception Still a Classic, 25 Years Later," *Fredericksburg (VA) Free Lance-Star*, 23 December 1997, p. B5.

3. Kevin Cook, "Rowdy and Rough," *ESPN*, 13 August 2012. http://www.espn.com/nfl/story/_/id/8203175/nfl-1970s-football-was-rowdy-rough.

4. "Steelers Pull Out Miracle Triumph," *Toledo Blade*, 24 December 1972, p. B-3.

5. Robert Markus, "Steelers Get Early Christmas 'Gift,'" *Chicago Tribune*, 24 December 1972, Section 3, p. 1.

6. Cook, "Rowdy and Rough."

7. Gene Collier, "Steelers' Immaculate Reception: 40 Years Later, It Still Thrills Us," *Pittsburgh Post-Gazette*, 23 December 2012. http://www.post-gazette.com/sports/steelers/2012/12/23/Steelers-Immaculate-Reception-40-years-later-it-thrills-us-still/stories/201212230196.

8. "Franco's Italian Army." https://www.watchyourbacknyc.com/blogs/news/run-piasano-run-franco-harris-and-his-italian-army.

9. Ruck, Patterson and Weber, *Rooney: A Sporting Life*, p. 414.

10. "Did Tatum Deflect the Pass?" *Eugene (OR) Register-Guard*, 24 December 1972, p. 3B.

11. *Ibid.*

12. "Oakland Raiders vs. Pittsburgh Steelers," *NBC*, 23 December 1972.

13. "Oakland Raiders vs. Pittsburgh Steelers," *Mutual Broadcasting Network*, 23 December 1972.

14. Gary Mihoces, "Rooney Missed Biggest Play in Team's History," *Lexington (NC) Observer-Reporter*, 26 December 1972, p. C-4.

15. "Freaky Touchdown Comes as Miracle," *St. Joseph (MO) Gazette*, 25 December 1972, p. 2D.

16. Ruck, Patterson and Weber, *Rooney: A Sporting Life*, p. 414.

17. "An 'Immaculate' Memory," steelers.com, 23 December 2018. https://www.steelers.com/news/an-immaculate-memory.

18. "No Tomorrow, Madden Declares," *Youngstown (OH) Vindicator*, 24 December 1972, p. D-1.

19. *A Football Life: The Immaculate Reception*, NFL Films, 2010.

20. "Steelers Pull Out Miracle Triumph," *Toledo Blade*, 24 December 1972, p. B-3.

21. Cook, "Rowdy and Rough."

22. Ed Bouchette, "Frenchy Fuqua: The Man Who Collided With History," *Pittsburgh Post-Gazette*, 16 September 2012. http://www.post-gazette.com/sports/steelers/2012/09/16/Frenchy-Fuqua-The-

man-who-collided-with-history/stories/
201209160228.

23. Timothy Gay, *The Physics of Football* (New York: HarperCollins, 2005).

24. Ruck, Patterson and Weber, *Rooney: A Sporting Life*, p. 415.

25. Dan Rooney, *My 75 Years With the Pittsburgh Steelers and the NFL* (Philadelphia: Da Capo Press, 2007), p. 5.

26. Ken Rappaport, "Four Games Down and Two to Go in Playoffs," *Portsmouth (OH) Times*, 26 December 1972, p. 22.

27. Personal communication, 28 November 2017.

28. Gola, "Immaculate Reception Still a Classic."

29. "Was the Reception Actually Immaculate?" *NBC Sports*, 19 December 2012. http://www.nbcsports.com/bayarea/raiders/was-reception-actually-immaculate.

30. Ed Bouchette, "Phil Villapiano: No Whining from Him," *Pittsburgh Post-Gazette*, 23 September 2012. http://www.post-gazette.com/sports/steelers/2012/09/23/Phil-Villapiano-No-whining-from-him/stories/201209230246.

31. *Fantastic Finishes, The Movie*, produced by Steve Sabol, *NFL Films*, 1988.

32. Tom Rose, "Immaculate Reception: 'Absolutely Unbelievable,'" *Greene Co. (PA) Observer-Reporter*, 19 December 1999, p. B7.

33. Al Abrams, "Sidelights on Sports," *Pittsburgh Post-Gazette*, 25 December 1972, p. 78.

34. Tom LaMarre, "Madden: Raiders Were Robbed," *Oakland Tribune*, 25 December 1972.

35. "Television Replay Had No Bearing," *Toledo Blade*, 24 December 1972, p. B4.

36. Gola, "Immaculate Reception Still a Classic."

37. *Ibid.*

38. Dan Rooney, *My 75 Years With the Pittsburgh Steelers and the NFL* (Philadelphia: Da Capo Press, 2007), p. 4.

39. *Fantastic Finishes, The Movie*, produced by Steve Sabol, *NFL Films*, 1988.

40. Ruck, Patterson and Weber, *Rooney: A Sporting Life*, p. 411.

41. *Ibid.*, p. 416.

42. Alan Robinson, "Twenty-five Years

Later, Franco's Catch Still Immaculate," *Gadsden (AL) Times*, 22 December 1997, p. D3.

43. "Immaculate Reception: The Facts and Fantasies," *Beaver (PA) County Times*, 21 December 1997, p. B4.

44. Bill Modoono, "Fleming Continues to do Double Duty Despite Insecurity," *Pittsburgh Press*, 1 September 1985, p. D3.

45. Vince Leonard, "THE Play: It's Torture to Madden and Raiders," *Pittsburgh Post-Gazette*, 25 December 1972, p. 79.

46. Gola, "Immaculate Reception Still a Classic," 1997.

Chapter 13

1. Personal communication, 16 January 2018.

2. Personal communication, 31 October 2017.

3. Perkins, *Winning the Big One*, p. 201.

4. "Vic Washington Gets Tryout as Defensive Back," *Washington (PA) Observer-Reporter*, 31 July 1974, p. D6.

5. Larry Bortstein, "The Year of the Rookie," *Rome (GA) News-Tribune*, 7 November 1971, p. 16.

6. Don Pierson, "Cowboys Arise, Nip 49ers 30–28," *Chicago Tribune*, 24 December 1972, Section 3, p. 4.

7. "Roger In, Craig Out; Lilly Ready to Play," *Pittsburgh Post-Gazette*, 29 December 1972, p. 14.

8. Don Pierson, "Cowboys Arise, Nip 49ers 30–28," *Chicago Tribune*, 24 December 1972, Section 3, p. 4.

9. Jerry Magee, "Receiving His Due," *San Diego Union-Tribune*, 20 November 2005. http://www.sandiegouniontribune.com/uniontrib/20051120/news_lz1s20sunspcl.html.

10. Perkins, *Winning the Big One*, p. 82.

11. "Rentzel, Alworth Keys to Seven-Player Trade," *Sarasota Journal*, 18 May 1971, p. 1D.

12. Brian Jensen, *Where Have All Our Cowboys Gone?* (Lanham, MD: Taylor Trade, 2001), p. 65.

13. "Frustrated Alworth Retires," *New London (CT) Day*, 2 July 1973, p. 11.

14. Bob St. John, "A Roger Rally Leaves SF in Tears," *Dallas Morning News*, 24 December 1972, p. B1.

15. Don Pierson, "Cowboys Arise, Nip 49ers 30–28," *Chicago Tribune*, 24 December 1972, Section 3, Page 4.

16. Jamie Aron, *Dallas Cowboys: The Complete Illustrated History* (Minneapolis: MVP Books, 2010), p. 68.

17. Bob St. John, "A Roger Rally Leaves SF in Tears," *Dallas Morning News*, 24 December 1972, p. B1.

18. Khari Murphy, "Staubach vs. 49ers in 1972 Playoffs," *USA Today*, 21 June 2016. http://cowboyswire.usatoday.com/2016/06/21/best-cowboys-decisions-subbing-in-staubach-vs-49ers-in-1972-playoffs/.

19. Peter Golenbock, *Cowboys Have Always Been My Heroes* (New York: Warner Books, 1997), p. 514.

20. Personal communication, 31 October 2017.

Chapter 14

1. Marty Ralbovsky, *Super Bowl* (New York: Hawthorn Books, 1971), p. 81.

2. Edwin Shrake, "Now the AFL Owns the Football," *Sports Illustrated*, 27 January 1969, p. 31.

3. Mark Mulvoy, "The AFL Has a Taste of Glory," *Sports Illustrated*, 4 September 1967, p. 14.

4. George Blanda and Jack Olsen, "That Impossible Season," *Sports Illustrated*, 2 August 1971, p. 32.

5. *Ibid.*, pp. 33–34.

6. *Ibid.*, pp. 35.

7. Jim Scott, "Over 40 Crowd Applauds Blanda, Mr. Big of the AFC," *The Sporting News*, 16 January 1971, p. 9.

8. Dave Eisenberg, "Football is Blanda's Life," *The Sporting News*, 14 November 1970, p. 46.

9. Phil Musick, "Gilliam Ready to Prove He's a Winner," *Pittsburgh Press*, 7 November 1973, p. 79.

10. Phil Musick, "The 'Bear' Facts: Gilliam Thinks He's Ready," *Pittsburgh Press*, 13 August 1974, p. 30.

11. Roy Blount, Jr., "Gillie Was a Steeler Driving Man," *Sports Illustrated*, 23 September 1974, p. 22.

12. Phil Musick, "Oakland Raid Wipes Out Steelers," *Pittsburgh Press*, 30 September 1974, p. 26.

13. Richard Goldstein, "Joe Gilliam is Dead at 49; Pioneer Black Quarterback," *New York Times*, 27 December 2000. http://www.nytimes.com/2000/12/27/us/joe-gilliam-is-dead-at-49-pioneer-black-quarterback.html.

14. Josh Katzowitz, "Remember When: Joe Gilliam Takes Terry Bradshaw's Starting QB Job," CBSsports.com, 10 October 2014. https://www.cbssports.com/nfl/news/remember-when-joe-gilliam-takes-terry-bradshaws-starting-qb-job/.

15. Phil Musick, "Jumbled Steelers Plunder Atlanta," *Pittsburgh Press*, 29 October 1974, p. 26.

16. Goldstein, "Joe Gilliam is Dead."

17. Paul Zeise, "Gilliam Paved the Way for Black Quarterbacks in the NFL," *Pittsburgh Post-Gazette*, 30 December 2000. http://old.post-gazette.com/steelers/20001230gilliam2.asp.

18. Musick, "Oakland Raid Wipes Out Steelers," 1974, p. 24.

19. "We're Going to Whip Those Guys—Villapiano," *Spartanburg (SC) Herald*, 23 December 1974, p. A6.

20. Phil Musick, "Steeler Teams Something Special," *Pittsburgh Press*, 8 November 1973, p. 35.

21. Phil Musick, "Greasy Kid Stuff, Etc. No Help to Raiders," *Pittsburgh Press*, 12 November 1973, p. 20.

22. "Steeler-Raider Rivalry is Gaining in Maturity," *Lexington (NC) Dispatch*, 13 December 1976, p. 9.

23. "Pittsburgh Steelers vs. Oakland Raiders: All-Time Great Games; Which Was the Best?" pennlive.com, 6 November 2015. http://www.pennlive.com/steelers/index.ssf/2015/11/steelers_vs_raiders_all-time.html.

24. Glenn Sheeley, "Noll Judges Raider Defense as Criminal," *Pittsburgh Press*, 14 September 1976, p. 20.

25. Milton Richman, "Pro Football Has Criminal Elements—Noll," *Boca Raton News*, 6 October 1976, p. 14A.

26. Donald B. Thackery, "Steeler Coach Noll Wins 'Criminal Element' Suit," *Baltimore Afro-American*, 26–30 July 1977, p. 9.

27. Phil Musick, "Raiders are Still Menace, But Not Like Bad Old Days," *Pittsburgh Press*, 16 December 1984, p. B1.

28. *Ibid.*

29. "Rozelle Calls Davis Outlaw, May Sue Him," *Boca Raton News*, 25 January 1981, p. 13A.

30. Ted Green, "Raiders Find Roster Spots for Other Team's Castoffs," *Sarasota Herald-Tribune*, 18 January 1981, p. 7C.

31. "Upshaw Supports Davis in Legal Dispute," *Ellensburg (WA) Daily Record*, 20 January 1981, p. 11.

32. Bruce Weber, "Al Davis, the Controversial and Combative Raiders Owner, Dies at 82," *New York Times*, 8 October 2011. http://www.nytimes.com/2011/10/09/sports/football/al-davis-owner-of-raiders-dies-at-82.html?_r=0.

33. "Steelers, Raiders Resume Football's Roughest Rivalry," *Spokane Spokesman-Review*, 22 September 1977, p. 18.

Chapter 15

1. Kristine Setting Clark, "Beard to Serve as Honorary Game Captain," 49ers.com, 28 August 2008. https://www.49ers.com/news/beard-to-serve-as-honorary-game-captain-492714.

2. Personal communication, 16 January 2018.

3. "Staubach Bought Sellers' Play," *Toledo Blade*, 24 December 1972, p. B4.

4. "Dallas Cowboys vs. San Francisco 49ers," *Mutual Broadcast Network*, 23 December 1972.

5. Roger Staubach and Frank Luksa, *Time Enough to Win* (Waco: Word Books, 1980), p. 100.

6. Peter Golenbock, *Cowboys Have Always Been My Heroes* (New York: Warner Books, 1997), p. 511, 517.

7. "Cowboys Parks Wants to be Traded," *Sarasota Herald-Tribune*, 31 March 1973, p. 3C.

8. Khari Murphy, "Staubach vs. 49ers in 1972 Playoffs," *USA Today*, 21 June 2016. http://cowboyswire.usatoday.com/2016/06/21/best-cowboys-decisions-subbing-in-staubach-vs-49ers-in-1972-playoffs/.

9. Perkins, *Winning the Big One*, p. 94.

10. Bob St. John, *Texas Sports Writers: The Wild and Wacky Years* (Plano: Republic of Texas Press, 2002), p. 59.

11. Perkins, *Winning the Big One*, p. 172–73.

12. Cliff Harris and Charlie Waters, *Tales From the Dallas Cowboys* (Champaign, IL: Sports Publishing, 2003), p. 138.

13. "Dallas: Roger—and In!" *St. Petersburg Times*, 25 December 1972, p. 4-C.

14. "Post Playoff Interviews with Staubach, Landry and Sellers," *KPIX-TV*, 23 December 1972.

15. Bob St. John, "A Roger Rally Leaves SF in Tears," *Dallas Morning News*, 24 December 1972, p. B1.

16. Personal communication, 31 October 2017.

17. "Dallas Cowboys vs. San Francisco 49ers," *Mutual Broadcast Network*, 23 December 1972.

18. "Post Playoff Interviews with Staubach, Landry and Sellers," *KPIX-TV*, 23 December 1972.

19. Don Pierson, "Cowboys Arise, Nip 49ers 30–28," *Chicago Tribune*, 24 December 1972, Section 3, p. 4.

20. *Fantastic Finishes, The Movie*, produced by Steve Sabol, *NFL Films*, 1988.

21. Joe Zagorski, *The NFL in the 1970s: Pro Football's Most Important Decade* (Jefferson, NC: McFarland, 2016), p. 100.

22. Bob St. John, *Texas Sports Writers*, p. 180.

23. Roger Staubach and Frank Luksa, *Time Enough to Win* (Waco: Word Books, 1980), p. 97.

24. "Post Playoff Interviews with Staubach, Landry and Sellers," *KPIX-TV*, 23 December 1972.

25. Eric Prewitt, "Miracle Finish Keeps Dallas in Playoffs," *Tuscaloosa News*, 24 December 1972, p. 2B.

26. Don Pierson, "Cowboys Arise, Nip 49ers 30–28," *Chicago Tribune*, 24 December 1972, Section 3, p. 4.

27. Austin Murphy, "The Greatest of Rivals," *Sports Illustrated*, 16 February 1995. http://www.si.com/vault/1995/02/16/133316/the-greatest-of-rivals-the-49ers-and-the-cowboys-have-dogged-one-another-for-the-last-25-years.

28. Art Spander, "Dick Nolan? He Turned the 49ers Into Winners," *East Bay Times*, 13 November 2007. http://www.eastbaytimes.com/ci_7449474?source=rss.

29. Don Pierson, "Cowboys Arise, Nip 49ers 30–28," *Chicago Tribune*, 24 December 1972, Section 3, p. 4.

30. Personal communication, 31 October 2017.

31. "Cowboys: The Comeback Kids of the Wild West," *Pittsburgh Post-Gazette*, 25 December 1972, p. 79.

32. "Post Playoff Interviews with Staubach, Landry and Sellers," *KPIX-TV*, 23 December 1972.

33. Don Pierson, "Cowboys Arise, Nip 49ers 30–28," *Chicago Tribune*, 24 December 1972, Section 3, p. 4.

34. *Top 10: Comebacks.*

35. Earl Caldwell, "Worried San Franciscans Take New Look at Quake Forecaster," *New York Times*, 26 December 1972. http://www.nytimes.com/1972/12/26/archives/worried-san-franciscans-take-new-look-at-quake-forecaster.html.

36. "Frisco Quake Predicted for Jan. 4," Associated Press, *Pittsburgh Post-Gazette*, 22 December 1972, p. 3.

37. *Ibid.*

Chapter 16

1. Mike Freeman, "Mike Freeman's 10-Point Stance: Tom Brady's the GOAT, But By How Much?" *Bleacher Report*, 17 January 2018. http://bleacherreport.com/articles/2754218-mike-freemans-10-point-stance-tom-bradys-the-goat-but-by-how-much.

2. Leviticus 16:10 (NIV).

3. Walter Trumbull, "Roy Riegels is Lucky; He Gets a Comeback," *Milwaukee Journal*, 9 January 1929, p. 2.

4. Personal communication, 31 October 2017.

5. *Ibid.*

6. *Ibid.*

7. David Bush, "Where Are They Now: Cedric Hardman," *San Francisco Chronicle*, 14 December 2003. http://www.sfgate.com/sports/article/WHERE-ARE-THEY-NOW-Cedrick-Hardman-Hardman-s-2525146.php.

8. Herb Caen, "In the Beginning," *San Francisco Chronicle*, 24 January 1995. http://www.sfgate.com/news/article/In-the-Beginning-3048728.php.

9. Eric Prewitt, "49ers Bid to Balance Attack," *Reading (PA) Eagle*, 7 September 1973, p. 24.

10. Matt Maiocco and David Fucillo, *Where Have You Gone? San Francisco 49ers* (New York: Sports Publishing, 2005), p. 101.

11. Jim Trotter, "Brandon Bostic Tries to Move on From NFC Title Blunder," *ESPN*, 20 September 2015. http://www.espn.com/nfl/story/_/id/13691819/brandon-bostick-former-green-bay-packers-player-moved-muffed-onside-kick-vs-seattle-seahawks-nfl.

12. Kevin Baker, "The Myth of the Home Run that Drove an Angels Pitcher to Suicide," *The Atlantic*, 27 October 2011. https://www.theatlantic.com/entertainment/archive/2011/10/the-myth-of-the-home-run-that-drove-an-angels-pitcher-to-suicide/247447/.

13. Ray Ratto, "NFL Playoffs, Full Day for the Faithful, Bay Area Teams own Spotlight," *San Francisco Chronicle*, 12 January 2003. http://www.sfgate.com/sports/article/NFL-Playoffs-Full-day-for-the-faithful-Bay-2680053.php.

14. Tom FitzGerald, "Baker's Boy Could Have Lent Giants' Snow a Helping Hand," *San Francisco Chronicle*, 7 October 2003. http://www.sfgate.com/sports/article/OPEN-SEASON-Baker-s-boy-could-have-lent-Giants-2584054.php.

15. Ron Fimrite, "Mind You, This Time It's Not All Over," *Sports Illustrated*, 25 January 1982, p. 34.

16. Amalie Benjamin, "Bill Buckner Welcomed Back to Fenway Park Warmly," *Boston Globe*, 9 April 2008. https://www.bostonglobe.com/sports/2008/04/09/bill-buckner-welcomed-back-fenway-park-warmly/VlEAI2I9YvosnDGviVMjpL/story.html.

17. *Ibid.*

18. Caen, "In the Beginning."

19. Personal communication, 31 October 2017.

Chapter 17

1. "Clemente Dies in Plane Crash," *Pittsburgh Post-Gazette*, 2 January 1973, p. 1.

2. "Omen? Griese on Bench," *Pittsburgh Post-Gazette*, 27 December 1972, p. 20.

3. "Nolan: Landry Will Start Roger," *Pittsburgh Post-Gazette*, 27 December 1972, p. 20.

4. Peter Golenbock, *Cowboys Have Al-*

ways Been My Heroes (New York: Warner Books, 1997), pp. 515–516.

5. *Ibid.*, p. 516.

6. Jimmy Miller, "Miracle Steelers Play it Straight," *Pittsburgh Post-Gazette*, 28 December 1972, p. 10.

7. "NFL Asks More Security," *Pittsburgh Post-Gazette*, 26 December 1972, p. 17.

8. Al Abrams, "Sidelights on Sports," *Pittsburgh Post-Gazette*, 27 December 1972, p. 20.

9. Nicholas P. Ciotola, "Spignesi, Sinatra, and the Pittsburgh Steelers: Franco's Italian Army as an Expression of Ethnic Identity, 1972–1977," *Journal of Sport History* 27, no. 2 (2000), p. 277.

10. Jimmy Miller, "Steelers Vow Comeback," *Pittsburgh Post-Gazette*, 1 January 1973, p. 61.

11. *Ibid.*

12. Bob Chick, "How the Playoffs Look with Confederate Money," *St. Petersburg Independent*, 22 December 1972, p. 1-C.

13. Karolyn Schuster, "Victory Postponed 'Until Next Year,'" *Pittsburgh Post-Gazette*, 1 January 1973, p. 51.

14. Charley Feeney, "Playing Games," *Pittsburgh Post-Gazette*, 1 January 1973, p. 62.

15. Pat Livingston, "The Greater Loss," *Pittsburgh Press*, 2 January 1973, p. 25.

16. Peter Golenbock, *Cowboys Have Always Been My Heroes* (New York: Warner Books, 1997), p. 517.

17. "Alworth, Hayes Benched for Test Against Lions," *Washington (PA) Observer-Reporter*, 30 October 1972, p. C-7.

18. *Ibid.*

19. Pat Putnam, "Jingle Joints Should Be Judged By His Cover," *Sports Illustrated*, 30 September 1968, p. 80.

20. Waters moved back to safety in 1975 and the next season made the first of three straight trips to the Pro Bowl. His nine playoff interceptions (including three in one game) are tied for the most in NFL history.

21. Bruce Lowitt, "Redskins Whip Cowboys, 26–3," *Owosso (MI) Argus-Press*, 2 January 1973, p. 13.

22. "Landry Says Redskins 'Deserved' Title Win," *Victoria (TX) Advocate*, 1 January 1973, p. 9A.

23. "Skins Say Morton Should Be Starter," *Wilmington (NC) Star-News*, 2 January 1973, p. 14.

24. "Cowboys' Staubach Becomes a Dolphin Fan," *Milwaukee Journal*, 10 January 1973, p. 18.

25. Roger Staubach and Frank Luksa, *Time Enough to Win* (Waco: Word Books, 1980), p. 98.

26. Tom Seppy, "Talbert-Staubach Rivalry Renewed," *Fredericksburg (VA) Free Lance-Star*, 1 November 1975, p. 11.

27. *Ibid.*

28. "Harsh Feelings Aired," *Victoria (TX) Advocate*, 27 November 1974, p. 1B.

Chapter 18

1. Tim Swanson, "The Hollow Man," *Sactown Magazine*, February-March 2012. http://www.sactownmag.com/February-March-2012/The-Hollow-Man/index.php?cparticle=3&siarticle=2.

2. *Ibid.*

3. Personal communication, 31 October 2017.

4. Eric Branch, "Forrest Blue Dies After Years of Dementia," *San Francisco Chronicle*, 20 July 2011.https://www.sfgate.com/sports/article/Forrest-Blue-dies-after-years-of-dementia-2354032.php.

5. John Branch, "Ken Stabler, a Magnetic N.F.L. Star, Was Sapped of Spirit by C.T.E.," *New York Times*, 3 February 2016. https://www.nytimes.com/2016/02/04/sports/football/ken-stabler-nfl-cte-brain-disease.html.

6. Elliott Almond, "Former Raiders All-Pro George Atkinson Struggles for Normalcy as his Mind Deteriorates," *San Jose Mercury-News*, 16 April 2016. https://www.mercurynews.com/2016/04/16/former-raiders-all-pro-george-atkinson-struggles-for-normalcy-as-his-mind-deteriorates/.

7. Personal communication, 16 January 2018.

8. *Ibid.*

9. "Supreme Court Leaves $1B NFL Concussion Settlement in Place," *Chicago Tribune*, 12 December 2016. http://www.chicagotribune.com/sports/football/ct-nfl-concussion-settlement-supreme-court-20161212-story.html.

10. Chris Ballard, "Zen and the Art of

Brain Maintenance," *Sports Illustrated*, 19–26 November 2018, p. 87.

11. *Ibid.*

12. "Correspondence," *Neurosurgery* 58, no. 5 (May 2006): E1003.

13. Kevin Seifert, "Dr. Bennet Omalu: CTE Obsession Obscuring Truth About Brain Health of Football Players," *ESPN*, 4 August 2017. http://www.espn.com/nfl/story/_/id/20245394/dr-bennet-omalu-says-obsession-cte-obscuring-larger-truth-brain-health-football-players.

14. Chris Mortensen, "NFL Adds Neurotrauma Consultants as Part of Revised Concussion Protocol," *ESPN*, 24 December 2017. http://www.espn.com/nfl/story/_/id/21864620/nfl-making-significant-changes-concussion-protocol.

15. Mark Lane, "Roger Staubach on CTE, Losing and More," *247Sports*, 19 March 2016. https://247sports.com/nfl/dallas-cowboys/Article/Roger-Staubach-Speaks-about-Concussions-CTE-and-Losing-103098769.

16. Chris Ballard, "Zen and the Art of Brain Maintenance," *Sports Illustrated* 19–26 November 2018, p. 87.

17. Juliet Macur, "For a Cowboys Star with Dementia, Time is Running Out," *New York Times*, 26 January 2014. https://www.nytimes.com/2014/01/27/sports/football/for-a-cowboys-star-with-dementia-time-is-running-out.html.

18. *Ibid.*

19. Personal communication, 31 October 2017.

20. Kevin Seifert, "Dr. Bennet Omalu: CTE Obsession Obscuring Truth About Brain Health of Football Players," *ESPN*, 4 August 2017. http://www.espn.com/nfl/story/_/id/20245394/dr-bennet-omalu-says-obsession-cte-obscuring-larger-truth-brain-health-football-players.

Chapter 19

1. "Dud Bowl II," *Married With Children*, Series 10, Episode 10, Fox Television, 1995.

2. "Raiders Still Can't Win the 'Big' One," *Park City (KY) Daily News*, 5 January 1976, p. 8.

3. "Dick Nolan Gets Axed," *Newburgh (NY) Evening News*, 26 December 1975, p. 8B.

4. Ron Kroichick, "Coach Established 49ers as a Winner," *San Francisco Chronicle*, 12 November 2007. http://www.sfgate.com/sports/article/Coach-established-49ers-as-a-winner-3235040.php.

5. *Top 10: Comebacks.*

6. Hubert Mizell, "Joe Thomas," *St. Petersburg* Times, 9 December 1978, p. 3C.

7. Art Spander, "Dick Nolan? He Turned the 49ers Into Winners," *East Bay Times*, 13 November 2007. http://www.eastbaytimes.com/ci_7449474?source=rss.

8. Bert Rosenthal, "Staubach or Morton?" *Bowling Green (KY) Daily News*, 13 July 1973, p. 12.

9. *Ibid.*

10. "Landry Chooses Staubach, Morton Reissues Trade Talk," *Pittsburgh Press*, 11 September 1973, p. 32.

11. Don Pierson, "Cowboys, Turnovers Crush Broncos," *Chicago Tribune*, 16 January 1978, Section 6, p. 2.

12. *Fantastic Finishes, The Movie*, produced by Steve Sabol, *NFL Films*, 1988.

13. *Ibid.*

14. *Ibid.*

15. "'Captain Comeback' leads '72 Cowboys past 49ers," *ESPN*, 8 October 2010. http://static.espn.go.com/nfl/playoffs98/news/1999/990104/01026665.html.

16. Johnette Howard, "Immaculate Reception Memories," *ESPN*, 23 December 2012. http://espn.go.com/nfl/story/_/id/8774529/remembering-immaculate-reception.

17. Mike Prisuta, "The Greatest Draft Class in NFL History," Steelers.com, 7 April 2014. http://www.steelers.com/news/article-1/The-greatest-draft-class-in-NFL-history/9cafed25-d4fb-4658-85f0-d2451b352f04.

18. Jim Dent, "Frustrated Cowboys Try to Break the Hex," *Pittsburgh Press*, 13 October 1985, p. D5.

19. Hubert Mizell, "The Hero of the Apes," *St. Petersburg Times*, 10 January 1975, p. C1.

20. "Franco Harris on Franco's Italian Army, the Immaculate Reception, and growing up in a multicultural family," *Italian American Experience*, 2 October 2016.

http://italianamericanexperience.com/
franco-harris-on-francos-italian-army-
the-immaculate-reception-and-growing-
up-in-a-multicultural-family/.

21. "Rozelle Questions Super Bowl Call,"
Deseret News, 23 February 1979, p. 2E.

22. Jim Martz, "Kiss of Death Came
From a Ref," *St. Petersburg Evening Independent*, 23 January 1979, p. 24C.

23. Peter Golenbock, *Cowboys Have Always Been My Heroes* (New York: Warner
Books, 1997), p. 643.

24. Jim Dent, "Frustrated Cowboys Try
to Break the Hex," *Pittsburgh Press*, 13 October 1985, p. D5.

25. *Ibid.*

26. Henry T. Stein, "Adlerian Overview
of Birth Order Characteristics." http://
www.adlerian.us/birthord.htm.

27. For the record, the ten games included are the Hail Mary game, the five
Super Bowl wins, and playoff wins over
Atlanta (1981), San Francisco (1992 and
1993), and Green Bay (1995). Another glar-
ing omission is the 1979 regular season finale in which Roger Staubach directed Dallas to two touchdowns in the final two
minutes to beat Washington, 35–34 and
win the NFC East.

28. Alan Robinson, "'Greatest Play'
Turns 40 Today," Steelers.com, 23 December 2012. http://www.steelers.com/news/
article-1/Greatest-play-turns-40-today/
1660205f-4849-4bbe-8fe4-357bf1870
d5b.

29. Nathan Francis, "Immaculate Reception Monument Debuts in Pittsburgh
on 40th Anniversary of Play," Inquisitr.
com, 23 December 2012. http://www.
inquisitr.com/452077/immaculate-
reception-monument-debuts-in-
pittsburgh-on-40th-anniversary-of-play/.

30. *Ibid.*

31. Alan Robinson, "'It's Caught Out of
the Air!'" *Beaver (PA) County Times*, 21
December 1997, p. B4.

32. Ed Bouchette, "Frenchy Fuqua: The
Man Who Collided With History," *Pitts-
burgh-Post Gazette*, 16 September 2012.
http://www.post-gazette.com/sports/
steelers/2012/09/16/Frenchy-Fuqua-The-
man-who-collided-with-history/stories/
201209160228.

33. Derek Burns, "Phil Villapiano's Plan
to Tackle Franco, the Immaculate Reception," *Talk of Fame Sports Network*, 19 December 2016. http://www.talkoffamenet
work.com/phil-villapianos-plan-tackle-
franco-immaculate-reception/.

34. *Ibid.*

Chapter 20

1. *Top 10: What Ifs.*

2. *Ibid.*

3. *Ibid.*

4. Lew Freeman, *Pittsburgh Steelers:
The Complete Illustrated History* (Minneapolis: MVP Books, 2009), p. 80.

5. Jimmy Miller, "Steelers Vow Comeback," *Pittsburgh Post-Gazette*, 1 January
1973, p. 62.

6. "Were '73 Dolphins Better Than '72
Perfect Team?" *Fox Sports*, 13 December
2012. https://www.foxsports.com/other/
story/were-73-dolphins-better-than-72-
perfect-team-121312.

7. Tom Flores coached the Raiders to
Super Bowl wins in 1980 and 1983.

8. Eric Prewitt, "Madden Calls it Quits,"
5 January 1979, *Hendersonville (NC) Times*,
p. 10.

9. Gordon W. Russell, *Aggression in
the Sports World: A Social Psychological
Perspective* (Oxford: University of Oxford
Press, 2008).

10. William F. Reed, "An Ugly Affair in
Minneapolis," *Sports Illustrated*, 7 February 1972, p. 18.

11. "'TV Call' on TD Irks Coach," *Pittsburgh Post-Gazette*, 26 December 1972, p.
17.

12. "Was the Reception Actually Immaculate?" *NBC Sports*, 19 December 2012.
http://www.nbcsports.com/bayarea/raid
ers/was-reception-actually-immaculate.

13. *Ibid.*

14. "History of Instant Replay," *NFL*,
2016. https://operations.nfl.com/the-game/
history-of-instant-replay/.

15. *Ibid.*

16. "Was the Reception Actually Immaculate?" *NBC Sports*, 19 December
2012. http://www.nbcsports.com/bayarea/
raiders/was-reception-actually-
immaculate.

17. "Morris Officially Gets His '1,000,'"

Fredericksburg (VA) Free-Lance Star, 22 December 1972, p. 6.

18. "Falcons' Dave Hampton Hits 1000-Yard Goal Then Loses It," *Baltimore Afro-American,* 23 December 1972, p. 10.

19. Milton Gross, "Weeb's Decision Entirely His Own," *St. Petersburg Evening Independent,* 23 December 1972, p. 3-C.

20. "Football Still Big With Mrs. Lombardi," *Lexington (NC) Dispatch,* 21 December 1972, p. 13.

21. *Ibid.*

22. Dink Carroll, "Ealey's Success With 'Cats May Change NFL's Attitude," *Montreal Gazette,* 19 December 1972, p. 32.

23. "Woody Stages Ho-Ho-Ho Act," *Owosso (MI) Argus-Press,* 23 December 1972, p. 14.

24. Bill Lucey, "The Day the Camera Blinked at the Rose Bowl," *Newspaper Alum,* 1 January 2014. http://www.newspaperalum.com/2014/01/the-day-the-camera-blinked-at-the-rose-bowl.html.

25. *Ibid.*

26. "Freshman Added Depth to 1972 Football Season," *Mt. Airy (NC) News,* 22 December 1972, p. 14.

27. "Pitt Acts to Solve Major Problem," *Washington (PA) Observer-Reporter,* 20 December 1972, p. D-4.

28. Ted Meier, "UCLA Batters Pitt for 50th Straight Win," *Owosso (MI) Argus-Press,* 23 December 1972, p. 14.

29. "NBC Protest Olympics TV," *Montreal Gazette,* 20 December 1972, p. 10.

30. "Shorter Tells it Like it Is," *Sarasota Journal,* 20 December 1972, p. C-1.

31. "AL Fights for Change," *St. Petersburg Evening Independent,* 19 December 1972, p. 2-C.

32. "'Gabby' Hartnett, Former Cub Catcher Dies at 72," *Washington (PA) Observer-Reporter,* 21 December 1972, p. C-7.

33. "Hockey Star Given Order of Canada," *Calgary Herald,* 23 December 1972, p. 11.

34. *Cold War on Ice: '72 Summit Series,* produced by Ross Greenburg, 2011.

35. *Ibid.*

36. Hal Bock, "Poor Attendance Problem for New Hockey Circuit," *Washington (PA) Observer-Reporter,* 21 December 1972, p. C-7.

37. "Billie Jean King Emotional Queen," *Spokane (WA) Daily Chronicle,* 20 December 1972, p. 35.

38. "Sports Executive Raps Apathy," *Montreal Gazette,* 22 December 1972, p. 16.

39. David Cicotello and Angelo J. Louisa, eds., *Forbes Field: Essays and Memories of the Pirates' Historic Ballpark, 1909–1971* (Jefferson, NC: McFarland, 2007), p. 153.

40. Steve Rotstein, "Good Times: Pirates Fans Celebrate Historic Home Run on Mazeroski Day," *The Pitt News,* 13 October 2016. https://pittnews.com/article/112289/sports/good-times-pirates-fans-celebrate-historic-home-run-on-mazeroski-day/.

Bibliography

This is not an exhaustive listing of every reference, but rather a representative bibliography of the most important sources used.

"American Central," *Sports Illustrated*, 18 September 1972.

"American West," *Sports Illustrated*, 18 September 1972.

Anderson, Dave. "Franco's 'Destiny' Survived Draft, Noll-Art Jr." *Pittsburgh Post-Gazette*, 16 January 1975.

Aron, Jamie. *Dallas Cowboys: The Complete Illustrated History.* Minneapolis: MVP Books, 2010.

Ballard, Chris. "Zen and the Art of Brain Maintenance," *Sports Illustrated*, 19–26 November 2018.

Blanda, George, and Jack Olsen. "That Impossible Season," *Sports Illustrated*, 2 August 1971.

Blount, Roy, Jr. "Gillie Was a Steeler Driving Man," *Sports Illustrated*, 23 September 1974.

Bouchette, Ed. "Cope Helped Draft Sinatra into Army," *Pittsburgh Post-Gazette*, 21 May 1998.

_____. "Frenchy Fuqua: The Man Who Collided with History," *Pittsburgh Post-Gazette*, 16 September 2012. http://www.post-gazette.com/sports/steelers/2012/09/16/Frenchy-Fuqua-The-man-who-collided-with-history/stories/201209160228.

_____. "Phil Villapiano: No Whining from Him," *Pittsburgh Post-Gazette*, 23 September 2012. http://www.post-gazette.com/sports/steelers/2012/09/23/Phil-Villapiano-No-whining-from-him/stories/201209230246.

Branch, Eric. "Forrest Blue Dies After Years of Dementia," *San Francisco Chronicle*, 20 July 2011. https://www.sfgate.com/sports/article/Forrest-Blue-dies-after-years-of-dementia-2354032.php.

Branch, John. "Ken Stabler, a Magnetic N.F.L. Star, Was Sapped of Spirit by C.T.E.," *New York Times*, 3 February 2016. https://www.nytimes.com/2016/02/04/sports/football/ken-stabler-nfl-cte-brain-disease.html.

Burns, Derek. "Phil Villapiano's Plan to Tackle Franco, the Immaculate Reception," *Talk of Fame Sports Network*, 19 December 2016. http://www.talkoffamenetwork.com/phil-villapianos-plan-tackle-franco-immaculate-reception/.

"Cadence in Cleveland." *Paesani Di Pittsburgh*, 2005. http://paesanidipittsburgh.omeka.net/exhibits/show/capturedmemories/francositalianarmy/cadenceincleveland.

"'Captain Comeback' Leads '72 Cowboys Past 49ers," *ESPN*, 8 October 2010. http://static.espn.go.com/nfl/playoffs98/news/1999/990104/01026665.html.

Carnicelli, Joe. "Greene: Didn't Think This Day Would Ever Come," *Windsor (ON) Star*, 22 December 1972.

Cartwright, Gary. "The Lonely Blues of Duane Thomas," *Texas Monthly*, February 1973. http://www.texasmonthly.com/the-culture/the-lonely-blues-of-duane-thomas/.

_____. "Turn Out the Lights," *Texas Monthly,* August 1997. https://www.texasmonthly.com/the-culture/turn-out-the-lights/.

Ciotola, Nicholas P. "Spignesi, Sinatra, and the Pittsburgh Steelers: Franco's Italian Army as an Expression of Ethnic Identity, 1972–1977," *Journal of Sport History* 27, no. 2 (2000).

Collier, Gene. "Steelers' Immaculate Reception: 40 Years Later, It Still Thrills Us," *Pittsburgh Post-Gazette,* 23 December 2012. http://www.post-gazette.com/sports/steelers/2012/12/23/Steelers-Immaculate-Reception-40-years-later-it-thrills-us-still/stories/20121223 0196.

Cook, Kevin. "Rowdy and Rough," *ESPN,* 13 August 2012. http://www.espn.com/nfl/story/_/id/8203175/nfl-1970s-football-was-rowdy-rough.

"Correspondence," *Neurosurgery* 58, no. 5 (May 2006: E1003.

Crain, Zac. "Tony Dorsett Is Losing His Mind," *D Magazine,* February 2014. https://www.dmagazine.com/publications/d-magazine/2014/february/dallas-cowboys-tony-dorsett-is-losing-his-mind/.

Crawley, Dave. "Man Who Scooped Up Immaculate Reception Football Tells Story," *KDKA-TV,* 21 December 2012. http://pittsburgh.cbslocal.com/2012/12/21/man-who-scooped-up-immaculate-reception-football-tells-story/.

"Dallas Cowboys Vs. San Francisco 49ers," *Mutual Broadcast Network,* 23 December 1972.

Daly, Dan. *The National Forgotten League.* Lincoln: University of Nebraska Press, 2012.

Fantastic Finishes, the Movie. Produced by Steve Sabol. *NFL Films,* 1988.

Feeney, Charles. "Early Steeler Defeats Cut Rooney Deeply," *Pittsburgh Post-Gazette,* 22 December 1972.

_____. "Playing Games," *Pittsburgh Post-Gazette,* 1 January 1973.

_____. "Playing Games," *Pittsburgh Post-Gazette,* 22 December 1972.

Fimrite, Ron. "Mind You, This Time It's Not All Over," *Sports Illustrated,* 25 January 1982.

_____. "When the Stars Cross," *Sports Illustrated,* 7 August 1972.

"A Flavor of Larimer Avenue." *Paesani Di Pittsburgh,* 2005. http://paesanidipittsburgh.omeka.net/exhibits/show/capturedmemories/herbamen/flavoroflarimeravenue.

A Football Life: The Immaculate Reception. NFL Films, 2010.

"Franco Harris on Franco's Italian Army, the Immaculate Reception, and Growing Up in a Multicultural Family." *Italian American Experience,* 2 October 2016. http://italianamericanexperience.com/franco-harris-on-francos-italian-army-the-immaculate-reception-and-growing-up-in-a-multicultural-family/.

"Franco's Italian Army." *NFL Films,* 2005. https://www.watchyourbacknyc.com/blogs/news/run-piasano-run-franco-harris-and-his-italian-army.

Freeman, Lew. *Pittsburgh Steelers: The Complete Illustrated History,* Minneapolis: MVP Books, 2009.

Gay, Timothy. *The Physics of Football,* New York: HarperCollins, 2005.

Georgatos, Dennis. *Game of My Life: San Francisco 49ers.* New York: Sports Publishing, 2007.

Gigler, Dan. "Immaculate Reception Football Means a Lot to Its Caretaker," *Pittsburgh Post-Gazette,* 18 November 2012. http://www.post-gazette.com/hp_mobile/2012/11/18/Immaculate-Reception-football-means-a-lot-to-its-caretaker/stories/201211180146.

Gola, Hank. "Immaculate Reception Still a Classic, 25 Years Later," *Fredericksburg (VA) Free Lance-Star,* 23 December 1997.

Golenbock, Peter. *Cowboys Have Always Been My Heroes.* New York: Warner, 1997.

_____. *Landry's Boys: An Oral History of a Team and an Era.* New York: Triumph, 2005.

Howard, Johnette. "An 'Immaculate' Memory," Steelers.com, 23 December 2018. https://www.Steelers.com/News/An-Immaculate-Memory.

_____. "Immaculate Reception Memories," *ESPN,* 23 December 2012. http://espn.go.

com/nfl/story/_/id/8774529/remem bering-immaculate-reception.

Jensen, Brian. *Where Have All Our Cowboys Gone?* Lanham, MD: Taylor Trade, 2001.

Kahler, Kalyn. "From Staubach to Dak: An Oral History of the Cowboys' Quarterbacks," *Sports Illustrated,* 1 November 2017. https://www.si.com/2017/11/01/dallas-cowboys-quarterbacks-oral-history-roger-staubach-troy-aikman-tony-romo-dak-prescott.

Karlovitz, Bob. "'Sports Detectives' Investigates Immaculate Reception Ball," *Pittsburgh Tribune-Review,* 20 April 2016. http://triblive.com/aande/moreaande/10296559-74/barrows-says-baker.

Kowet, Don. *Franco Harris.* New York: Coward, McCann & Geoghegan, 1977.

LaMarre, Tom. *Oakland Raiders: Colorful Tales of the Silver and Black.* New York: Globe Pequot, 2003.

Lane, Mark. "Roger Staubach on CTS, Losing and More," *247sports,* 19 March 2016. https://247sports.com/nfl/dallas-cowboys/Article/Roger-Staubach-Speaks-about-Concussions-CTE-and-Losing-103098769.

Macur, Juliet. "For a Cowboys Star with Dementia, Time Is Running Out," *New York Times,* 26 January 2014. https://www.nytimes.com/2014/01/27/sports/football/for-a-cowboys-star-with-dementia-time-is-running-out.html.

Maiocco, Matt, and David Fucillo. *Where Have You Gone? San Francisco 49ers.* New York: Sports Publishing, 2005.

Maule, Tex. "Champion Blahs in Big D," *Sports Illustrated,* 18 December 1972.

_____. "The Cowboys Take It on the Lam," *Sports Illustrated,* 10 January 1972.

_____. "Old Brodie Went Witcher-Way," *Sports Illustrated,* 25 December 1972.

Mihoces, Gary. "It's 'Steeler-Mania' for Fun and Profit," *Lexington (NC) Observer-Reporter,* 21 December 1972.

_____. "Rooney Missed Biggest Play in Team's History," *Lexington (NC) Observer-Reporter,* 26 December 1972.

Murphy, Austin. "The Greatest of Rivals," *Sports Illustrated,* 16 February 1995. http://www.si.com/vault/1995/02/16/133316/the-greatest-of-rivals-the-49ers-and-the-cowboys-have-dogged-one-another-for-the-last-25-years.

Murphy, Khari. "Staubach Vs. 49ers in 1972 Playoffs," *USA Today,* 21 June 2016. http://cowboyswire.usatoday.com/2016/06/21/best-cowboys-decisions-subbing-in-staubach-vs-49ers-in-1972-playoffs/.

Musick, Phil. "Bad Day All Around for Steelers," *Pittsburgh Press,* 9 October 1972.

_____. "The 'Bear' Facts: Gilliam Thinks He's Ready," *Pittsburgh Press,* 13 August 1974.

_____. "Could '72 Be Year of the Steelers?" *Pittsburgh Press,* 18 September 1972.

_____. "Gilliam Ready to Prove He's a Winner," *Pittsburgh Press,* 7 November 1973.

_____. "Greasy Kid Stuff, Etc. No Help to Raiders," *Pittsburgh Press,* 12 November 1973.

_____. "Jumbled Steelers Plunder Atlanta," *Pittsburgh Press,* 29 October 1974.

_____. "Oakland Raid Wipes Out Steelers," *Pittsburgh Press,* 30 September 1974.

_____. "Raiders Are Still Menace, but Not Like Bad Old Days," *Pittsburgh Press,* 16 December 1984.

_____. "Steeler Teams Something Special," *Pittsburgh Press,* 8 November 1973.

"National East," *Sports Illustrated,* 18 September 1972.

"No Tomorrow, Madden Declares," *Youngstown (OH) Vindicator,* 24 December 1972.

"Oakland Raiders Vs. Pittsburgh Steelers," *Mutual Broadcasting Network,* 23 December 1972.

_____, *NBC,* 23 December 1972.

_____, *Pittsburgh Steelers Radio Network,* 23 December 1972.

Pearson, Barry. Personal communication, 28 November 2017.

Perkins, Steve. *Winning the Big One,* New York: Grossett & Dunlap, 1972.

Pierson, Don. "Cowboys Arise, Nip 49ers 30–28," *Chicago Tribune,* 24 December 1972.

"Post Playoff Interviews with Staubach, Landry and Sellers," *KPIX-TV,* 23 December 1972.

Prewitt, Eric. "Miracle Finish Keeps Dallas in Playoffs," *Tuscaloosa News,* 24 December 1972.

Ralbovsky, Marty. *Super Bowl.* New York: Hawthorn, 1971.

"Redskins Whip Cowboys, 26–3," *Owosso (MI) Argus-Press*, 2 January 1973.

Reed, William F. "An Ugly Affair in Minneapolis," *Sports Illustrated*, 7 February 1972.

Reid, Ron. "Black and Gold Soul with Italian Legs," *Sports Illustrated*, 11 December 1972.

Ribowsky, Mark. *The Last Cowboy: A Life of Tom Landry*. New York: Liveright, 2013.

Richman, Milt. "Pro Football Has Criminal Elements—Noll," *Boca Raton News*, 6 October 1976.

Ritenhouse, Duke. "49ers' Historic 'Catch' Anniversary Is Sunday," *Reno Gazette-Journal*, 9 January 2016. http://www.rgj.com/story/sports/2016/01/09/ers-historic-catch-anniversary-sunday/78576594/.

Robinson, Alan. "'Greatest Play' Turns 40 Today," Steelers.com, 23 December 2012. http://www.steelers.com/news/article-1/Greatest-play-turns-40-today/1660205f-4849-4bbe-8fe4-357bf1870d5b.

_____. "'It's Caught Out of the Air!'" *Beaver (PA) County Times*, 21 December 1997.

_____. "Twenty-Five Years Later, Franco's Catch Still Immaculate," *Gadsden (AL) Times*, 22 December 1997.

Rooney, Dan. *My 75 Years with the Pittsburgh Steelers and the NFL*. Philadelphia: Da Capo, 2007.

Rose, Tom. "Immaculate Reception: 'Absolutely Unbelievable,'" *Greene Co. (PA) Observer-Reporter*, 19 December 1999.

Roth, Mark. "Earlier Immigrants Reshaped the Region, Then Blended In," *Pittsburgh Post-Gazette*, 19 May 2014. http://www.post-gazette.com/local/city/2014/05/19/Pittsburghs-new-immigrants-Earlier-immigrants-reshaped-region-then-blended-in/stories/201405180230.

Rotstein, Gary. "Ethnic Neighborhoods Becoming Thing of Past," *Pittsburgh Post-Gazette*, 25 May 2003. http://old.post-gazette.com/localnews/20030525ethnicreg3p3.asp.

Ruck, Rob, Maggie Jones Patterson and Michael P. Weber. *Rooney: A Sporting Life*. Lincoln: University of Nebraska Press, 2010.

Russell, Gordon W. *Aggression in the Sports World: A Social Psychological Perspective*. Oxford: University of Oxford Press, 2008.

St. John, Bob. "A Roger Rally Leaves SF in Tears," *Dallas Morning News*, 24 December 1972.

_____. *Texas Sports Writers: The Wild and Wacky Years*. Plano: Republic of Texas, 2002.

"'Same Old Steelers' Tag May Be Dispelled in '72," *Rome (GA) News-Tribune*, 20 August 1972.

Schumann, Mike. "Mike Schumann Honors Teammate, Friend, Dwight Clark After Emotional Reunion," *KGO-TV*, 23 October 2007. http://abc7news.com/sports/mike-shumann-honors-teammate-friend-dwight-clark-after-emotional-reunion/2560032/.

Schuster, Karolyn. "Victory Postponed 'Until Next Year,'" *Pittsburgh Post-Gazette*, 1 January 1973.

Sell, Jack. "Guy Names Art Missed 'Work of Art,'" *Pittsburgh Post-Gazette*, 25 December 1972.

75 Seasons. Atlanta: Turner, 1994.

Silver, Michael. "Candlestick Moments: Iconic San Francisco 49ers Reminisce," NFL.com, 19 December 2013. http://www.nfl.com/news/story/0ap200000030092900/article/candlestick-park-moments-iconic-san-francisco-49ers-reminisce.

_____. "A Tale of Two Cities," NFL.com, December 2015. http://www.nfl.com/twocities.

Simers, T.J. "Dallas Dynasty Shows First Signs of Crumbling," *Los Angeles Times*, 16 January 1995. http://articles.latimes.com/1995-01-16/sports/sp-20568_1_nfc-championship-game.

Spander, Art. "Dick Nolan? He Turned the 49ers into Winners," *East Bay Times*, 13 November 2007. http://www.eastbaytimes.com/ci_7449474?source=rss.

Staubach, Roger. Personal communication, 16 January 2018.

Staubach, Roger, and Frank Luksa. *Time Enough to Win*. Waco: Word Books, 1980.

"Steeler-Raider Rivalry Is Gaining in Maturity," *Lexington (NC) Dispatch*, 13 December 1976.

"Steelers Pull Out Miracle Triumph," *Toledo Blade*, 24 December 1972.

"Steelers, Raiders Resume Football's Roughest Rivalry," *Spokane Spokesman-Review,* 22 September 1977.

Stein, Henry T. "Adlerian Overview of Birth Order Characteristics." http://www.adlerian.us/birthord.htm.

Stellino, Vito. "NFL Confidential: Rules at the Time Made Immaculate Reception Legendary," *Florida Times-Union,* 22 December 2012. http://jacksonville.com/sports/premium-sports/2012-12-22/story/nfl-confidential-rules-time-made-immaculate-reception.

"Supreme Court Leaves $1b NFL Concussion Settlement in Place," *Chicago Tribune,* 12 December 2016. http://www.chicagotribune.com/sports/football/ct-nfl-concussion-settlement-supreme-court-20161212-story.html.

Swanson, Tim. "The Hollow Man," *Sactown Magazine,* February-March 2012. http://www.sactownmag.com/February-March-2012/The-Hollow-Man/index.php?cparticle=3&siarticle=2.

Thackery, Donald B. "Steeler Coach Noll Wins 'Criminal Element' Suit," *Baltimore Afro-American,* 26–30 July 1977.

Togneri, Chris. "'Immaculate' Football Holds Special Meaning for West Mifflin Father Who Scooped It Up," *Pittsburgh Tribune-Review,* 20 June 2015. http://triblive.com/news/projects/ourstories/8541621-74/baker-ball-sam.

Tomaso, Bruce. "NFL Network Presents— 'Tom Landry, a Football Life," *Dallas Morning News,* 2 November 2011. http://thescoopblog.dallasnews.com/2011/11/nfl-network-presents-tom-landr.html/.

Top 10: Comebacks, NFL Films, 2008.

Top 10: What Ifs, NFL Films, 2017.

Trotter, Jim. "Brandon Bostic Tries to Move on from NFC Title Blunder," *ESPN,* 20 September 2015. http://www.espn.com/nfl/story/_/id/13691819/brandon-bostick-former-green-bay-packers-player-moved-muffed-onside-kick-vs-seattle-seahawks-nfl.

Vanderbundt, Skip. Personal communication, 31 October 2017.

"Wait Worth It, Declares Owner of Steelers," *Spokane Daily Chronicle,* 18 December 1972.

"Was the Reception Actually Immaculate?" *NBC Sports,* 19 December 2012. http://www.nbcsports.com/bayarea/raiders/was-reception-actually-immaculate.

Weber, Bruce. "Al Davis, the Controversial and Combative Raiders Owner, Dies at 82, *New York Times,* 8 October 2011. http://www.nytimes.com/2011/10/09/Sports/Football/Al-Davis-Owner-Of-Raiders-Dies-At-82.Html?_R=0.

Zagorski, Joe. the *NFL in the 1970s: Pro Football's Most Important Decade.* Jefferson, NC: McFarland, 2016.

Zeise, Paul. "Gilliam Paved the Way for Black Quarterbacks in the NFL," *Pittsburgh Post-Gazette,* 30 December 2000. http://old.post-gazette.com/steelers/20001230gilliam2.asp.

_____. "Steelers Receiver Barry Pearson Came Away from 'The Play' with a Great Story to Tell," *Pittsburgh Post-Gazette,* 14 October 2012. http://www.post-gazette.com/sports/steelers/2012/10/14/Steelers-receiver-Barry-Pearson-came-away-from-The-Play-with-a-great-story-to-tell/stories/201210140211.

Index